HARPERCOLLINS
ATLAS OF
BIBLE HISTORY

HARPERCOLLINS
ATLAS OF
BIBLE HISTORY

HarperOne
An Imprint of HarperCollins*Publishers*

HarperOne

HarperCollins books may be purchased for educational, business, or sales promotional use. For information please write: Special Markets Department, HarperCollins Publishers, 10 East 53rd Street, New York, NY 10022.

HarperCollins Web site: http://www.harpercollins.com

First published in the United Kingdom in 2008 by Collins UK

FIRST EDITION

Edited by James Pritchard and Nick Page
Atlas prepared by Martin Brown
Editorial direction: Louise Stanley
Editing and proof-reading: Jodi Simpson
Indexing: Joan Dearnley

Library of Congress Cataloging-in-Publication Data is available.

ISBN: 978-0-06-145195-9

08   09   10   11   12   PE   10   9   8   7   6   5   4   3   2   1

Foreword

The aim of this book is to provide a general overview of the events of Bible times; the wars, journeys, migrations, rebellions, and invasions which, both recorded in the text of the Bible and beyond, throw light on the people, lands, and culture of the biblical world.

The foreword to the original edition of this Atlas, written in 1990, emphasized the extent to which archaeology was having an impact on the field of biblical studies. Since then, its impact has only gained momentum, with scholars drawing on data from a wide range of archaeological disciplines.

Whereas, in its early days, apologetics supplied one of the main motivations behind archaeology, in recent years the driving force has been a desire to explore the wider context of the world in which the characters from the Bible lived. Discoveries relating to travel, commerce, living conditions, and social and religious activities have given new life to the accounts in both the Old and New Testaments.

Recent archaeological finds are continuing to redefine the relationship between the Bible and history. For example, the publication of the Cave 4 fragments of the Dead Sea Scrolls in the 1990s gave a new angle to early Judaism and the origins of Christianity. Even during the preparation of this edition, there came claims of the discovery of Herod the Great's tomb at the Herodion, a possible mention of a Babylonian official mentioned in Jeremiah on a clay tablet in the British Museum, and the discovery of an ancient village just to the north of Jerusalem.

Of course, archaeology is a matter of interpretation and opinion as well as investigation; and such opinions become particularly acute when the Bible is involved. For example, the issue of ancient chronology – especially Egyptian – excites much debate and discussion. Ancient dating was by means of regnal years of different rulers, rather than the kind of dating we are used to today. So, absolute dates are hard to determine, and have to be established through other means. Some dates can be checked by cross-referencing the same event as dated by two different cultures; others by means of astronomy. However, there remain huge areas of uncertainty, especially beyond the seventh century BC. For the most part the dating preferences of the original edition have been kept. However, for the dates of the Egyptian rulers, this new edition follows the preferred chronology of the Department of Egyptian Antiquities in the British Museum.

One of the most important factors for understanding the Bible, whether as an historian, a theologian, or a general reader, is an understanding of the historical context. The aim of the *HarperCollins Atlas of Bible History* is to provide the reader with all the information they need to acquire this understanding, in a way that is accessible, informed, and visually stimulating.

Contents

ONE

SETTING
THE SCENE

Monastery of Saint George of Koziba, near Jericho.
Clinging to the walls of the Wadi Qelt, this monastery,
(founded in the fifth century AD), stands on the place
where, according to tradition, Elijah stopped on his way
to the Sinai.

The land

Palestine has always been something of a "gateway." Geographically, it serves as a land-bridge between Asia and Africa; historically, it was an important route between the two centers of ancient civilization: Mesopotamia and Egypt.

The land has a basic relief of rounded mountains and incised valleys, which have determined the pattern of major roads. Seen from the west, Palestine consists of a coastal plain, a lowland, and two lines of mountains, divided by the great rift that runs southward from Syria to the source of the African river Zambezi.

The river Jordan runs through the Palestinian section of this rift. Indeed, the Jordan depression is a unique feature of the physical geography of Palestine. The point where the river enters the Dead Sea is the lowest point on the land surface of the Earth, some 393 m (1280 ft) below sea level. Appropriately, the name Jordan means "the descender."

Palestine lies in a subtropical zone, with a long dry summer and a short rainy season in winter. Precipitation varies greatly. The northern mountains of Carmel, Upper Galilee and northern Samaria were once covered with dense woodland sustained by the fair amount of rain. Now, however, only a narrow strip along the Mediterranean enjoys a relatively large amount of rainfall. Desert surrounds Palestine on the south and east.

The geography of the country is directly related to the quality of the soil (*map right*). Palestine's most fertile soil derives from the Cenomanian limestone, which, with adequate rainfall, breaks down into the rich terra rossa. The Senonian chalk is easily eroded and is infertile. Numbers indicate elevations in feet.

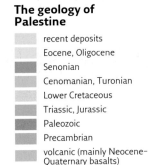

The geology of Palestine

- recent deposits
- Eocene, Oligocene
- Senonian
- Cenomanian, Turonian
- Lower Cretaceous
- Triassic, Jurassic
- Paleozoic
- Precambrian
- volcanic (mainly Neocene–Quaternary basalts)

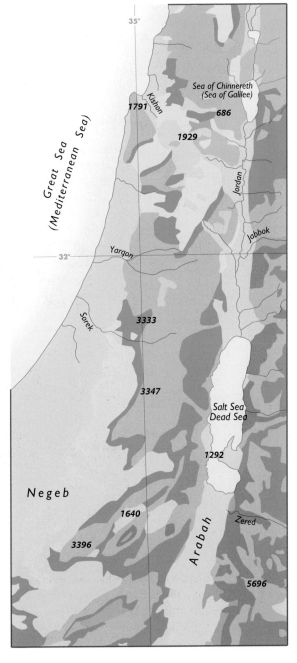

The geology of the land has had a huge impact on human activities. The hard limestone in the hills of Palestine weathers into a rich red-brown soil called terra rossa, ideal for farming. However, the soft limestone (the intermediate Senonian rock) tends to erode into a gray infertile soil. Building stone was quarried from the limestone rocks of Cenomanian, Turonian, and Eocene formations. Quarries have been found at Megiddo, Samaria, and Ramat Rahel in Iron Age contexts. Basalt exists in eastern Galilee and in the Golan; since prehistoric times, it has been the basic material for making querns and mortars.

Palestine is not very rich in mineral resources. A thick layer of red Nubian sandstone, containing deposits of copper, is known from southern Transjordan and around the river Jabbok; iron is mined in the mountains of Transjordan. Salt is obtained from the Mediterranean or from the Dead Sea.

Agriculture

The economy of Palestine has generally been pastoral-agrarian in character. Some plant species have migrated from as far away as Western Europe, Central Asia, and Central Africa. Agriculture has traditionally been based on grain, wine, and olive oil. Barley was usually grown in areas of poor soil and limited precipitation. Supplementing these were figs, pomegranates, dates, and almonds. Terraces were frequently built in

serried fashion on the slopes of hills for farming. Easy access between fields and the marketplaces was vital, and in many areas of Palestine a complex network of regional and rural roads was established.

The great variety of soil and rainfall makes for a diversity of flora. In the narrow belt of land known as the Mediterranean zone, the climate is characterized by a short, wet winter with an annual total rainfall of between 15.5 and 47.25 in. The zone originally supported evergreen woodlands and high maquis vegetation, but this has now been destroyed. The typical trees are the Aleppo pine, the

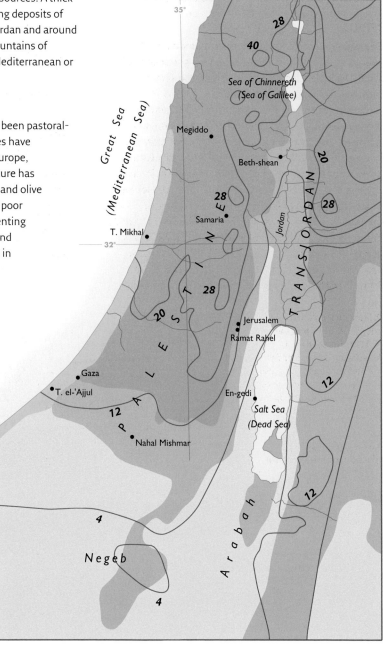

Main phytogeographic regions in Palestine

- coastal dune vegetation
- Mediterranean zone
- Irano-Turanian zone
- Saharo-Arabian zone

28 annual precipitation (inches)

Major climatic and floral zones in Palestine (*map right*). Lines show average yearly rainfall in inches.

common oak, the Palestine terebinth, the laurel, the carob, and the mastic terebinth.

Loess or thin calcareous soils exist in the Irano-Turanian zone. The climate is characterized by a low rainfall with an annual total ranging between 7.5 and 11.5 in. Since this is the absolute limit for dry-farming, only sparse trees and shrubs are to be found, notably the lotus jujube and the Atlantic terebinth.

The Saharo-Arabian zone has the poorest flora in the Levant. The rainfall does not exceed 7.5 in and can be much less. The soils are not conducive to plant growth, but thorny acacias of African-savannah origin grow in the wadi beds and survive on the water of the occasional flash flood.

Fauna

The region supports a great variety of animals including over 100 species of mammals and almost 500 species of birds. The Bible refers to many different wild animals, including the lion, tiger, bear, antelope, wild ox, Mesopotamian fallow deer, ostrich, crocodile, and hippopotamus. Some of these - such as the lion, ostrich, and bear – are no longer found in the region, mainly due to intensive hunting. At the turn of the nineteenth century, the crocodile, which originally inhabited the river Jordan, could still be seen in Nahal Tanninim ("the crocodile river") in the coastal plain of Palestine. The ibex and hyrax, mentioned in the Bible as living in the high hills (*Ps 104.18*), are common today in a number of rocky locations in Sinai and Negeb and at En-gedi near the Dead Sea. In nearby Nahal Mishmar, objects decorated with ibex horns were found in the bronze hoard dating back to the Chalcolithic

period. The Sinai leopard referred to in a number of biblical passages is critically endangered, if not already extinct. Ancient representations of the leopard have come to light on a Neolithic wall painting in Anatolia, in stone constructions in the desert floor next to a structure of the late 6th millennium BC at Biqat Uvda in southern Palestine, and in ancient wall carvings in Sinai (Wadi Abu-Jada).

Domesticated animals are also frequently mentioned in the Bible. Among them are horses, donkeys, goats, sheep, and cattle. Insects too, such as fleas, mosquitoes, and locusts, feature in biblical passages.

Agriculture and the Bible

The importance of agriculture is reflected throughout the Bible. Two out of the three major Israelite festivals were connected with agriculture: the Feast of Weeks, with the end of the grain harvest and the arrival of the first fruits, and the Feast of Booths, which celebrated the completion of the fruit harvest. (The date of Passover may also have been linked with the start of the grain harvest.)

Similarly, the Bible abounds in agricultural imagery. In the later chapters of Isaiah, the renewal of the land is couched in agricultural terms; Jesus' teaching often featured farms, vineyards, and agricultural laborers, while poems such as the Song of Solomon are rich in agricultural metaphors.

Most significantly, God's blessing could be measured by the success of the harvest, while events such as droughts or plagues of locusts (*Joel 1:2–4*) were seen as signs of his displeasure.

Palestine not only forms a bridge between Egypt and Arabia to the south and Anatolia and Mesopotamia to the north and east, but is also at the end of sea routes across the Mediterranean and up the Gulf of Suez (*map right*).

The convergence of routes in Palestine

plateau

desert

→ sea route

→ land route

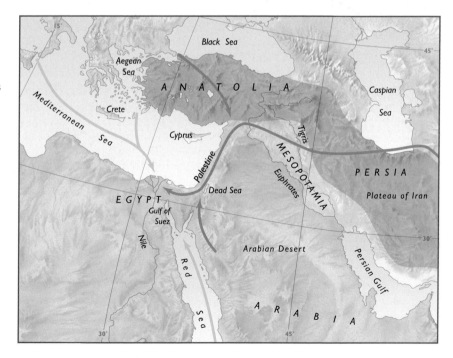

The topography of Palestine

— main road

— minor road

⤳ pass

The contours of the land obviously had their effect on travel (*map below*). The map shows major lines of communication in biblical times, the biblical names for the major highways, and the position of the passes through high ground. These roads were important both for troop movements and for trade and commerce.

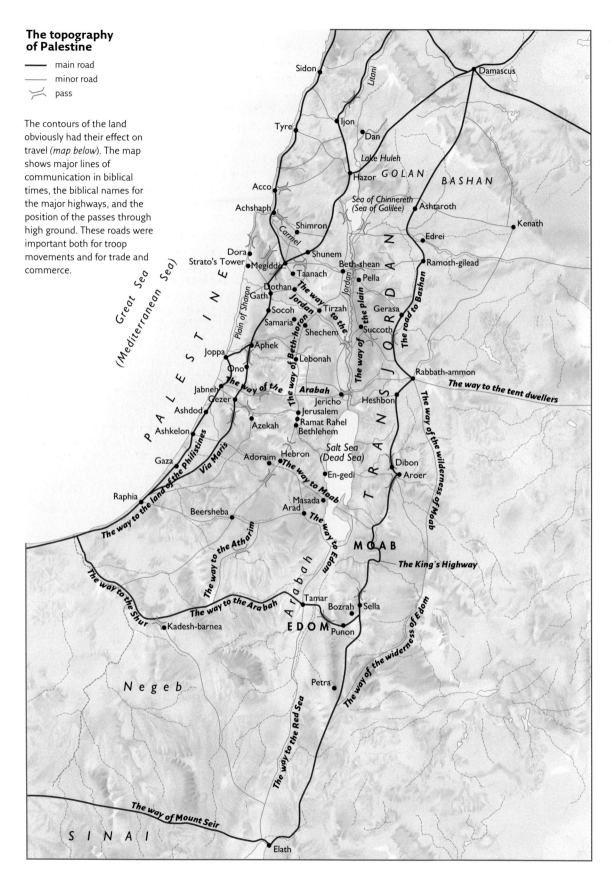

Sidon

Litani

Damascus

Tyre

Ijon

Dan

Lake Huleh

Hazor

GOLAN

BASHAN

Acco

Achshaph

Sea of Chinnereth
(Sea of Galilee)

Ashtaroth

Kenath

Shimron

Carmel

Edrei

Dora

Shunem

Beth-shean

Ramoth-gilead

Strato's Tower

Megiddo

Taanach

Pella

Great Sea

Dothan

The way to the plain

Gerasa

(Mediterranean Sea)

Gath

Socoh

Jordan

Tirzah

Succoth

The road to Bashan

Samaria

Shechem

The way of the Jordan

Plain of Sharon

Aphek

Lebonah

Rabbath-ammon

Joppa

Ono

The way of Beth-horon

The way to the tent dwellers

Jabneh

The way of the Arabah

Gezer

Jericho

Heshbon

Ashdod

Jerusalem

Azekah

Ramat Rahel

Ashkelon

Bethlehem

The way of the wilderness of Moab

Via Maris

Adoraim

Hebron

Salt Sea
(Dead Sea)

Dibon

Gaza

The way of the land of the Philistines

The way to Moab

En-gedi

Aroer

Raphia

Masada

Beersheba

Arad

The way to Edom

MOAB

The way to the Atharim

The King's Highway

The way to the Shur

The way to the Arabah

Arabah

Tamar

Bozrah

Sella

Kadesh-barnea

EDOM

Punon

The way of the wilderness of Edom

N e g e b

Petra

The way to the Red Sea

The way of Mount Seir

S I N A I

Elath

Mapping Biblical narratives

At first sight, the account of the travels of the ark (*1 Sam 4.1–7.2*) is the ideal subject for a map. Yet the complexities of the account and the difficulty of identifying the site illustrate some of the problems inherent in mapping Biblical narratives.

It begins with the ark at Shiloh in the charge of Eli and his two ill-behaved sons (*1 Sam 8.1–3*). Then the ark is taken to Aphek and Ebenezer, where the Philistines rout the Israelites, capture the ark, and take it to Ashdod, one of their chief cities. At Ashdod the ark brings trouble upon the Philistines - the statue of their god Dagon collapses before it and the people of Ashdod are struck by a plague. So they transfer it to Ekron, another Philistine city, with similar results. Finally, in desperation, the Philistines place the ark on a cart yoked to two cows who pull it to Beth-shemesh, where it is taken into custody by Levites. They take it to the house of Abinadab at Gibeah (or "the hill") near Kiriath-jearim. There it remains until David transfers it to Jerusalem.

It seems pretty clear. But there are difficulties. For a start, it's not certain where Ebenezer is, let alone "the hill" near Kiriath-jearim. Secondly, although the narrative implies the ark stayed at Kiriath-jearim for 20 years (*1 Sam 7.2*), it must have been there for longer, if we are to fit it in to the accepted chronology. Was it housed elsewhere during that time?

The most fundamental problem in mapping Bible narratives is simply identifying the locations. The books of the Bible refer to numerous places that, although well known to the ancient Israelites, have become lost to us. The locations of the major cities of ancient Palestine can be established with a reasonable degree of certainty, but, when it comes to less-prominent villages and landmarks, there is far less certainty. The story of Saul's search for his father's asses, for example, describes how he passes through the hill country of Ephraim, the lands of Shalishah, Shaalim, and Benjamin and eventually reaches the land of Zuph (*1 Sam 9.4*). Except for the references to Benjamin and Ephraim, none of the other "lands" can be located with any confidence.

This lack of certainty can strike even sites of major significance: in modern scholarship, at least a dozen different sites have been proposed for Mount Sinai. Nor is it restricted to Old Testament sites: the village of Emmaus (*Luke 24.13–35*) has also never been definitely identified.

The problems are further exacerbated by difficulties with translating the manuscripts, or where there are variant

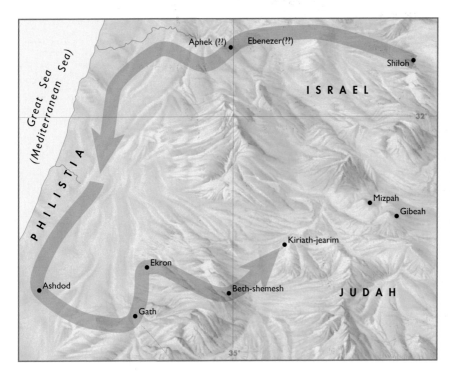

The route of the ark of the covenant from Shiloh, where it was in possession of the old priest Eli, to the Philistine cities and its return to the house of Adinadad at Gibeah near Kiriath-jearim (*map left*). The account in 1 Samuel 4–7 though seemingly straightforward, presents both geographical and chronological difficulties.

Route of the ark according to 1 Samuel 4-7

 route of the ark

readings. For example, 2 Samuel 24.5–7 describes the area covered by officials during the census conducted by David. Yet these verses are difficult to untangle, and it is unclear whether some of the words should be translated as proper names, such as Tahtim Hodshi and Dan Jaan (NIV).

Finally, there is the issue of dealing with stories where there are conflicts of opinion over the historicity. In the ark narrative, different scholars would argue over what is history and what is legend.

The net result of all this is that almost all Bible maps are hypothetical to some degree, reflecting not only the best guesses as to location, but also a degree of textual interpretation, and even the mapmaker's view on the historicity of the narrative.

The journey of Edward Robinson

In 1838, and again in 1852, Edward Robinson, an American Bible scholar, traveled through Palestine and the Sinai recording the names of towns and villages. Robinson believed that the ancient Hebrew names could still be heard in the modern names by which villagers identified their homes. For example, in the name of Anata he could hear Anathoth, the home of Jeremiah; er-Ram was Ramah; Jeba was probably the site of Geba; Mukhmas was Michmash, the place of Jonathan's victory over the Philistines; Beitin, the site of Bethel.

Robinson's studies, and the development of rules for comparing ancient Hebrew geographical terminology with modern Arabic, helped to establish biblical geography as a serious, academic pursuit.

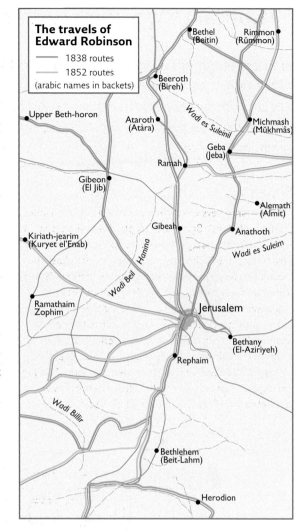

The description of Saul's search for his father's asses found in 1 Samuel 9.10 located the area around Ephraim and Benjamin and mentions several familiar cities (*map right*). However, the three lands of the Shalishah, Shaalim, and Zuph cannot be located on the map, since they are not metioned elsewhere in the Bible.

The route taken on May 4–5 1838, by Edward Robinson and Eli Smith over the area imediately north of Jerusalem (*map above right*).

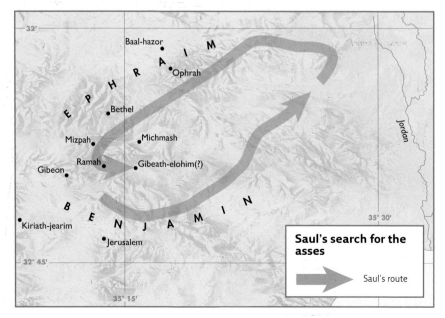

Historical geography and archaeology

Numerous pilgrims, travelers, and explorers have sought to unearth the past of the lands of the Bible, beginning, perhaps, with Helena, mother of the emperor Constantine, and her claim to have discovered remnants of the cross in the 4th century. However, true archaeological research in Palestine and the near East really dates back only to the nineteenth century.

Surveys

The earliest surveys were made by Edward Robinson and Eli Smith in 1838 and 1852 to identify places mentioned in the Bible. During the years 1872–1877, a team of Royal Engineers of the British Army, sponsored by the Palestinian Exploration Fund, compiled the *Survey of Western Palestine*, a 26-sheet set of maps covering the entire country.

In more recent times, surveys have widened their focus to look also at the advantages offered by a particular location. Was the spot favorable for defense, subsistence, trade, and transport? Did it have a good water supply? Was it close to other settlements connected by bonds of kinship or religion? Answers to these and other questions have prompted many careful surveys of large areas.

Excavation

Scientific excavations began in 1890 with Sir Flinders Petrie's stratigraphic excavations at Tell el-Hesi. He demonstrated that the ancient mound, or tell, was composed of layers of debris deposited by successive occupations, often over long periods of time. In general, it could be assumed that, unless the deposits had been

The horizontal bird's-eye view of the superimposed architectural remains uncovered by archaeologists at T. Arad in the Negeb desert. The architectectural remains shown in this plan represent different stages of the Iron Age fortress (c. 120–600 BC) with a square tower of the Hellenistic date built above earlier remains (*plan below*).

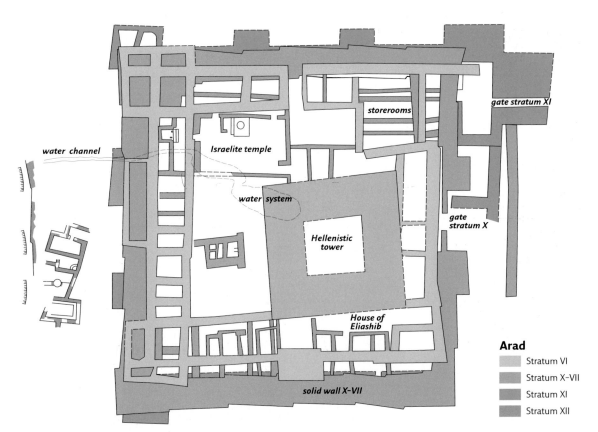

water channel

Israelite temple

storerooms

gate stratum XI

water system

gate stratum X

Hellenistic tower

House of Eliashib

solid wall X-VII

Arad

- Stratum VI
- Stratum X-VII
- Stratum XI
- Stratum XII

Quantitative comparison of settlements in Palestine

 Early Bronze II-III settlements

Middle Bronze IIA settlements

Middle Bronze IIB settlements

settlements along the coastal plain

- Early Bronze II-III settlements
- Middle Bronze IIA settlements
- Middle Bronze IIB settlements

The change in settlement patterns has been charted for the sites of the coastal plain for the three periods of ocupation: Early Bronze II-III (c. 2850–2350 BC), Middle Bronze IIA (c. 2000–1750 BC), and Middle Bronze IIB (c. 1750–1550 BC) (*map right*). The bar charts show comparisons of settlements for each of these periods for three different areas - the Central Mountains, the Middle and Lower Jordan Valley, and the coastal plain.

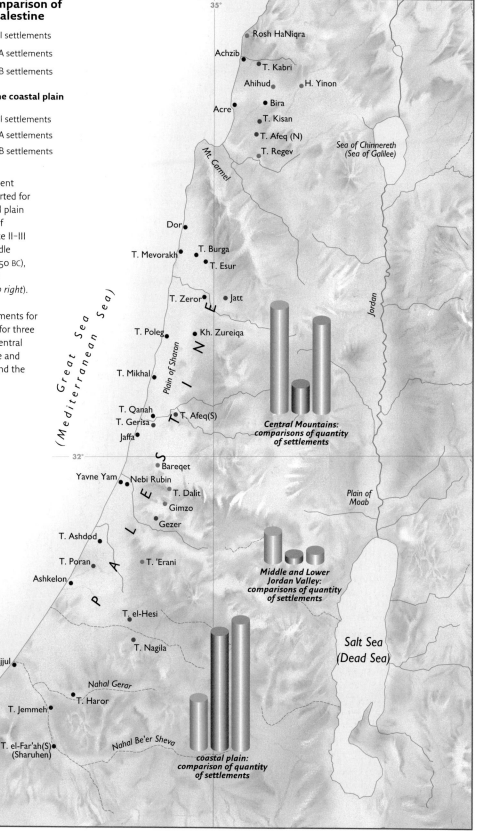

35°

Rosh HaNiqra

Achzib

• T. Kabri

Ahihud • • H. Yinon

• Bira

Acre • T. Kisan

• T. Afeq (N)

Sea of Chinnereth (Sea of Galilee)

• T. Regev

Mt. Carmel

Dor •

• T. Burga

T. Mevorakh • • T. Esur

Jordan

T. Zeror • • Jatt

T. Poleg • • Kh. Zureiqa

Plain of Sharon

T. Mikhal •

Central Mountains: comparisons of quantity of settlements

T. Qanah • • T. Afeq(S)

T. Gerisa •

Jaffa •

32°

• Bareqet

Yavne Yam • • Nebi Rubin

• T. Dalit

• Gimzo

• Gezer

Plain of Moab

T. Ashdod •

Middle and Lower Jordan Valley: comparisons of quantity of settlements

T. Poran • • T. 'Erani

Ashkelon •

T. el-Hesi •

Salt Sea (Dead Sea)

• T. Nagila

T. el-'Ajjul •

Nahal Gerar

• T. Haror

T. Jemmeh •

T. el-Far'ah(S) • *Nahal Be'er Sheva*
(Sharuhen)

coastal plain: comparison of quantity of settlements

Great Sea

(Mediterranean Sea)

PALESTINE

disturbed (for example, by earthquakes), the upper layer was later in time than the lower. Layers containing burnt debris and broken artifacts may be the result of warfare or disaster in the region, and might therefore be datable according to other historical records. The principle of stratigraphy established in 1890 is still the basic practice of modern archaeology.

Excavation reveals, in general, four distinct elements: architecture (buildings, walls, etc.), artifacts (tools, pots, and other objects), various kinds of deposit (ashes, building debris, etc.), and floors (beaten earth, paving stones, street surfaces, etc.). Architecture and artifacts are normally straightforward to identify, but distinguishing layers of deposits from the floor level requires careful judgment.

Pottery and dating

The most common artifact found in excavations is the ceramic vessel, or potsherds from it. Because pots were fragile, they would often break; therefore, they had to be replaced. Styles were often changed as potters sought to attract buyers, and these stylistic shifts, with such wide differences in form and decoration, provide various kinds of information about ancient life. One is the dating of the stratum in which they were found. Since changes in styles were gradual and some survived longer than others, a quantitative record of the number of sherds of a type provides an accurate picture of change from one period to another.

Such changes can be observed in other objects as well. Tools, weapons, jewelery, and ivory and bone carvings are useful in charting changes through time and serve to strengthen chronological conclusions based on pottery types. More precise means for dating are provided by coins of a known mint, scarabs, inscriptions, and datable imported goods from neighboring civilizations. Destructions wrought by invaders such as Shishak, Sennacherib, or Nebuchadnezzar, or others for whom written records are available, are useful in pinpointing dates for artifacts found in the ruins, yet even here there is debate among scholars over identification of a particular destruction with a specific event mentioned in the Bible or other texts.

Use of science in archaeology

Science has provided new means for surveying sites and dating objects. Techniques such as aerial surveys and archaeological geophysics can be used to reveal hidden structures below the ground. Indeed, archaeological field work is no longer restricted to the land. Wrecks of ancient ships, filled with valuable cargo, have documented ancient trade and revealed the construction methods. Underwater surveys can use geophysical or other remote-sensing devices.

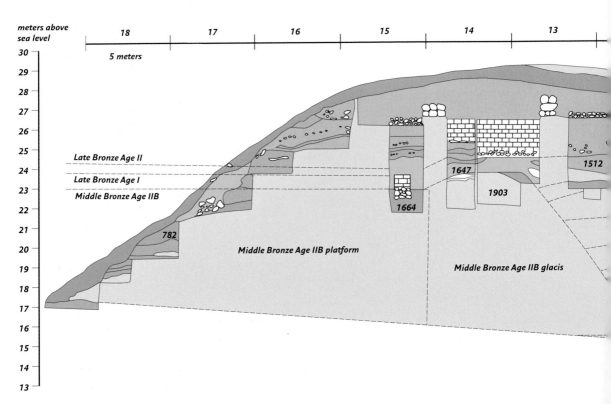

Radiocarbon and tree-ring dating (dendrochronology) are now commonplace in dating sites and objects (although the lack of an established continuous sequence in Palestinian archaeology limits the use of the latter). Thermoluminescence can determine how much time has elapsed since the original firing of the pottery. Metal analysis can identify trace elements within alloys, revealing information about ore deposits and even trading activity.

Professionals with specific expertise are increasingly used in archaeology. Osteoarchaeologists study animal bones and can tell us much about the development of domestic animals and the fauna of a region. Archaeobotanists and palynologists study plant life and pollen from the soil, throwing valuable light on the vegetation of a region or of a particular period of occupation at a site.

Excavations have become smaller in terms of the size of the site being excavated, but more intensive in terms of the information being gleaned from the sites. Such attention to detail requires longer excavation projects and more time before findings are published. This, combined with the need for technologically advanced specialist equipment, can make archaeological digs extremely expensive.

New objectives

While archaeology continues to result in spectacular finds (such as the recent discovery of the tomb of Herod the Great), there has been a shift towards smaller sites and a

concern to explore the lives of ordinary people. Was there a stratification of society? What evidence is there about the accumulation of wealth, power, and position? How has society adapted to its environment at various periods of its history?

The increased use of ethnographic and environmental data reveals a great deal about ancient societies, while the distribution of the mundane objects of daily living - those used for cooking, weaving, and metalworking - enables a more precise study of households and the relationships between those who work at various activities within a city or settlement.

Knowledge of human society and its organization in ancient Palestine has become an important objective of archaeological research, and one that draws on an increasing range of disciplines, such as zoology, botany, hydrology, and geology. This new approach, which has been termed "socio-archaeology" or "contextual archaeology," is an activity that draws on many specialists from a wide range of disciplines. "Excavation is both art and science," wrote W. F. Allbright, one of the pioneers of biblical archaeology; in modern times, it is also, above all, teamwork.

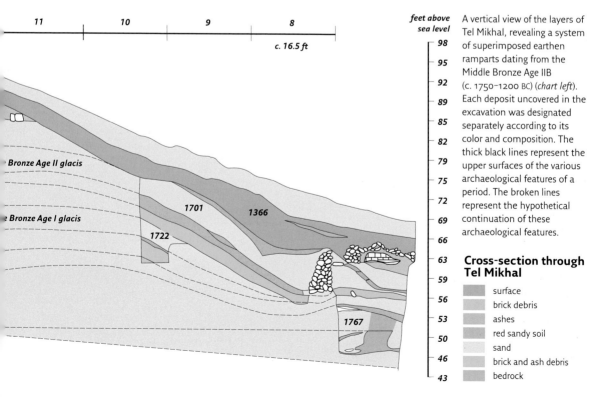

| | | | |
| 11 | 10 | 9 | 8 |

c. 16.5 ft

Bronze Age II glacis

Bronze Age I glacis

1701 1366

1722

1767

feet above sea level

98
95
92
89
85
82
79
75
72
69
66
63
59
56
53
50
46
43

A vertical view of the layers of Tel Mikhal, revealing a system of superimposed earthen ramparts dating from the Middle Bronze Age IIB (c. 1750–1200 BC) (*chart left*). Each deposit uncovered in the excavation was designated separately according to its color and composition. The thick black lines represent the upper surfaces of the various archaeological features of a period. The broken lines represent the hypothetical continuation of these archaeological features.

Cross-section through Tel Mikhal

surface
brick debris
ashes
red sandy soil
sand
brick and ash debris
bedrock

Writing, archives, and libraries in the ancient Near East

The ancient Near East - the lands of Egypt and Mesopotamia - formed the cradle of civilization. And key to any civilization is, of course, writing.

Some of these ancient writing systems were kept alive - Hebrew and Greek, for example - but many more were forgotten, and it is only relatively recently that scholars have been able to translate the ancient texts. Deciphering these "dead" languages only really began in the 1750s, when Phoenician was first read. In the 1820s, the Rosetta stone provided Champollion with the key to Egyptian hieroglyphs; Assyrian cuneiform was fairly well understood by 1857, and Ugaritic was read in 1930, just a year and a half after the first tablet was found.

Whether written records survive depends on what they were written on. Most literate societies of the ancient Near East left inscriptions on stone, or sometimes on metal. These texts, however, are limited in their subject matter, usually proclaiming the greatness of a king, recording his victories, entreating the favor of a god, or displaying the laws of the land.

The clay tablet, which originated in Mesopotamia, is also extremely durable. (Fire, for example, which destroys papyrus and wood, simply bakes clay hard). Cheap and easily produced, such tablets filled the great libraries and archives of the ancient Near East, mainly written in Sumerian and Akkadian. Although 15 libraries can be listed, some important archives have simply never been discovered (for example, Carchemish and Aleppo). Archives were essentially practical collections of law, diplomacy, and economics, relating to their own generation. Libraries were more permanent collections, containing literary texts, epics, poetry, and "wisdom" (including texts on religion, mythology, rituals, festivals, and incantations), as well as scientific and scholastic texts dealing with medicine, mathematics, and astrology.

Other documents were written on less-permanent material. In Egypt, and in places under its influence, writing was normally on papyrus or wood, neither of which survive well enough to preserve a full library or archive, though fragmentary hoards sometimes imply the existence of a larger collection.

The alphabet

14 N. and S. Arabian scripts appear at an uncertain date (c. 500 BC), the latter giving rise to Ethiopic. These scripts may have split off the developing alphabetic tradition as early as the Proto-Canaanite stage (i.e. before 1000 BC).

15 Scattered graffiti in a linear pictographic script on various objects (c. 1500–1100 BC) come from Canaan. Termed Proto-Canaanite, the signs are found arranged in alphabetic order c.1150 BC. The cursive letters imply a system of witting for papyrus or skin.

16 In Ugarit a "cuneiform alphabet" was used c. 1400–1200 BC to write the local language – also found in Canaan. Signs were arranged in alphabetic order, linking the script to the Proto-Canaanite linear alphabet.

17 An undeciphered "Pseudo-Hieroglyphic" script on stone and metal comes from Byblos. The earliest readable inscriptions in the true alphabet are found here, in a group of Phoenician inscriptions on scripture.

18 The Hebrews adopted the alphabet (c.1150–1050 BC). Preserved contemporary documents from the Hebrew kingdoms (c. 620–595 BC) are sparse: ostraca, seals, and very few stone inscriptions.

19 The Aramaeans adopted the Phoenician-Hebrew alphabet after 900 BC and established their script and language in Mesopotamia. Aramaic became the administrative language of the Persian Empire (c. 500–330 BC) disseminating their alphabet from Anatolia to India.

20 Phoenician colonization (c. 1000–700 BC) took their language and script west, to Carthage, Malta, Sardinia, and Spain. Surviving examples are mostly stone inscriptions.

21 By c. 800 BC, the Greeks had adopted the Phoenician alphabet and remodeled it for their language. By 400 BC, the Ionic alphabet had become the common script.

22 In Anatolia, several peoples adopted a variant of the alphabet and left stone inscriptions, etc. Phrygian (from c. 750 BC), Lydian, Carian (from c. 600), and Lycian (from c. 500). These Anatolian writings continued until they were superseded by Greek.

23 Greek colonization of the west, Sicily, southern Italy, and southern France in the period c. 800–500 BC effectively Hellenized the coastal areas and established the Greek language and script. Each colony used its own variant of the alphabet.

24 The Etruscans began writing after 700 BC. The earliest inscriptions are from c. 650 BC. They maintained their script and language until the 1st century AD. Only a few hundred words of Etruscan have been translated with any certainty.

25 Early Rome was under strong Etruscan influence, and borrowed much, including the alphabet. Most of the letters of the alphabet passed directly from Greek through Etruscan, though some in variant forms. Three were later additions (G, Y, and Z), as were the medieval J, V, and W.

Sardinia

Carthage

Sicily

Rome

Cumae

24

Hieroglyphic

9 The earliest writing in Egypt is on stone monuments of c. 3100 BC, where the signs already show the characteristic "hieroglyphic" forms. The use of hieroglyphic expanded in the Early Dynastic period (c. 3100–2900 BC), surviving largely as tomb inscriptions.

10 In Crete, c. 2000 BC, a native "hieroglyphic" script appeared on seals and clay dockets. This developed into two linear scripts, A and B. Linear B (c. 1400–1200 BC) has been deciphered and shown to write Mycenaean Greek.

11 Cyprus has two indigenous scripts, the undeciphered Cypro-Minoan, written on clay (c. 1500–1200 BC), and the Cypriot syllabary (c. 750–300 BC), descended from the earlier script and used for writing monumental inscriptions in Greek and an unknown language.

12 The Hittites employed a hieroglyphic script for seals and monumental inscriptions (c. 1500–700 BC), but the language written was Luvian not Hittite.

13 Many Egyptian hieroglyphic inscriptions (dated c. 2700–1000 BC) were discovered at Egyptian mines in Sinai. There is also a small group of linear pictographic inscription, "Proto-Sinaitic," connected both with hieroglyphic and with the Proto-Canaanite alphabet.

Mesopotamian cuneiform

1 The earliest writing – pictographic signs on clay tablets from Uruk – dates from the "Protoliterate" period (c. 3200–2800 BC).

2 In the Early Dynastic period (c. 2800–2400 BC), inscriptions in Sumerian are found on many sites, including Ur and Lagash. The script developed from pictographic to "cuneiform," i.e., signs made of wedge (Latin *cuneus*)-shaped strokes.

3 The Ebla archive (c. 2500–2300 BC) contains some 15,000 tablets, written in Sumerian cuneiform but also Eblaite, a Semitic language.

4 The Semitic Dynasty of Akkad (c. 2400–2250 BC), borrowed cuneiform for its inscriptions. Akkadian replaced Sumerian as the spoken language of Mesopotamia.

5 At Susa, a large group of tablets was found, inscribed in a pictographic script. The script has only partially been deciphered.

6 After 2000 BC, cuneiform Akkadian on clay tablets was widely used as an international means of communication. Other peoples used the script and the tablet for writing their own languages, including the Elamites (c. 2250–350 BC), Hurrians (c. 2200–1300 BC), Hittites (c. 1650–1200 BC) and Urartians (c. 8500–600 BC).

7 The Indus Valley cities have produced many short, undeciphered inscriptions (c. 2500–1800 BC). Links with Mesopotamia may have spread the idea of writing and led to the local invention of the script.

8 In the Persian empire (c. 550–330 BC) a "cuneiform" script was used on monumental stone inscriptions. The script was modeled on the Aramaic alphabet with influence from Akkadian.

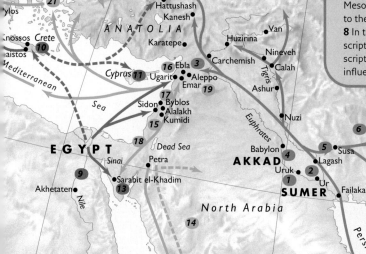

The spread of writing

→ Mesopotamian cuneiform

→ Egyptian hieroglyphic

→ Alphabetic script

Solid arrows indicate definite transmission, dashed arrows indicate possible transmission.

The Bible and ancient history

In the surviving literature of the great empires that surrounded ancient Israel, there is hardly any mention of the characters and events of the Bible. Famous characters such as Abraham, Isaac, Joseph, Saul, David, and Solomon are known only from the pages of the Bible. This is not surprising, for, compared to powers like Assyria and Egypt, Israel played a minor role in the military and commercial affairs of the time.

However, the discovery of the ancient palaces of the Assyrian kings at Khorsabad, Nineveh, and Nimrud revealed, for the first time, details about ancient Israel from sources outside the Bible. The Assyrian kings' boastful accounts of their military triumphs include the names of some monarchs of Israel and Judah.

Carved in stone or written on clay, these documents are contemporaneous with the campaigns, battles, and conquests to which they bear witness. The boxed sections contain accounts of these events, written shortly after they occurred and discovered in the mounds of Assyria and Babylonia, on a stela found in Transjordan, and on a temple wall at Karnak. There are agreements and disagreements between the accounts. Some sources, such as the inscription of Shalmaneser III mentioning Ahab; list events not referred to in the Bible; others contain information supplementary to the biblical account.

For example, Sheshonq I's (Shishak of the Bible) long list of cities conquered in Palestine, not only confirms the biblical account of the invasion but also provides a valuable source for the geography of the 10th century BC. The details on the sources naturally reflect the bias of those who caused the inscriptions to be made. A stela erected by King Mesha of Moab proclaims to his subjects that "Israel hath perished forever!" But even the wishful thinking of Israel's enemies serves to integrate events and kings - otherwise known only in the religious history of ancient Israel - with the history of the larger world.

Perhaps the most important aspect of these discoveries is that they make possible a chronology for the kingdoms of Israel and Judah. The Assyrian kings kept records of the years of their reigns, covering the period from the beginnings of the 9th through to the end of the 6th century BC. Among the important events recorded is a solar eclipse in a certain year of the reign of Ashur-Dan. With a high degree of certainty, astronomical calculations fix the year this eclipse (as observed from Nineveh) at 763 BC. This date makes possible the assignment of dates to the biblical kings whose history was interwoven with that of the kings of Assyria.

Comparison of biblical and non biblical texts

1 c. 924 BC
(Victories of Seshonq I over the) Asiatics of distant foreign countries [with list of cities in Palestine and Syria]).
Amon Temple, Karnak.

In the fifth year of King Rehoboam, King Shishak of Egypt came up against Jerusalem...
(1 Kings 14.25)

2 853 BC
He brought along to help him... 200 chariots, 10,000 foot soldiers of Ahab the Israelite... I fought with them... I did inflict a defeat upon them... With their corpses I spanned the Orentes before there was a bridge.
Shalmaneser III, on monolith from Kurkh.

No mention of this battle in the Bible.

3 c. 830 BC
As for Omri, king of Israel, he humbled Moab many years... And his son followed him... but I have triumphed over him... while Israel hath perished forever!
Mesha, king of Moab, on stela found at Dibon.

Now King Mesha of Moab was a sheep breeder, who used to deliver to the king of Israel one hundred thousand lambs, and the wool of one hundred thousand rams. But when Ahab died, the king of Moab rebelled against the king of Israel.
(2 Kings 3.4–5)

4 732 BC
They overthrew their king Pekah and I placed Hoshea as king over them.
Tiglath-pileser III, inscription at Nimrud.

In the days of King Pekah of Israel, King Tiglath-pileser of Assyria came... and he carried the people captive to Assyria. Then Hoshea son of Elah made a conspiracy against Pekah son of Remaliah, attacked him, and killed him; he reigned in place of him...
(2 Kings 15.29–30)

5 722 BC
I besieged and conquered Samaria, led away as booty 27,290 inhabitants of it.
Sargon II, inscription at Khorsabad.

In the ninth year of Hoshea the king of Assyria captured Samaria; he carried the Israelites away to Assyria...
(2 Kings 17.6)

6 712 BC
Azuri, king of Ashdod, had schemed not to deliver tribute (any more)... I besieged and conquered the cities of Ashdod, Gath (and) Asdudimmu.
Sargon II, inscription at Khorsabad.

In the year that the commander-in-chief, who was sent by King Sargon of Assyria, came to Ashdod and fought against it and took it...
(Isa 20.1)

7 701 BC
As to Hezekiah, the Jew, he did not submit to my yoke, I laid siege to 46 of his strong cities... I drove out (of them) 200,150 people... Himself I made a prisoner in Jerusalem... like a bird in a cage... Hezekiah himself... did send me, later... 30 talents of gold, 800 talents of silver...
Sennacherib, text from Nineveh.

King Hezekiah of Judah sent to the king of Assyria at Lachish, saying, "I have done wrong; withdraw from me; whatever you impose on me I will bear." The king of Assyria demanded of King Hezekiah of Judah three hundred talents of silver and thirty talents of gold.
(2 Kings 18.14)

8 597 BC
The king of Akkad... laid siege to the city of Judah... and the king took the city... He appointed in it a [new] king of his liking, took heavy booty from it and brought it into Babylon.
Nebuchadnezzar II, on tablet from Babylon.

King Nebuchadnezzar of Babylon came to the city, while his servants were besieging it; King Jehoiachin of Judah gave himself up to the king of Babylon... The king of Babylon took him prisoner in the eighth year of his reign. He carried off all the treasures of the house of the LORD, and the treasures of the king's house... The king of Babylon made Mattaniah, Jehoiachin's uncle, king in his place, and changed his name to Zedekiah.
(2 Kings 24.11-17)

Comparison of biblical and non-biblical texts

● Egyptian   ● Assyrian
● Moabite   ● Babylonian

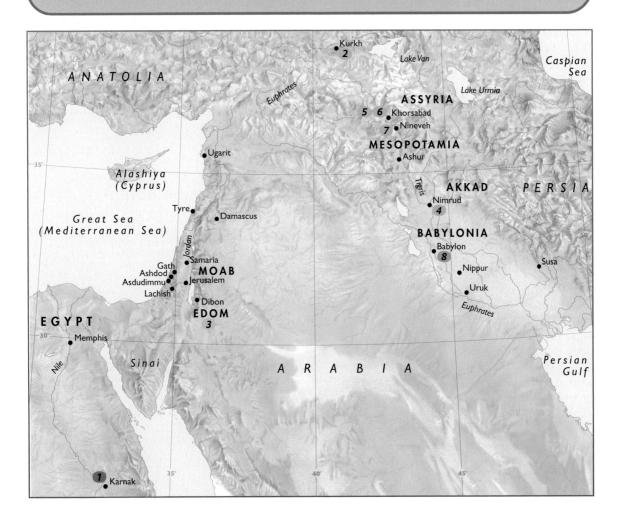

Pagan cults and religious practice

The monotheistic Hebrew religion faced a constant challenge from Canaanite polytheism and its practices. The diversity of religious allegiances is evident from discoveries at Kuntillet Ajrud to the south of Kadesh-barnea, where inscriptions record the names of Baal, Asherah, and El, as well as Yahweh "and his consort." Clearly, the popular cults did not die easily.

The practices and imagery of the religions of the time were characterized by naturalistic symbols such as standing stones, trees, the bull, the cow, and serpents.

A basalt upright stone found at Jericho shows that the custom of setting up a stone for religious purposes reaches back to Neolithic times. Biblical accounts of memorial stones are many: a stone marks Jacob's covenant with Laban (*Gen 31.45*); another is used as a cult object at Bethel (*Gen 28.18-19*).

Altars were for slaughtering animals and burning offerings. They were made of mud brick or unquarried stone (*Exod 20.24-26; Deut 27.5*), and examples have been found at Megiddo and Lachish. Altars from the Iron Age have also been found, one from Beersheba having "horns" at the four corners and a snake engraved on one side.

Trees were also important. Late Bronze Age cylinder seals often show a worshipper standing in front of a tree; other seals

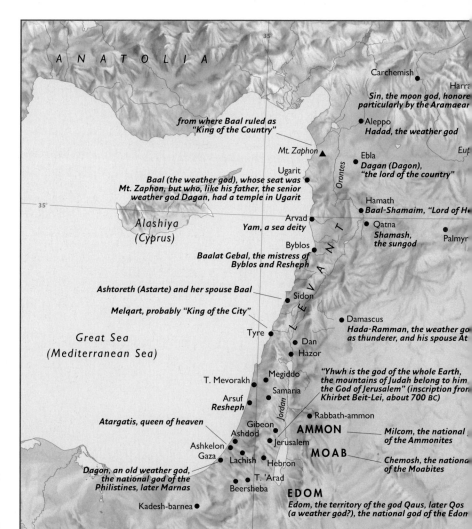

National gods in the Levant and Mesopotamia, 2000–500 BC

● city

"You shall have no other gods before me," declared the god of Israel. The countries and culture surrounding Israel, however, worshipped a huge number of different gods. The map shows the distribution of religious cults throughout Palestine, Phoenicia, Syria, and Mesopotamia.

ANATOLIA

Carchemish
Harra
Sin, the moon god, honore particularly by the Aramaear
●Aleppo
Hadad, the weather god
Mt. Zaphon ▲
Eu
Ebla
Dagan (Dagon), "the lord of the country"
from where Baal ruled as "King of the Country"
Ugarit
Baal (the weather god), whose seat was Mt. Zaphon, but who, like his father, the senior weather god Dagan, had a temple in Ugarit
Orontes
Hamath
Baal-Shamaim, "Lord of H
Arvad●
Yam, a sea deity
●Qatna
Shamash, the sungod
Palmyr
Alashiya (Cyprus)
Byblos
Baalat Gebal, the mistress of Byblos and Resheph
Ashtoreth (Astarte) and her spouse Baal
●Sidon
Melqart, probably "King of the City"
●Damascus
Hada-Ramman, the weather go as thunderer, and his spouse At
Tyre ●
Great Sea (Mediterranean Sea)
●Dan
●Hazor
Megiddo
T. Mevorakh●
Samaria
Arsuf ●
Resheph
Jordan
"Yhwh is the god of the whole Earth, the mountains of Judah belong to him, the God of Jerusalem" (inscription from Khirbet Beit-Lei, about 700 BC)
Atargatis, queen of heaven
Gibeon
Ashdod
Ashkelon ●
Gaza ●
Lachish
Jerusalem
●Rabbath-ammon
AMMON
Milcom, the national of the Ammonites
MOAB
Chemosh, the nationa of the Moabites
Hebron
T. 'Arad
Dagon, an old weather god, the national god of the Philistines, later Marnas
Beersheba
EDOM
Edom, the territory of the god Qaus, later Qos (a weather god?), the national god of the Edon
Kadesh-barnea ●
Kuntillet 'Ajrud ●

dating from the 10th to the 8th centuries BC depicting a tree flanked by worshippers have been found at Tel Halif, Lachish, Beth-shemesh, Gibeon, Samaria, and elsewhere. Gold pendants from Tel el-Ajjul and Ugarit even display trees growing out of the navel or the genitals of some kind of goddess. Sexual intercourse took place under holy trees and was considered a part of the sacrifice to the goddess (*Hosea 4.13–14*).

Numerous Canaanite bronzes of a young man with his right hand raised in a gesture of victory are thought to represent Baal. Bronze bulls, also possibly representing Baal, are known from Hazor, Ugarit, and Samaria. Jeroboam is said to have violated the law by setting up images of golden calves in the temples at Dan and Bethel (*1 Kings 12.28–30*).

The female deity is referred to as the consort of Baal (*Judg 3.7; 2 Kings 23.4*), and Ashtoreth (Astarte) is often described as a fertility goddess. Maternal traits were usually expressed in animal, rather than human, form. The cow suckling her calf,

> "You shall not make gods of silver alongside me, nor shall you make for yourselves gods of gold."
> **(Exod 20.23)**

familiar from Phoenician ivories, can be regarded as the counterpart of the god in the form of a bull.

Small bronze snakes found in Late Bronze Age temples at Hazor, Megiddo, Tel Mevorah, Gezer, and in the Early Iron Age shrine at Timnah, may have been votive offerings to a goddess, since a figurine of a female has been found holding a serpent in her hands. This same image, or one like it, may be the "Nehushtan" worshipped by the Israelites (*2 Kings 18.4*).

The pantheon was as large and varied as the natural world, with deities for the sky, sun, moon, storm, and sea, as well as for more abstract concepts such as war, love, healing, wisdom, and writing.

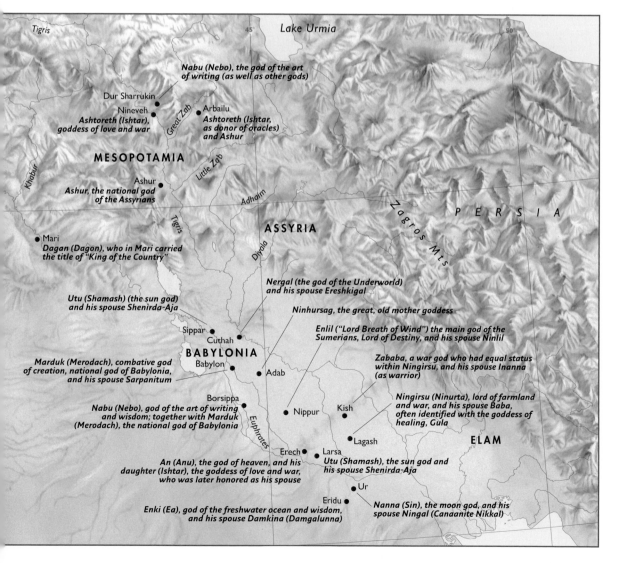

Routes and distances

Most people walked. Wheeled vehicles need roads; walkers need only tracks. There were ancient roads, such as the road between Babylon and Larsa in the days of Hammurabi, but they would not have been paved. Bridges, too, were rare; rivers had to be forded or travelers carried across on ferries. Only the rich few had horses, and even then, the ancient world used neither horseshoes nor stirrups, which made traveling on horseback far less convenient. Animals were used mainly for transporting goods or equipment. The most common pack animals were donkeys or asses. Camels were used by desert tribes and traders making long journeys. Traveling to Jerusalem after the exile, the returning exiles used 435 camels (*Neh 7.69*) and David appointed an expert - Ofil the Ishmaelite - to look after his (*1 Chron 27.30*).

By Roman times, a traveler might make fifteen to twenty miles a day on foot, perhaps twenty-five to thirty in a carriage. In emergencies, forty to fifty might be possible.

For long distances, sailing, where possible, was the best. With a good wind, a ship could make up to one hundred miles a day. Sea travel was risky, however. Unless absolutely vital, no sailor would travel between November and March. The account of Paul's shipwreck shows just how dangerous such travel could be (*Acts 27*).

The following list gives the distances in miles between places mentioned in biblical accounts of journeys, marches, and other movements of people. A selection of distances outside Palestine has also been added to the list to set journeys mentioned in the New Testament in a wider context. Since the routes taken from one point to another are not generally known, distances are those of a straight line. This approximation serves for comparative purposes and to provide an idea of the length of a journey. Only those ancient places that can be identified with reasonable certainty are included.

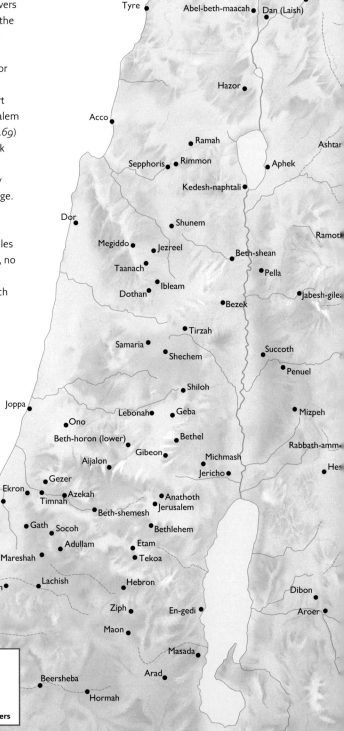

Main towns and villages in Palestine

scale

| 0 | 10 | 20 | 30 | 40 | 50 miles |

| 0 | | | | | 80 kilometers |

Index of Distances

Antioch	Acco	235
	Caesarea	55
	Ephesus	575
	Damascus	195
	Dura-Europas	310
	Jerusalem	330
Ashkelon	Azotus	10
	Gaza	12
	Joppa	30
	Timnah	23
Athens	Corinth	62
	Ephesus (by sea)	230
	Philippi	310
	Thessalonica	230
Babylon	Asshur	210
	Damascus	471
	Jerusalem	540
	Megiddo	536
	Nineveh	273
Beersheba	Bethel	53
	Dan	146
	Gerar	17
	Hebron	25
Bethel	Beersheba	53
	Bethlehem (Judah)	16
	Gibeah	5
	Haran	410
	Hebron	29
	Ramah (Benjamin)	5
	Shechem	19
	Shiloh	9
	Tekoa	20
Bethlehem	Adullam	13
	Bethel	16
	Jerusalem	4
Beth-shemesh	Ekron	7
	Jerusalem	16
	Kiriath-jearim	9
Caesarea Philippi	Damascus	40
	Capernaum	37
	Tyre	25
	Philadelphia	90
	Petra	260
Capernaum	Bethsaida	3
	Cana	17
	Jericho	71
	Jerusalem	79
	Nazareth	20
	Samaria	48
Corinth	Alexandria (by sea)	600
	Caesarea (by sea)	750
Damascus	Antioch	195
	Dura-Europas	295
	Hamath	110
	Jerusalem	140
	Palmyra	135
	Tyre	65
Dan (a/c Laish)	Beersheba	146
	Hebron	123
	Shechem	75
	Sidon	28
Ephesus	Antioch	508
	Athens	194
	Corinth	236
	Miletus	31
	Philippi	264
	Rome	808
	Tarsus	424
	Thessalonica	295
Gath	Adullam	10
	Ashdod	12
	Ekron	5
	Jerusalem	23
Gaza	Alexandria	270
	Hebron	38
	Hormah	36
	Jerusalem	48
	Joppa	38
	Petra	100
	Zorah	36

Gezer	Eglon	24
	Geba (Benjamin)	20
	Gibeon	15
	Jerusalem	19
	Lachish	21
Gibeah	Bethel	5
	Bezek	36
	Jabesh-gilead	45
	Jerusalem	6
	Mizpah (Benjamin)	3
	Ramah (Benjamin)	1
	Rimmon	2
	Ziph	28
Gibeon	Abel-beth-maacah	103
	Gezer	15
	Jerusalem	6
	Kiriath-jearim	6
	Mahanaim	38
Hebron	Beersheba	25
	Bethel	29
	Beth-shean	72
	Dan	123
	Eglon	23
	Gaza	38
	Jerusalem	19
	Marisa	13
	Shechem	48
Jabesh-gilead	Beth-shean	13
	Bezek	17
	Gibeah	45
	Rabbath-ammon	35
	Shiloh	33
Jericho	Abel-shittim	14
	Ai	11
	Gazara	32
	Jerusalem	14
	Samaria	31
Jerusalem	Abel-beth-maacah	105
	Alexandria	320
	Anathoth	3
	Antioch	330
	Ashdod	34
	Ashkelon	42
	Baalah	8
	Baal-hazor	14
	Beth-horon (lower)	12
	Bethlehem (Judah)	4
	Beth-shemesh (Judah)	16
	Bethzur	16
	Bezek	42
	Caesarea	54
	Damascus	140
	Dora	60
	Elephantine	740
	Gath	23
	Gazara	19
	Geba (Benjamin)	6
	Gezer	19
	Gibeah	6
	Gibeon	6
	Hebron	19
	Jamnia	30
	Jericho	14
	Jezreel	54
	Joppa	34
	Lachish	27
	Mahanaim	39
	Mareshah	23
	Masada	33
	Megiddo	57
	Michmash	8
	Mizpah (Benjamin)	8
	Modein	18
	Panion	102
	Persepolis	1020
	Rabbath-ammon	43
	Ramoth-gilead	67
	Samaria	35
	Shechem	30
	Succoth	37

	Tekoa	10
	Tyre	104
Jezreel	Ibleam	8
	Jerusalem	54
	Ramoth-gilead	40
	Samaria	21
Kiriath-jearim	Beth-shemesh	9
	Eshtaol	6
	Gibeon	6
	Laish	103
	Zorah	7
Mizpah	Bethel	3
	Gibeah	3
	Jerusalem	8
	Ramah	3
	Samaria	27
	Shechem	23
	Shiloh	13
Nazareth	Bethlehem	69
	Cana	8
	Capernaum	20
	Jerusalem	64
	Sepphoris	4
Philippi	Athens	212
	Beroea	114
	Corinth	224
	Thessalonica	74
	Troas	128
Ramah	Bethel	5
	Geba (Benjamin)	2
	Gibeah	1
	Jerusalem	6
	Kedesh-naphtali	88
	Mizpah (Benjamin)	3
	Shiloh	14
	Tirzah	30
Samaria	Dothan	10
	Jericho	31
	Jerusalem	35
	Jezreel	21
	Mizpah (Benjamin)	27
	Ramoth-gilead	50
	Tirzah	9
Sepphoris	Acco	19
	Caesarea	24
	Capernaum	20
	Gischala	22
	Nazareth	4
	Tiberias	15
Shechem	Arumah	5
	Bethel	19
	Dan	75
	Dothan	14
	Haran	390
	Hebron	48
	Jerusalem	31
	Mizpah (Benjamin)	23
	Penuel	24
	Shiloh	11
	Succoth	20
	Tirzah	7
Shiloh	Aphek (Sharon)	22
	Bethel	9
	Jabesh-gilead	33
	Mizpah (Benjamin)	13
	Ramah (Benjamin)	14
Succoth	Abel-meholah	13
	Jerusalem	37
	Penuel	5
	Shechem	20
Tirzah	Gibbethon	41
	Ramah (Benjamin)	30
	Samaria	9
	Shechem	7
Ur	Haran	590
Zorah	Eshtaol	2
	Gaza	36
	Kiriath-jearim	7
	Laish	111
	Timnah	5

TWO

THE PATRIARCHS

Abraham and Isaac, Chartres Cathedral.
Abraham looks up, stopped in the act of
sacrificing his son. To his right is Melchizedek;
beyond Abraham stand statues of Moses,
Samuel, and David.

Hunters, farmers, and metalworkers

The list of sons of Adam and Eve and their occupations reflects all the elements of the beginnings of human culture. Cain tills the ground and Abel is a shepherd, Enoch builds a city, Jabal is a nomad, Jubal is a musican, and Tubal-cain is a smith (*Gen 4.2, 17, 20-22*). Their skills have been investigated at numerous sites in the Holy Land.

It is around 11,000 BC that we first find settled societies with houses, storage facilities, decorative art, pounding and grinding tools, and tools made from bone. The people of the Natufian period (named after Wadi en-Natuf, in central Palestine, where remains were first discovered) hunted gazelles, fallow deer, and wild boar; they also fished, trapped birds, and gathered a wide variety of wild cereals, pulses, and nuts. Their settlements feature circular houses (there is one even with lime-plastered walls at Ena). Other discoveries include carved gazelles on sickle handles of bone from el-Wad and animal and human figurines from a cave near Kebara.

As their population increased, Late Natufian communities established new sites (e.g., Mureybat and Abu Hureira on the Middle Euphrates and Rosh Zin and Rosh Horesha in the Nageb highlands). In the Early Natufian period, there were common group burials and frequent use of bone and shell pendants; In the Late Natufian period, single burials were more common and body ornaments were rare.

More permanent settlements began to appear as early as the 9th and 8th millennia BC (e.g., Jericho and Nahal Oren in Palestine, and Mureybat in Syria). Agriculture and animal husbandry developed further during the 7th millennium, although most communities continued to rely on hunting and gathering to supplement their diet.

Neolithic

The most intensive Neolithic settlement in Palestine occurred between about 7500 and 6000 BC (known as the Pre-Pottery Neolithic B period). Major settlements at Jericho, Munhata, Beidha, and Ain Ghazal feature well-built, multiroomed rectangular buildings with burnished lime plaster on walls and floors. A group of male and female figures at Ain Ghazal suggests ancestor worship. The large presence of flint blades probably indicate an increasing use of wood; flint arrowheads point to continuation of hunting. Most of these sites were abandoned around 6000 BC, with cultivated cereals and domesticated animals becoming more important in the Late Neolithic period.

Chalcolithic

During the Chalcolithic period (5th-4th millennia BC) new building techniques, art, and skills appeared, the most notable of which was metallurgy. The large

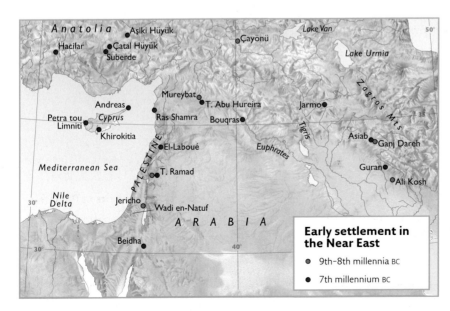

Early settlement in the Near East

- ● 9th-8th millennia BC
- ● 7th millennium BC

Permanent settlement increased greatly in the 7th millennium BC due to the development of cultivated cereals and domesticated animals (*map left*).

Chalcolithic site at Tuleilat Ghassul has two spectacular buildings with wall paintings. One shows a procession of worshippers approaching two gods on a dais. Another painting has three figures hand in hand, their leader holding a sickle-shaped object, similar in shape to an ivory sickle found at Horbat Zafad, near Beersheba. The lack of fortifications at the site lead experts to believe the settlements saw a time of peace and prosperity.

Recently, discoveries near Beersheba and at En-gedi and Nahal Mishmar have enlarged the earlier picture of Chalcolithic culture. Beersheba had a highly sophisticated metal industry, and a remarkable hoard of copper objects was found at Nahal Mishmar. Other sites, such as those at Azor, Gilat, and Megiddo, have produced clay ossuaries, domestic house shrines, and human and animal figurines.

Domesticated sheep and goats began to replace gazelle as the dominant meat source in Jericho c. 7000 BC. In the period before this date, 38% of bones found were of gazelle, and 7% were of sheep and goats; in the following period, only 14% of bones found were of gazelle, and 40% were of sheep and goats (chart below).

Permanent settlement occurred in Palestine as early as the 10th–9th millennia BC (map right).

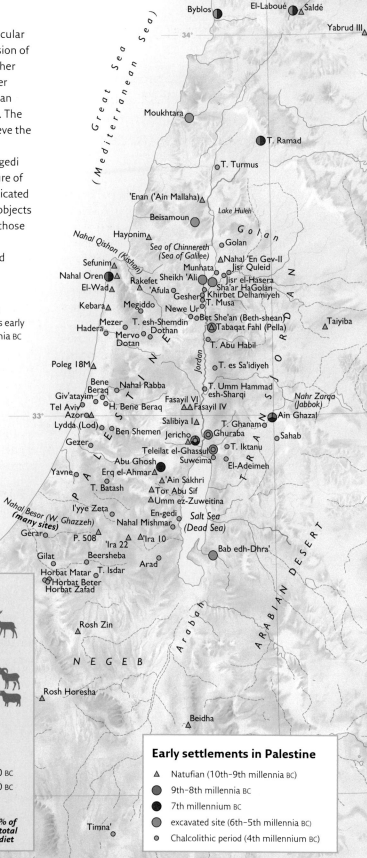

Jericho: development of farming, 8000-6000 BC

gazelle

small ruminant

goat/sheep

cattle

pig

horse

c.8000-7000 BC
c.7000-6000 BC

fox

0   10   20   30   40   % of total diet

Early settlements in Palestine

△ Natufian (10th–9th millennia BC)

● 9th–8th millennia BC

● 7th millennium BC

● excavated site (6th–5th millennia BC)

∘ Chalcolithic period (4th millennium BC)

Noah's descendants

Before the rise of Greek scholarship, there was no science of geography in the ancient world. What maps were made were not necessarily drawn on two-dimensional planes; some were linear, consisting of individual roads (later known as itinerae), which provided information useful to a traveler. Some maps were religious and cosmological, but most were for practical purposes such as trade, taxation, and welfare.

Genesis 10 is a map: albeit of a different kind, the chapter gives, in the briefest fashion, an ethnographic lineage of the peoples of the Earth, information that can be superimposed on a modern map. The lineage descends from Noah and his three sons, Ham, Shem, and Japheth; in the narrative of Genesis, all other males are said to have perished in the flood.

Scholars identify two broad streams of tradition in this larger narrative: an early epic story, which existed in its essential form by the time of the Hebrew United Monarchy in the 10th century BC, and priestly traditions, added to the older narrative as late as the 7th–6th centuries BC, which

systematized and embellished the earlier material in ways reflecting the knowledge and theological views of the later period.

Because they lived at a time when tribal relationships were still a major concern in Hebrew religious thought, the authors of the old patriarchal epic in Genesis tended to see the world from an ethnic perspective. People are categorized not by their geographical locations or their linguistic affinities but by their ethnic origins. In their society, kinship played an important role, and it was possible to build up a picture in which the relationships between peoples could be expressed as family relationships.

The basis for the map is Genesis 10 (*map right*). The names of the descendants of Noah have been identified as far as possible with the names of cities, tribes, and geographical areas of the ancient world. Hecataeus of Miletus described the world like this in his *Periodos* (c. 520 BC) (*map far right top*). The world as seen by Strabo in his *Geography* (1st century BC) (*map far right bottom*).

The spread of writing
regions of the sons of Noah

—— **HAM**

—— **SHEM**

—— **JAPHETH**

⊙   city

(Nimrud)   modern form of an ethnic or tribal name

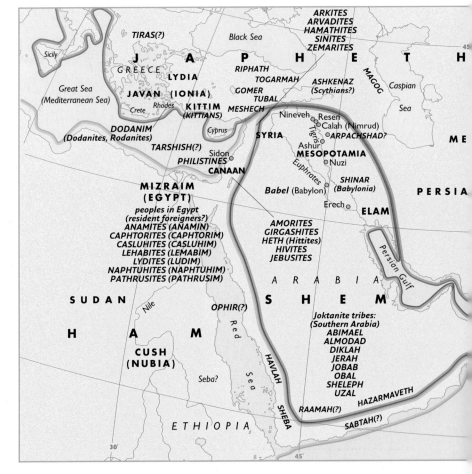

Each ethnic group, therefore, is represented eponymously, by a single person who bears the name of the group and is said to be that group's ancestor. The use of such figures led easily to the arrangements of the persons into a single, comprehensive lineage. This method was not unique to the Hebrews; it was employed, with variations, throughout the ancient Near East.

The later editors of the earlier epic tradition retained this ethnographic structure but added to the list some names that reflected their awareness of the larger world - peoples of Anatolia to the north, Media and Elam to the east, and Cush to the south. They seem to have had some interest in geography in its own right, but their concerns were primarily theological. The center of the world was, as in the epic narrative, Canaan, the land that the Israelites had taken as their home. The extent of the inhabited Earth known to priestly editors was not more than 1500 miles in any direction from the hub of Canaan/Palestine, less than one-twentieth of the Earth's actual surface.

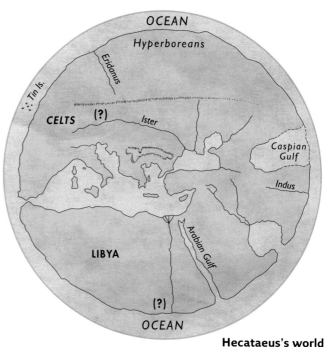

Hecataeus's world

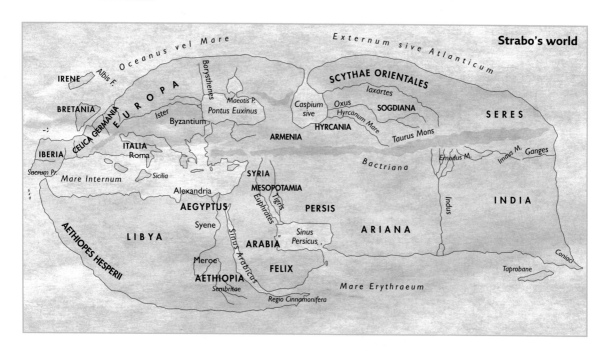

The flood

Details of the great flood (*Gen 6.8*) resemble those found in the *Epic of Gilgamesh*, in which the hero, Utnapishtim, is instructed by one of the gods to build a ship to save himself and "the seed of all living beings." After six days of storm, the sea grew quiet and the ship came to rest on a high mountain. A dove was released, then a swallow, and finally a raven, which found the waters diminished enough for Utnapishtim to disembark and offer a sacrifice to the gods.

The first cities

Towards the end of the 4th millennium, developments took place in the Levant that led, at the beginning of the Early Bronze Age, to the appearance of towns. By about 3000 BC, many Chalcolithic villages had been abandoned, to be replaced by a smaller number of walled towns, functioning, probably, as centers in a trading network linking Canaan with Egypt.

The evolution of these urban societies had a profound effect on civilization. Large buildings, such as fortifications and temples, required a complex system of social, economic, and political organizations.

The most imposing feature of these early towns was a defensive wall built of rough stones and mud bricks. At Arad, one of the best-preserved sites, semicircular bastions appear at regular intervals, exactly as those depicted in an Egyptian tomb of the 5th dynasty. At Jericho, there were both rounded and square towers; and at T. el-Far'ah (North) two square, mud-brick towers flanked the gateway. Some early town planning may be seen at Arad, where a palace and a double temple appear to have been separated by a wall from the rest of the town. A large artificial reservoir to conserve the winter rains was also incorporated into the plan.

The buildings themselves are diverse, both in design and size, but one basic plan does seem to have been popular for temples and houses alike: a rectangular structure with the entrance in the long side and often with benches along the other three.

Within these towns, crafts and industries were at a comparatively low level. Artistic design was limited to cylinder and stamp seals, and copper tools and weapons were cast in simple open molds. Only in pottery was any real technological progress made through the use of better clay, the development of the potter's wheel, and better firing in a controlled kiln. Ovoid jars of the period have been found in Egypt, providing tangible proof of the oil trade between the two areas.

These towns needed their walls, for the Early Bronze Age was not a peaceful period. Judging from the frequency of repair and strengthening of fortifications at places such as Jericho and Ai, intertown rivalry and the military intervention mentioned in Egyptian texts led to conflict and insecurity.

Some towns seem to have been abandoned before the end of the period, possibly due to the gradual decline in Egyptian trade. Discoveries at T. Mardikh (ancient Ebla), south of Aleppo, have established that the city maintained some sort of hegemony after about 2400 BC as far south as Damascus and commercial relations even farther afield.

The rise of Ebla may have been detrimental to Egypt's role in the Levant.

Just as trade with Egypt had been the stimulus for the urbanization of Canaan about 3000 BC, its demise was to bring about the end of the urban interlude. In the final centuries of the Early Bronze Age, the archaeological record shows that city walls and public buildings were destroyed or fell into disuse. New groups of nomadic peoples (identified by some scholars as the biblical Amorites) may have appeared and contributed to the decline of urbanism. Whatever the cause, the country became once again a land of agricultural villages and pastoral encampments, as it had been in the 4th millennium.

Urbanization in the Early Bronze Age (*map below*). Information about Early Bronze Age Canaan comes from Pharaoh Pepy I's (c. 2321-2287 BC) descriptions of his campaigns there.

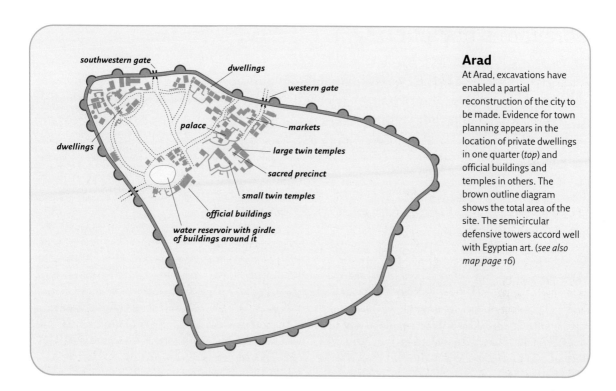

Arad

At Arad, excavations have enabled a partial reconstruction of the city to be made. Evidence for town planning appears in the location of private dwellings in one quarter (*top*) and official buildings and temples in others. The brown outline diagram shows the total area of the site. The semicircular defensive towers accord well with Egyptian art. (*see also map page 16*)

southwestern gate

dwellings

western gate

palace

markets

dwellings

large twin temples

sacred precinct

small twin temples

official buildings

water reservoir with girdle of buildings around it

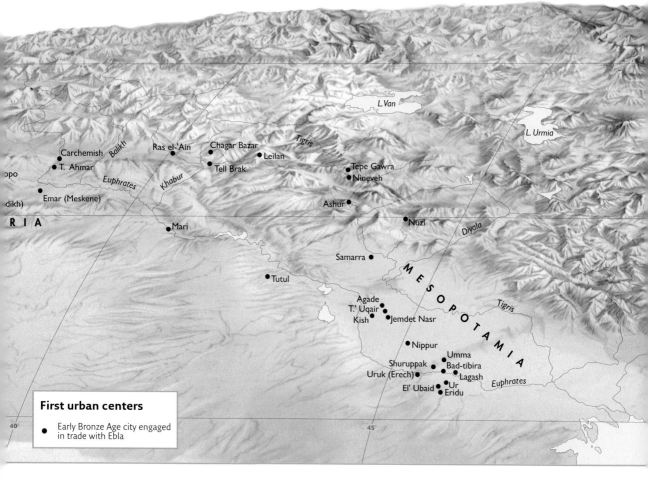

Carchemish
T. Ahmar
opo
dikh)
Emar (Meskene)
Balikh
Ras el-'Ain
Chagar Bazar
Leilan
Tell Brak
Euphrates
Khabur
Tigris
L. Van
L. Urmia
Tepe Gawra
Nineveh
Ashur
R I A
Mari
Nuzi
Diyala
Samarra
M E S O P O T A M I A
Tutul
Agade
T.' Uqair
Kish
Jemdet Nasr
Tigris
Nippur
Umma
Shuruppak
Bad-tibira
Lagash
Uruk (Erech)
El' Ubaid
Ur
Eridu
Euphrates

First urban centers

● Early Bronze Age city engaged in trade with Ebla

40

45°

Abraham's migration

Abraham, the earliest of the Hebrew patriarchs, left his home in Ur, one of the principal cities of southern Mesopotamia, and journeyed to Haran ("crossroads") in the north and from thence to Canaan. From the biblical account of this decisive journey (*Gen 11.31–12.5*), it is impossible to trace his specific route.

However, commonly used trade routes between cities that flourished in the 2nd millennium BC are known from cuneiform sources, and a patriarchal caravan would probably have followed one of these. One detailed surviving itinerary describes an army or caravan moving by named stages from near Ur and up the Tigris, via Ashur and Nineveh, before striking westwards to Haran in the early 18th century BC . Another text describes the nine-month journey by Zimri-Lim, king of Mari, (c. 1760 BC), up the Euphrates and river Khabur, thence to Haran, and on to Aleppo (Khalab). There is a well-attested route extended from the river Balikh to Haran, south to Aleppo, and then via Qatna, Damascus, and Hazor, along the Palestine ridge to Shechem, Hebron, and Beersheba.

Scholars disagree about the date of Abraham's journey to Canaan, but the milieu of the biblical accounts suggests that the Middle Bronze Age provides the most suitable background. Most of the cities mentioned in the stories were occupied during this period, especially those along the central mountain ridge, such as Shechem, Bethel, and Hebron.

Trade routes

In the 2nd millennium, major cities recorded a range of imports of nonlocal items such as gold, silver, precious stones, and wine, together with the commodities essential to their industrial and technological processes (e.g., copper, tin, and oil). They also imported luxury items, such as textiles, precious objects, and furnishings. Valuable wood from Lebanon was floated down the coast or dragged to major streams for transport to eastern cities as tribute. In the north, tin from sources east of Mesopotamia was exchanged for copper, some tin reaching Canaan via Hazor and Mari. The main route followed in and near Palestine was the "Way of the Sea," the Philistine road from Egypt. It was supplemented by sea routes to both the Philistine coastal cities and the northern ports, such as Byblos, Tyre, and Ugarit.

From Ur to Canaan

The tradition of Abraham's coming from Ur in Mesopotamia is matched by more general links between the great center of civilization to the east and the Bible.

From a wider perspective, there is the influence of Mesopotamian culture found in Israel. The tower "with its top in the heavens" (*Gen 11.4*) is a reference to the stepped temple tower, or ziggurat, that was seen throughout Mesopotamia. The flood story of Gilgamesh and the laws of Hammurabi also attest these links.

Abraham's journey from Ur to Canaan has left no visible traces along the route. For later writers, this memorable trek was an example of a bold adventure in obedience to a divine command. God is called "the God of Abraham," while the land that Israel later came to occupy is that that "Yahweh gave unto Abraham." The story of Abraham's response to a call when he was "beyond the River," therefore, casts a long shadow over Jewish centuries, and even over those of the other faiths of Christianity and Islam.

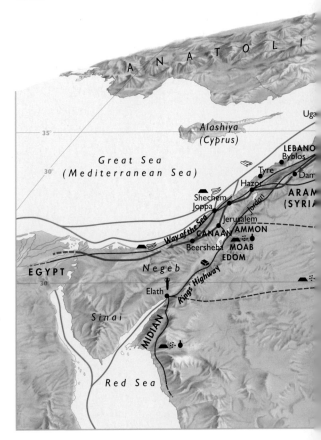

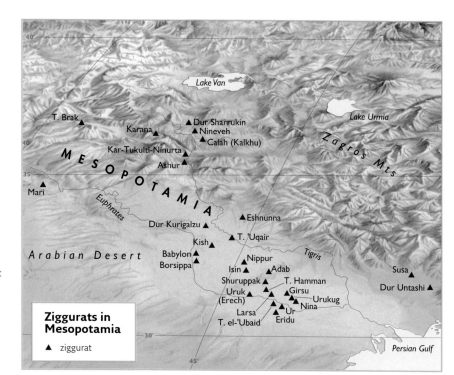

Ziggurats in Mesopotamia

▲ ziggurat

The ancient Near East was not a trackless waste but was covered with an extensive network of trade routes (*map below*). Distribution of ziggurats, or stepped temple towers, in Mesopotamia (*map right*).

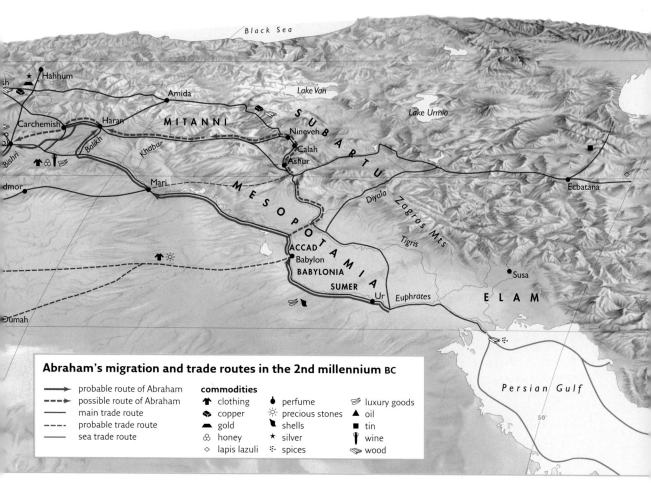

Abraham's migration and trade routes in the 2nd millennium BC

➡	probable route of Abraham	**commodities**	
┅➡	possible route of Abraham	↟ clothing	⬥ perfume	≋ luxury goods
─	main trade route	⬗ copper	☼ precious stones	▲ oil
┄	probable trade route	◣ gold	↘ shells	■ tin
─	sea trade route	⊛ honey	★ silver	⚘ wine
		◇ lapis lazuli	⁂ spices	≋ wood

Wanderings and journeys of the patriarchs

The patriarchal stories mention only a few cities in Palestine, and only about a dozen of these can be identified on a map. In general, the patriarchs are portrayed as pastoralists who avoided the urban life of Canaan.

The patriarchs Abraham and Isaac generally confined their wanderings to the central hill country of Palestine, along the watershed route from Shechem to Hebron via Bethel and on to the biblical Negeb at Beersheba. The only forays toward the coast were to Gerar (*Gen 20.26*). Abraham also made a military expedition to Dan (Laish) and near Damascus (*Gen 14.14–15*).

However, Abraham still had strong links with Haran. His son, Isaac, found his wife nearby (*Gen 24*), and Jacob spent 20 years of his life around Haran. Haran had two claims to fame: its position on international trade routes and its reputation as the center for the worship of Sin, the moon god.

Jacob's journeys

After falling out with his brother Esau (*Gen 27.41–46*), Jacob fled from Beersheba to Bethel (Luz), where he dreamt of the staircase reaching to heaven (*Gen 28.10–22*). He traveled to Haran, where he married his cousin Leah and her sister, Rachel (*Gen 29–30*). After a dispute with his father-in-law Laban, Jacob fled towards Palestine (*Gen 31.17–21*). Laban caught up with him in the region of Gilead, where, after a tense meeting, they marked their agreement by heaping up stones (*Gen 31.22–55*). Jacob continued toward Mahanaim and Penuel, where, after a divine encounter, he became reconciled with Esau (*Gen 32–33*). He proceeded on to Succoth, where he built accommodation for himself and his cattle (*Gen 33.17*). At Shechem, he bought some land and built an altar (*Gen 33.18–20*). He returned to Bethel, where God changed Jacob's name to Israel (*Gen 35.1–15*). When Rachel died,

Jacob buried her in Bethlehem and finally settled where his father had lived, at Hebron (*Gen 35.27–29, 37.1–2*).

Archaeology at Mari and Ebla

Excavations at Mari on the Upper Euphrates and at Ebla in northern Syria reveal a high culture and extensive trade in the Levant. The Palace of Zimri-Lim at Mari, discovered in 1933, provides a record of life in this region during the first half of the 2nd millennium BC. Cuneiform tablets - some 25,000 texts have been found - show that Mari traded with the cities of Canaan, Hattusha in Anatolia, and even with the centers of commerce in Alashiya (Cyprus) and Crete. Shipments of tin from Hazor and Laish (Dan) are also mentioned.

Contemporary with Mari was Ebla, discovered in 1964 at T.Mardikh (see p.34). The site contained thousands of cuneiform tablets providing details about international trade and politics from Mesopotamia to Palestine between about 2400 and 2250 BC. T. Mardikh was also occupied in the later Old Syrian period (c. 2000–1600 BC). Architectural features from this later period demonstrate significant connections with Canaan.

Genesis 28-29 describes how Jacob left Canaan and went to Haran, where he married his two cousins, Leah and Rachel. He eventually returned home over 20 years later and was united with Isaac at Hebron (*map right*).

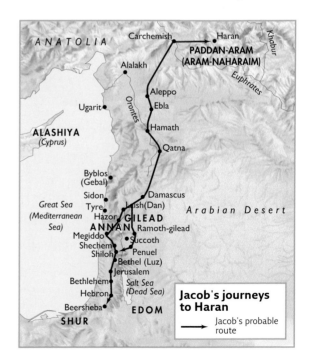

Jacob's journeys to Haran

→ Jacob's probable route

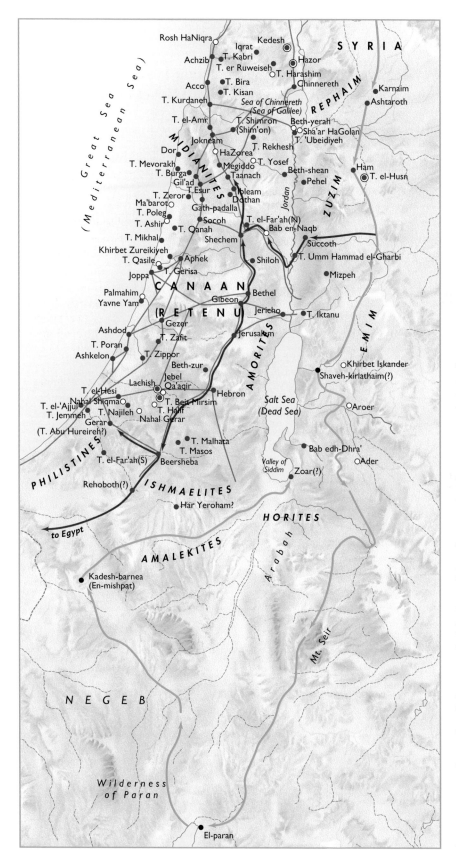

The wanderings of Abraham in Canaan, the wars of Chedorlaomer in Transjordan, the Dead Sea area and the south (exact locations of peoples are conjectural), and settlement patterns in the Middle Bronze Age (*map left*). According to Genesis 14, Chedorlaomer led a coalition of four kings against the Rephaim, Zuzim, Emim, Horites, Amalekites, and Amorites. The coalition finally put down a rebellion by five other kings in a battle in the Valley of Siddim. After plundering Sodom and Gomorrah and capturing Abram's nephew Lot, they were defeated by Abram on their way back.

Patriarchal routes in Canaan according to Genesis

→ Abraham's journeys in Canaan (*Gen 12–13*)

→ Chedorlaomer's campaign against the Canaanite king's (*Gen. 14*)

○ Middle Bronze Age I site, (2200–2000 BC)

● Middle Bronze Age II site, (2000–1550 BC)

— major route

Jacob and Joseph

Genesis 37–50 tells how Joseph came to Egypt and rose to power. Eventually, his family - the progenitors of the tribes of Israel - settled in Egypt to escape famine in Canaan.

These events cannot be dated with any certainty, since Joseph is not mentioned in any Egyptian writings and the biblical narratives do not give the names of the pharaohs or any datable events. However, the stories do depict aspects of Egyptian society that are paralleled by other sources.

Joseph was taken to Egypt by Midianite or Ishmaelite traders, one of many groups that visited Egypt during the first half of the 2nd millennium BC.

The Canaanite towns of Shechem and Dothan, which feature in Joseph's travels, are also attested in external sources for this general period.

The list of one large Egyptian household (c. 1740 BC) contains the names of 79 domestic servants, over half of them "Asiatic" with Semitic names. While many Asiatics spent their life in Egypt in service, others are known to have reached high office, just as Joseph is said to have done.

The Papyrus D'Orbiney, dated about 1225 BC, tells of the attempted seduction of a moral young man by his elder brother's wife. When her advances are rejected, she accuses the young man of attempted rape, an episode that bears a marked resemblance to Joseph's rejection of the advances of Potiphar's wife (Gen 39).

This rejection landed Joseph in jail. A section of an ancient prison register and other monuments reveal that major prisons had a director, whose role was like that of the captain of the guard (Gen 40.3), and keepers, similar to the chief jailer (Gen 39.21–22).

Butlers or cupbearers were prominent at the courts of the pharaohs, often playing important administrative roles at the king's direct command. Joseph's ability to interpret

dreams accords with Egyptian beliefs in the importance of such practices; there exist instruction manuals in this art.

When he was appointed to high office, he was given a collar of gold and the royal seal. This was a regular custom.

Joseph's brothers arrive in Egypt to buy grain. A fertile country, Egypt normally produced surplus crops, and there are records of starving foreigners arriving to ask for assistance. Sometimes the harvest failed repeatedly – an event that may be the basis for the tradition of "seven lean years" (Gen 41).

Finally, the manner in which Joseph was embalmed and laid in a coffin was not a Hebrew custom but was typical of the practices of the Egyptians (Gen 50.26).

Egyptian execration texts

The execration texts are the earliest known lists of cities, regions, and governors of Palestine and Syria. These are three groups of short inscriptions written on small bowls

Places identified from Egyptian execration texts

- ● town from c. 1900 BC text
- ◉ town from c. 1800 BC text

unidentified locations from c.1900 BC text	from c.1800 BC text
'Ahumuta	'Aqlaya/'Aqraya
Anharu	'As'apa
Arhanu	'Enya
As'annu	'-f-r-?-a
Mutara	Haramu
Qahlamu	Harimu
Raqaha	Hasasum
Yamu'aru	Marsih-ki (North & South)
Ya'nuqa	Masha
Yarimuta	Mash'ala
Yas'apa	Qarqarum
	Rayata
	Sa'pum
	Shalam-'il(?)
	Shariyanu
	Surudanu
	Yabilya

and figurines, which include curses directed at Egypt's enemies. The objects were then smashed and buried, symbolizing their defeat and destruction. Only a few cities are mentioned in the first of the lists (written c. 1900 BC) including Jerusalem, Ashkelon, and Rehob. The appearance of more cities on a later list (c. 1800 BC) illustrates the urbanization of the region. Among the names mentioned are the foreign rulers of Retenu (Canaan) and cities such as Shechem, Ashtaroth, Hazor, and Acre. Along with the personal names are their towns, many of which are known from the Bible and other texts. The texts reflect a pattern of settlement similar to that which continues into the Late Bronze Age, with a concentration of towns in the plains. Only Shechem and Jerusalem are listed in the hill country.

The coming of the Hyksos

In Egyptian history the best remembered influx of a Semitic people into Egypt was that of the Hyksos. Although some scholars have attempted to connect the entry of Joseph with the Hyksos invasion, all we really know is that foreigners migrated to Egypt from c. 1800 to c. 1650 BC, finding places in Egyptian society. About 1674 BC, one of these Hyksos rulers finally took the Egyptian throne, founding a new regime, the so-called 15th or Hyksos dynasty. The extent of their authority in Canaan is uncertain; certainly Apepi was termed "Ruler of Retenu" by his opponent Kamose of Thebes; this could imply rule of part of Palestine. Archaeological finds suggest a sphere of direct rule as far north as Joppa, and reaching along the western foothills of Canaan from Gezer to Tell Beit Mirsim.

Joseph and the Hyksos empire

→ route of Midianite traders
→ route of Joseph
←→ route of the Hyksos
◉ Hyksos capital
• scarab with Hyksos name
—— extent of Hyksos rule
- - - extent of Hyksos influence

Joseph was sold by his brothers to the Midianites, who were traveling from Gilead to Egypt (*map below*). There, Joseph's purchaser could have been in royal service at Rowaty/Avaris.

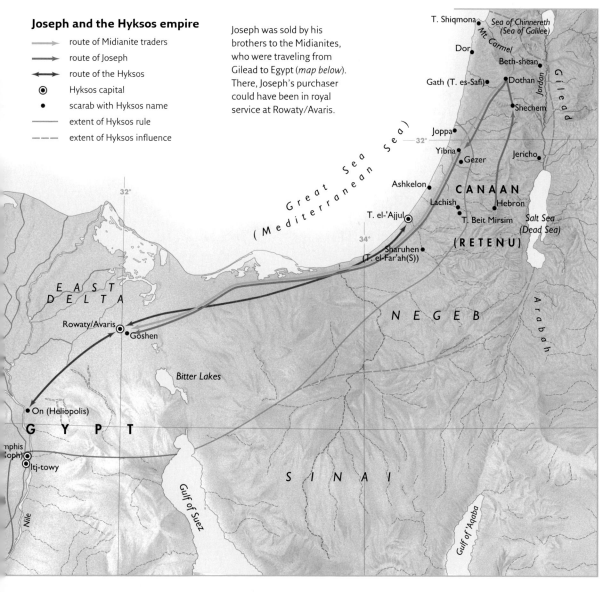

THREE

EGYPT AND THE EXODUS

Ramesses II at Abu Simbel.
One of four colossal statues of the Pharaoh
at the entrance to the "Temple of Ramesses,
beloved by Amun." Each statue is some
20 meters high.

Egyptian expansion into Canaan

The book of Genesis ends with the Hebrews settling down to live in Egypt, where they stayed, according to their tradition, for 400 years (*Gen 15.13*). However, the Bible contains no information about Palestine or its patterns of settlement during this time.

The records of eight pharaohs, who made military expeditions into Palestine and Syria over a period of about 300 years (c. 1450–1200 BC), allow us to fill in some of the blanks. Their lists of conquered cities and the routes of their marches feature the names of about 90 cities and towns of Canaan, many of which feature in the subsequent history of Israel.

Tuthmose III

Tuthmose III (1479–1425 BC) established Egypt's control of Canaan by making campaigns into Asia almost annually from the 22nd to the 42nd year of his reign. Through the "annals," carved on the walls of the Temple of Amon at Thebes as a memorial to the god who had given him victory, Tuthmose is responsible for one of the most factually reliable sources for the geography and history of Palestine.

In the 23rd year of his reign (c. 1457 BC), he won a dramatic and daring victory at Megiddo over a league of Canaanite rulers. The Canaanite coalition had occupied the best tactical position on the plains and, not knowing by which of the three possible routes the Egyptians intended to cross the Carmel range, chose to block the two most obvious routes. Tuthmose rejected his officers' advice and marched his army single file though the narrow pass directly to Megiddo, taking the enemy completely by surprise. Eventually, the Canaanites broke ranks and ran. Megiddo was placed under siege, and six months later it capitulated.

Amenhotep II

Amenhotep II, son of Tuthmose III, began his "first campaign" (as sole ruler) against his archrival Mitanni. The first encounter took place at Shemesh-adam (Shamshu-'Adam), and the northernmost town mentioned is Aleppo (Khalab). He arrived at Niyi where he received intelligence about an attempt to dislodge an Egyptian garrison at a place, which was possibly Ugarit. Amenhotep went in person to that city and quelled the rebellion. He then camped at Salqa, a town known to belong to the kingdom of Alalakh. After plundering the village of Mansatu, Amenhotep was cordially received at two unidentified towns north of Qadesh. Afterwards, Amenhotep went hunting in the forest of Lebo (Lebo-hamath) and then proceeded to put down resistance at Khashabu, in the Lebanese Beqaa Valley.

In the ninth year of his reign, Amenhotep II was again on the road to Retenu (Canaan), visiting Aphek, Socoh, Yaham, and Adoren and traveling through the Valley of Jezreel to Anuhartu and Geba-somen, where he was summarily arrested and a new ruler was appointed.

In addition to geographical information, the inscriptions of Amenhotep II also give a glimpse into the social strata of the Levant during the 15th century BC. Along with lists of booty are also the names of rulers; the oligarchs who supported them, including the chariot warriors; and geographical groups such as Canaanites, the people of Nukhashshe (Syria north of Tunip), Bedouin, and the "outcasts" ('apiru).

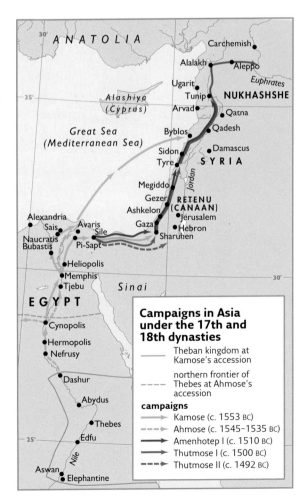

Campaigns in Asia under the 17th and 18th dynasties

— Theban kingdom at Kamose's accession

---- northern frontier of Thebes at Ahmose's accession

campaigns

→ Kamose (c. 1553 BC)

--→ Ahmose (c. 1545–1535 BC)

→ Amenhotep I (c. 1510 BC)

→ Thutmose I (c. 1500 BC)

--→ Thutmose II (c. 1492 BC)

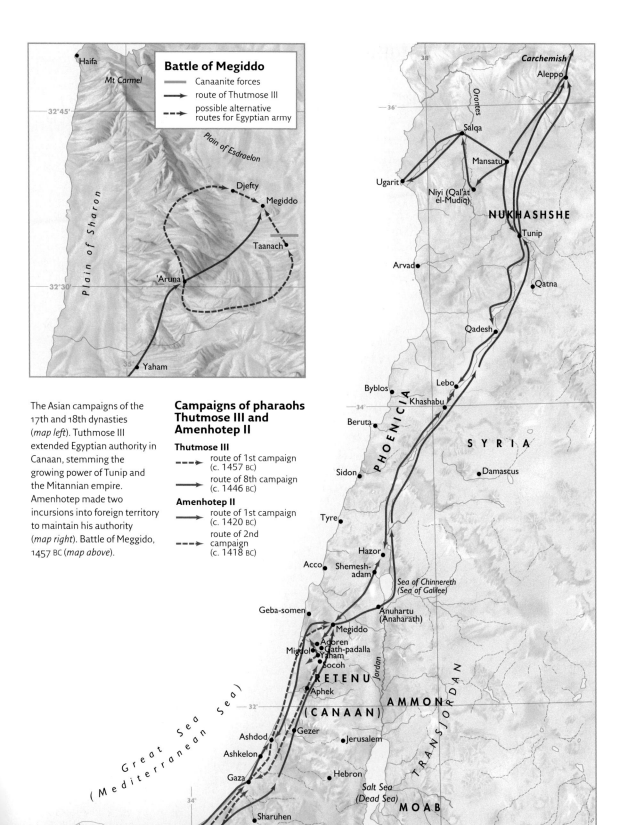

Battle of Megiddo

━━━ Canaanite forces

──▶ route of Thutmose III

- - -▶ possible alternative routes for Egyptian army

Haifa

Mt Carmel

32°45'

Plain of Esdraelon

Plain of Sharon

Djefty

Megiddo

32°30'

Taanach

'Aruna

35°

Yaham

The Asian campaigns of the 17th and 18th dynasties (*map left*). Tuthmose III extended Egyptian authority in Canaan, stemming the growing power of Tunip and the Mitannian empire. Amenhotep made two incursions into foreign territory to maintain his authority (*map right*). Battle of Meggido, 1457 BC (*map above*).

Campaigns of pharaohs Thutmose III and Amenhotep II

Thutmose III

- - -▶ route of 1st campaign (c. 1457 BC)

──▶ route of 8th campaign (c. 1446 BC)

Amenhotep II

──▶ route of 1st campaign (c. 1420 BC)

- - -▶ route of 2nd campaign (c. 1418 BC)

Carchemish

Aleppo

38

Orontes

36

Salqa

Mansatu

Ugarit

Niyi (Qal'at el-Mudiq)

NUKHASHSHE

Arvad

Tunip

Qatna

Qadesh

Byblos

Lebo

Khashabu

Beruta

34

PHOENICIA

SYRIA

Sidon

Damascus

Tyre

Hazor

Acco

Shemesh-adam

Sea of Chinnereth (Sea of Galilee)

Geba-somen

Megiddo

Anuhartu (Anaharath)

Adoren

Gath-padalla

Migdol

Yaham

Jordan

TRANSJORDAN

Socoh

RETENU

AMMON

Aphek

(CANAAN)

32

Ashdod

Gezer

Jerusalem

Ashkelon

Gaza

Hebron

Salt Sea (Dead Sea)

Great Sea (Mediterranean Sea)

34

MOAB

Sharuhen

YPT

NEGEB

EDOM

Ugarit - center of trade and influence

During the two documented centuries of Ugarit's civilization (1400–1200 BC), no city of the ancient Near East provides such a diverse and rich profile as Ugarit's. Destroyed by the disasters at the end of the 13th century - disasters that brought to an end most of the great Bronze Age civilizations of the Levant - it would be centuries before the Phoenician cities of the south would once again match the sophistication of Ugarit's culture.

Ugarit was first discovered in 1928, when a Syrian farmer accidentally uncovered some ancient tombs. The ensuing archaeological excavation resulted in one of the greatest finds ever: the archives of the ancient kingdom of Ugarit. There were thousands of cuneiform tablets in an alphabetic script that, when deciphered, proved to be part of a family of Semitic languages that included Hebrew and Aramaic. Subsequent excavations have revealed many more tablets: in 1958, archaeologists discovered another library; in 1973, rescue excavations revealed around 120 tablets; in 1994, over 300 tablets covering the final years of the city's existence were discovered.

The tablets not only proved invaluable in enhancing our understanding of biblical Hebrew, they also contributed hugely to our knowledge of Canaanite religion, revealing much more about Canaanite deities such as Baal, El, and Asherah (Athirat in Ugaritic). They also revealed details of a society that formed the center of a trading network covering the Levant, Anatolia, and Greece. The remarkable Near Eastern culture is known from archaeological records discovered at Ras Shamra itself, and from written records found in Ebla, Mari, Egypt, and the Hittite capital of Hattushash (modern Boğazköy). The city was already established in the 25th century BC, when it was referred to in the Early Bronze Age records of the city of Ebla. The kingdom of Ugarit, with a heavily fortified capital of over 52 acres, extended over some 1300 square miles of fertile countryside.

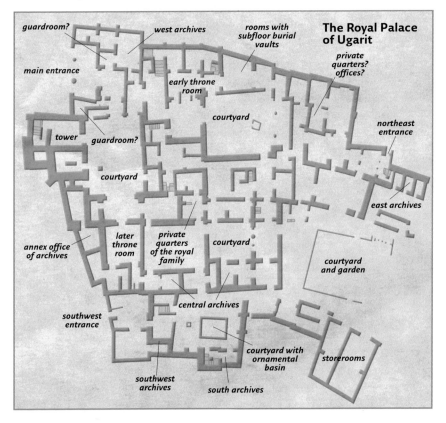

The Royal Palace of Ugarit

- guardroom?
- west archives
- rooms with subfloor burial vaults
- private quarters? offices?
- main entrance
- early throne room
- courtyard
- northeast entrance
- tower
- guardroom?
- courtyard
- east archives
- annex office of archives
- later throne room
- private quarters of the royal family
- courtyard
- courtyard and garden
- southwest entrance
- central archives
- courtyard with ornamental basin
- storerooms
- southwest archives
- south archives

The Late Bronze age (1550–1200 BC) Royal Palace of Ugarit was a cluster of rooms and courtyards covering an area of over 3000 square yards (*plan left*). Ugarit had the finest natural harbor on the eastern Mediterranean coast. Its unique strategic location linked land and sea routes (*map right*).

Donkey caravans converged on the city from Syria, Mesopotamia, and Anatolia to exchange goods with merchants from Canaan and Egypt as well as the maritime traders who arrived by ship from Alashiya (Cyprus) and Kaptaru (Crete) and the Aegean. Ugarit's industries - textiles, ivory, metal, agriculture products, timber, ceramics, and handicrafts - converted raw materials into goods for further trade and export on hundreds of ships, controlled by the Crown, that ventured to markets as far afield as Egypt and Crete, and perhaps beyond. Two recent excavations of ships from the 14th and 13th centuries BC off the south coast of Turkey (at Kas and at Cape Gelidonya) illustrate the variety of goods carried: copper, tin, tools, chemicals, glass ingots, faience and amber beads, ceramics (Canaanite, Cypriot and Mycenaean), ivory, jewelery, semiprecious stones, timber, and foodstuff. Merchants also carried weights reflecting standards in different areas, personal seals,

and equipment for manufacturing metal goods en route.

Goods were exchanged by barter, but values were calculated by the equivalent value of silver. Tin, essential in the production of bronze, was transshipped from Ugarit in ingot form. Ships also transported livestock and, occasionally, more exotic animals. Ugarit was a cosmopolitan city formed by diverse ethnic and linguistic groups. There were ten different languages in five different scripts, one of which, alphabetic cuneiform, was probably developed in the local scribal academy. Through international treaties and via a sophisticated legal system, the merchants were assured safety and correct dealings. The political skills of Ugarit's rulers allowed the kingdom to participate in international trade by walking a tightrope between the two major powers of the era, Hatti and Egypt, although bound to the former by vassal treaty for much of the period.

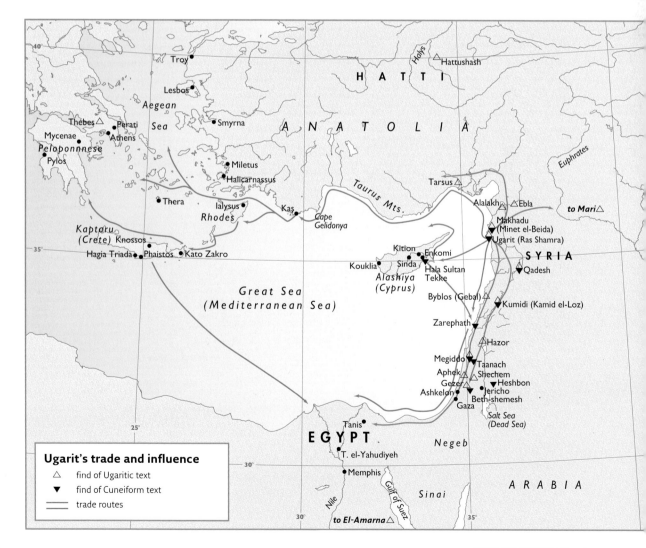

Ugarit's trade and influence

△   find of Ugaritic text

▼   find of Cuneiform text

──   trade routes

The Amarna tablets and Sety I's campaigns

The archive of about 380 texts and fragments from the ruins of El-Amarna (the official modern name of Akhetaten) tells us much about Canaan during a time about which the Bible is silent (c. 1400–1350 BC).

The clay tablets include letters from Canaanite rulers describing the turbulent local situation in Palestine. The documents are written in the cuneiform script, and almost all are in various dialects of the Akkadian language, the language commonly used for international correspondence. The texts from Canaan contain examples of local inflection and syntax. The documents are mostly letters written to or by Pharaohs Amenhotep III (1390–1352 BC), Amenhotep IV (better known as Akhenaten; 1352–1336 BC), and Tutankhamun (1336–1327 BC). The tablets were discarded when Akhetaten was destroyed by Horemheb.

Canaan

The Amarna tablets show that the area of direct Egyptian control conformed more or less to the biblical description of the borders of Canaan (*Num 34.1–12*), with the addition of the states of Qatna, Qadesh (on the Orontes), and Amurru (on both sides of the Nahr el-Kebir, the classical Eleutherus). Canaan's international status as a legal-political entity is confirmed by a document from Ugarit in which the "sons [citizens] of Canaan" had to pay an indemnity to the "sons [citizens] of Ugarit." The Egyptians maintained administrative centers in Canaan, with commissioners posted at Gaza, Sumur (Simyra), and Kumidi. They also had a supply base at Yarimuta (unidentified) and a major ordnance base at Joppa. Troops posted at Beth-shean protected the caravan route that crossed the Jordan on the way to Damascus. Other units were stationed at city-states such as Jerusalem, and were recruited from Nubian (Cushite) and other subject peoples.

City-states

Canaanite society consisted of small city-states with one town at the center, often with subordinate neighboring towns. All the villages nearby were subject to this local king and his noblemen. The land was cultivated by tenant farmers who also served as infantry. Every city-state was subject to tribute payments, and its fighting men were subject to call-up whenever the Egyptian king required them to march with his army.

Clay tablets from El-Amarna name places in Canaan, thus proving their existence in the 14th century BC (*box left*). Sety I's campaign to restore Egyptian authority (*map right*).

The Amarna tablets

The following text is a translation of an Amarna tablet. Yahtiri, governor of Gaza and Joppa (c. 1400 BC), writes to the pharaoh for permission to come to Egypt to serve in his army:

"To the king my lord, my pantheon and my Sun god I speak: thus says Yahtiri, your servant, the dust of your feet. At the feet of the king my lord, my pantheon and my Sun god, seven and seven times I fell. Moreover, I am a faithful servant of the king my lord. I looked here and I looked there, but there was no light; I look to the king my lord and there is light. And even though one brick might move from beneath its neighbor, I will not move from beneath the feet of the king my lord. And let the king my lord ask Yanhamu, his deputy! When I was young he brought me to Egypt, and I served the king my lord, and I stood in the gate of the king my lord. And let the king my lord ask his deputy whether I guard the gate of Azzati and the gate of Yapu. And I, with the troops of the king my lord, will go wherever they go. And now indeed have I set the front of the king's yoke upon my neck, and I will bear it."

The 'apiru

The 'apiru ("outlaws" or "renegades") were runaways who, for various reasons, had to flee from their home regions or city-states. They tended to band together in isolated places like the forested hillsides of the Lebanon, the sparsely settled hill country around Shechem, or on the ridges of Upper Galilee. Whenever they appear in the Amarna letters, they are engaged in violent or subversive activity on behalf of one or other of the city-state rulers. They had a major role in founding the state of Amurru on the northern border of Canaan.

Campaign of Sety I

In about 1294 BC, Pharaoh Sety I received intelligence that the headman of Hammath, in concert with the town of Pella, was harassing the towns of Beth-shean and Rehob. He also heard that a large number of bedouin Sutu (Shasu) had moved into the Negeb and north Sinai, thus posing a threat to Egypt's land route to Asia. The army easily defeated the Sutu, took Gaza, and moved up the coast, probably to Acco, where Sety despatched three divisions to successfully quell the Hammath disturbance.

Reliefs at Karnak show more of the campaign, including the felling of timber in the Lebanon by Canaanite chiefs, and a sequence of places along the Phoenician coast (Tyre, Uzu, and Ullaza being the best known). Probably these mark the main itinerary of the expedition (a stela of Sety was, in fact, recovered from Tyre).

The campaign of Pharaoh Sety I, 1294 BC

route of Sety's army
1 first division of Amun
2 first divison of Re
3 first division of Sutekh
route of armies from Hammath and Pella
route of Sutu

cities named in the Amarna tablets
■ city
■ city governed by Egyptian ruler
■ center of Egyptian authority

Ramesses II of Egypt in contest with the Hittite empire

In the early part of the 13th century BC, the Egyptians and the Hittites, two major world powers, struggled to control the Syro-Palestinian area. Bas-reliefs on the Ramesseum at Thebes record six campaigns of Pharaoh Ramesses II in the Levant, as well as a detailed description of the battle of Qadesh. As well as data on the geography of Canaan, the records include information about espionage, surprise attacks, and skillful military maneuvers - the kind of military tactics that were later used by the Israelites against the Canaanites, as told in the book of Joshua.

Pharaoh Ramesses II spent at least a decade trying to recapture Egypt's Syrian possessions. In the fourth year of his reign (c. 1275), he swept north through the Egyptian province of Canaan and along the Lebanese coast through Tyre and Byblos. Ramesses then struck a surprise attack on Amurru itself, forcing its ruler to acknowledge Egyptian overlordship. The following year, he returned, but the Battle of Qadesh proved inconclusive (*see box*). In 1271 BC, Ramesses led a campaign to crush unrest in Galilee (and probably in Transjordan), recover the province of Upe, and strengthen his hold on the Phoenician coastlands. Two years later, he was back north again, leading an attack on Dapur.

Battle of Qadesh, 1274 BC

☐ Egyptians   ☐ Hittites

Prior to the battle, Ramesses II divided his force into two parts at Gaza. An elite corps - the Ne'arim - went up the coast to rendezvous with Ramesses from the north. The pharaoh led the main force to the Qadesh ridge, from which he could see the city. He encountered two bedouin, planted by the Hittites to give false information, that mis-led Ramesses to cross the Orontes and set up camp, unaware that his foe was just to the east of Qadesh.

Phase 1
Ramesses soon became aware of his predicament, and aides were sent to hasten the arrival of the division of Ptah and Seth. However, the Hittite chariot force swept west over the Orontes and scattered the 2nd Egyptian division of Re.

Phase 2
The Hittites then attacked the Amun division and plundered Ramesses' camp. Egyptian chariot units escaped and reformed to the north.

Phase 3
The elite force of the Ne'arim then arrived from the north and joined with Ramesses' reserves to push the Hittites back to the river Orontes.

Phase 4
The Egyptians then pushed the Hittites in a mad scramble across the Orontes. The next day, Ramesses launched his own counterattack, but the Hittite infantry stood firm. The

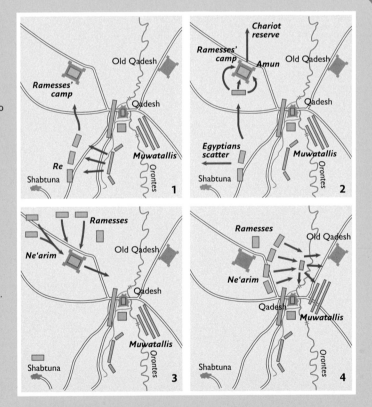

Hittite king, Muwatallis, proposed peace; Amurru and Qadesh would remain Hittite, while Egypt retained the coastland up to Simyra. When Ramesses returned to Egypt, Muwatallis reclaimed Amurru and Qadesh and even proceeded to invade the Egyptian province of Upe (including Damascus).

As long as the powerful Hittite centers at Aleppo and Carchemish remained untouched, raids on lesser city-states like Dapur were doomed to failure. When the Hittite king Mursil III was ejected from office by his uncle (who took power as Hattusil III), the dethroned king fled to Egypt. When extradition was refused, Hattusil threatened war, and Ramesses II made an expedition northwards as far as Beth-shean. In 1261 BC, Hattusil opened negotiations and, eventually, a treaty of peace and alliance was drawn up. Egypto-Hittite relations became so close that Hattusil III married off two of his daughters to the pharaoh.

The Egyptian empire in the Levant, 13th century BC, and the campaigns of Ramesses II of Egypt (*map right*).

The Egyptian empire in the Levant, 13th century BC

- —— limit of Egyptian rule
- —— approximate limit of the three main provinces of Egypt
- —— Transjordan state subject to Egypt
- ■ Egyptian capital
- ■ provincial center and Levant possessions

campaigns of Ramesses II of Egypt

- ——▶ Year 4 (1275 BC) to Amurru
- ——▶ Year 5 to Qadesh (main force)
- – – ▶ Year 5 (elite Ne'arim forces)
- ——▶ Year 8 to Galilee
- – – ▶ to Edom and Moab (undated)
- ——▶ Year 10 to Phonecia
- – – ▶ to North Syria (undated)

Map labels:

HITTITE EMPIRE
NIYI
TUNIP
Ugarit
Dapur
Arvad
Simyra (of Ramesses?)
Nahr el-Kebir
Qadesh
Byblos
Kawil
Beruta
AMURRU
Beqa'a
SYRIA
Kumidi
Year 5
Damascus
Sidon
UPE
Nahr el-Kalb
Tyre
Year 8
Beth-anath
Acco
Merom
Kanah
Sea of Chinnereth (Sea of Galilee)
Sheikh Sa'd
GALILEE
Beth-shean
Megiddo
'Ain Na'm
Jordan
TRANSJORDAN
CANAAN
(Mediterranean Sea) Great Sea
Year 5
Year 4
MOAB
Ashkelon
Dibon
Salt Sea (Dead Sea)
Gaza
Butartu
SEIR (EDOM)
NEGEB
Ramesses
Sile
Year 10
Pi-Ramesse
LOWER EGYPT
SINAI
Timna' copper mines
polis

Routes of a scribe and Pharaoh Merneptah

In the 19th century, a Greek merchant, Anastasi, who lived in Alexandria, discovered a document written by an Egyptian scribe. The document is in the form of a satirical letter from one scribe (Hori) to another (Amenemope), in which Hori shows up the ignorance and incompetence of his colleague in matters of Syrian geography.

Unlike the pompous accounts of victories so characteristic of the pharaohs, this source of geographic information is often humorous and informative about other matters of human interest. In the sixth section, the scribe pictures his rival penetrating the rocky ravine (through the Carmel ridge) on his way to Joppa: "The narrow ravine is infested with bedouin hiding in the bushes, men seven or nine feet tall from head to toe, ferocious and merciless, heedless of pleas. You're on your own, no one to help you.... Your path is strewn with boulders and pebbles, overgrown... the abyss yawns on one side, and the mountain towers up on the other..."

The final geographical section is a gazetteer of 12 principal forts and wells along the Sinai coastal road from Sile on the Egyptian border to Gaza in Canaan.

Pharaoh Merneptah

When Ramesses II died in his sixty-seventh year of sole reign, the throne passed to his thirteenth son Merneptah,

The author of the "Satirical Letter" picks out the main coast-roads from Phoenicia to Egypt (map right).

Routes in Papyrus Anastasi I

——	Section I
----	Section II
——	Section III
----	Section IV
——	Section V
——	Section VI
----	Section VII
■	Egyptian captial
●	Egyptian administrative center
⛫	fort
╱╱	ford

to Hatti

Ugarit

Orontes

S Y R

Dapur

Simyra

the Magur

Mt. Shawi

Hermil

Qadesh

TAMINTA

Byblos

TAKHSI

Beirut

Beqaa

PHOENICIA

Kumidi

Litani

Sidon

Damascus

Sarepta

Tyre
Uzu

U P E

Selaim

Hazor

Adurun

Acco

Hammath

Achshaph

Sea of Chinnereth (Sea of Galilee)

Adummim

Yenoam

Megiddo

Qiryat-'Aanab

Rehob

Beth-shean

Bedouin Ravine

Shechem

Jordan

(M e d i t e r r a n e a n   S e a)
G r e a t   S e a

Joppa

CANAAN
(RETENU)

Salt Sea (Dead Sea)

Gaza

Rapah

El-'Arish

A r a b i a n   D e s e r t

L O W E R

N E G E B

E G Y P T

Arabah

Sile

S I N A I

Pi-Ramesse

a man already in his fifties. Although almost half a century of peace had elapsed since the famous Hittite treaty, Merneptah dispatched an expedition to put down any unrest following his succession. The blows fell on the towns of Ashkelon, Gezer, and Yenoam, and defeat was inflicted on a "new" people, Israel, apparently still settling in the hill country. This allusion, in a triumphal hymn of Merneptah to his fifth year (inscribed on the Merneptah stele), is the earliest mention of Israel in ancient documents. It sets that people's initial entry into Canaan at an undetermined date prior to the first five years of Merneptah's reign - that is before 1208 BC - or other dates adopted for his accession.

By year 3 of the pharaoh, a register shows the arrivals and departures of royal messengers based at the Delta capital of Pi-Ramesse and traveling via the border port of Sile. Besides the expected links with Gaza, a letter goes to the Prince of Tyre, and three centers of royal rule are mentioned. The "Wells of Merneptah" (doubtless with a fort) were probably the "Waters of Nephtoah" of the Bible (Josh 15.9, 18.15), being "on the [mountain] ridge" at Lifta, just northwest of Jerusalem. Such a strongpoint would have enabled Merneptah's agents to keep an eye on the growing conflicts between the Canaanites and the Israelites.

A second center of rule was the Castle of Merneptah near Selalim (a slip for Selaim?), probably a new fort to guard the coastal pass at Ras en-Nakura just south of Tyre. A third center, "the Town of Merneptah in the district of Pi-Aram," is most likely the Beqa'a center Kumidi, renamed from its former epithet "Town of Ramesses II in the Cedar Valley."

Pharaoh Merneptah and the Levant

➡	Merneptah's campaign, year 1–2
➡	route of royal messenger
➡	tribute taken from Lachish to Gaza
➡	direction of Egyptian expansion
✕	battle
■	Egyptian capital
●	Egyptian administrative center
▥	fort
≲	ford
—	approximate boundary of Egyptian rule

Pharaoh Merneptah quickly crushed any signs of revolt in Canaan after his father's death. His forces struck successively at Ashkelon, Gezer, and Yenoam, engaging also with elements from the people of Israel, then settling in the hill country of Canaan (*map right*).

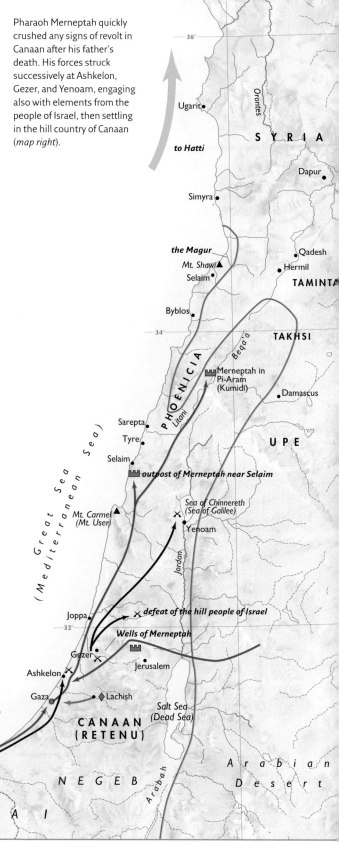

Canaan's trade with Mycenae and Cyprus

The era before the coming of the Israelites was marked by a cosmopolitan culture in Canaan. From archaeological discoveries in Syria and Palestine, it is possible to chart the routes from ports to inland cities and to date more precisely the layers of debris by the types of imported pottery found within them.

Mycenaean pottery is found at about 100 excavated sites in the Levant and Egypt. The distinctive wheel-made pots are usually found with large deposits of Cypriot hand-made wares, illustrating international commerce in goods, people, and ideas in the Late Bronze Age.

Archaeological research shows that the need for improved defenses and weapons in Mycenae led to sustained efforts to obtain copper from Cyprus, and tin and luxuries from further east. Mycenaean (and a few Minoan) goods were perhaps distributed through the international market of Ugarit, where palace archives list commodities of likely Aegean origin, but Cyprus was always the prime target. Exported Mycenaean pottery traveled far beyond Cyprus as part of shipments of Cypriot handmade base-ring and white-slip wares (base-ring juglets may have been containers for opium). Since Mycenaeans needed the trade, it is likely that Aegean ships carried the metals home, together with exotic goods, known from excavation at Aegina, Athens, Mycenae, Gournia, and Kommos in Crete.

The excavation of a Late Bronze Age shipwreck off Kas, in southwest Turkey (now called the Ulu Burun wreck),

revealed a truly international cargo including copper, tin, and glass ingots; Syro-Palestinian amphorae, one packed with Cypriot pottery, others with traces of grapes, olives, and unidentified seeds; Mycenaean and Syrian pottery; artifacts and ornaments in faïence, amber, gold, and silver; and bronze weapons and tools.

Except at El-Amarna, the capital of Egypt under Akhenaten, and at Deir el-Medina, the artisan village at Thebes, no varied or large deposits of Mycenaean pottery have been found in Egypt, perhaps because it was at the end of the trade route.

In the cities of the Levant, menaced by hostility among Hittites and Egyptians, by internal faction, and external attack, Aegean imports were comforting luxuries that gave social status in life and death.

Mycenaean pottery

Mycenaean pottery was a highly organized industry. Pots were usually thrown, but some special shapes and most figurines were handmade. All Mycenaean pottery was unglazed and porous, and although burnishing before firing could reduce porosity, containers used for long-term

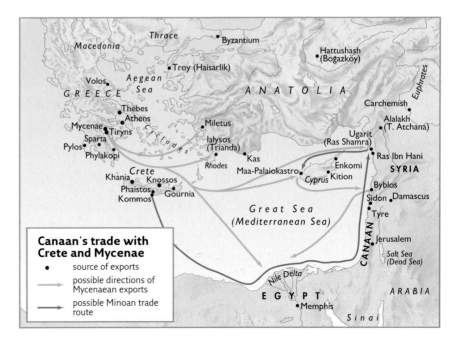

Trade routes for importing pottery from Crete and Greece (*map right*). The import of pottery from Cyprus to the Levant began in the Middle Bronze Age and reached its zenith in the late fifteenth and fourteenth centuries BC.

Canaan's trade with Crete and Mycenae

- •   source of exports
- →   possible directions of Mycenaean exports
- →   possible Minoan trade route

http://www.metmuseum.org/toah/hd/myce/hd_myce.htm
Examples of Mycenaean pottery and ceramics
http://projectsx.dartmouth.edu/history/bronze_age/lessons/
les/22.html
Aspects of Mycenaean trade
http://www.thebritishmuseum.ac.uk/explore/galleries/
ancient_greece_and_rome/room_12b_greece_mycenaeans.aspx
Mycenaean art in the British Museum

storage or transport had to be lined with resin, easily
obtainable in the Aegean. Color variation in body and
decoration show that kilns were vertical, like the Late
Bronze Age kilns excavated at Sarafand in Lebanon
or like simple modern kilns in the Mediterranean.
The stirrup or false-necked jar, Minoan in origin,
was designed for liquids, with a narrow pouring
spout and handle across the top like an inverted
stirrup. This popular shape was a hallmark of
Mycenaean activity, and survived after the
Mycenaeans were forgotten. Some pottery
was custom-made for the export market,
particularly the Mycenaean version of the
eastern "pilgrim flask" and the amphoroid
krater. The krater seems too big to drink
from, too small to use for burial. Its
decoration often celebrates a social,
religious, or official event, in which
chariots and horses
are prominent.

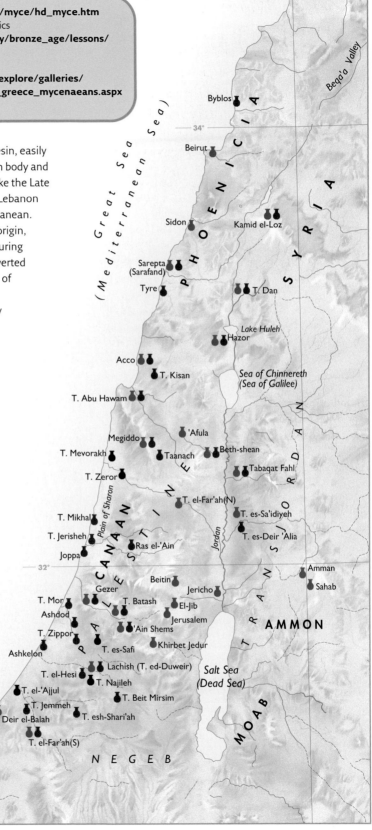

Late Bronze Age sites with
imported Minoan, Mycenaean,
or Cypriot pottery (*map right*).
As well as being a major
exporter of copper, Cyprus
acted as a commercial
"middleman" between the
Aegean world and the Levant.

**Finds of Minoan/
Mycenaean/Cypriot
pottery in Palestine**

🏺 settlement
🏺 tomb
🏺 undetermined

Changes beyond Israel's borders in the 13-12th centuries BC

At the end of the Late Bronze Age (c. 1200 BC), Israel was securing a foothold in Canaan. Little is said in the Bible of the movement of people and tribes in other parts of the Mediterranean, but there is reason to believe that in the eastern Mediterranean, the end of the Late Bronze Age was a time of mass movement of peoples and consequent warfare.

Texts from Boğazköy (Hattushah, the Hittite capital) and Ras Shamra (ancient Ugarit) show that, in the 12th century BC, invaders came into the area of the eastern Mediterranean by sea. Many place-names in the Mediterranean owe their origins to the Sea Peoples: Sardinia (from the Sherden), Sicily (the Sheklesh), Palestine (the Philistines or Peleset), Achaia (the Akwash or Akaiwasa), and Lycia (the Lukka).

Destruction levels are recorded at sites on Cyprus and along the Levantine coast. There is evidence that during the 12th century BC there were extensive migrations of peoples in the Levant and also in the Aegean. On the Greek mainland these destructions have been attributed to invaders from the north; in Cyprus and along the Levantine coast the destruction is seen as the work of the Sea Peoples. In Palestine, on the other hand, destructions that can be assigned to the same period have been seen as archaeological evidence for the conquest of Canaan by the Israelites in some areas and by the Philistine in others.

The Neo-Hittites

When the Hittite empire fell, the capital of Hattushah was burned to the ground in a massive conflagration. Archaeology does not tell us who was responsible for this destruction; however, following the defeat, the main centers of power moved from central Anatolia, at Boğazköy, Alaca Hüyük, and Masat, to the southeast, to the areas surrounding Melitene (Malatya), Carchemish, and Aleppo. It is there that the post-1200 BC development of the so-called Neo-Hittite (or Syro-Hittite) civilization arose. The Neo-Hittites are almost certainly the Hittites of the Bible, such as Uriah the Hittite, the husband of Bathsheba (2 Sam 11). Solomon brought horses from Kue (Cilicia) and chariots from Egypt

and sold them to "all the kings of the Hittites and to the kings of Syria" (1 Kings 10.28–29). Kue was known to the Bronze Age Hittites as Kizzuwadna, and the kings of Aram ruled over an Aramaean state that developed only after 1200 BC.

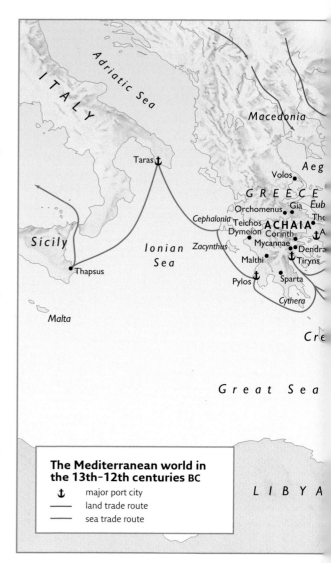

The Mediterranean world in the 13th–12th centuries BC

⚓   major port city
——   land trade route
——   sea trade route

The end of the Mycenaean civilization

The invaders who put an end to Mycanaean civilization at the end of the 13th century BC brought with them bronze weapons and a hitherto unknown type of crude, handmade pottery. Bronze helmets, corselets, and greaves became more popular than before. (Greaves were of special importance, offering protection against the new cut-and-thrust sword.) The most interesting aspect is the remarkable parallel between these new weapons and armor and the new style of fighting they must have entailed. Certain details in the story of David and Goliath, as recorded in 1 Samuel 17 may reflect these developments. The bronze armor worn by Goliath (1 Sam 17.5–7) fits the description of the "northern" warriors, whose path across the eastern Mediterranean seems to coincide with the destruction of all the major Late Bronze Age sites in the area.

> "He had a helmet of bronze on his head, and he was armed with a coat of mail; the weight of the coat was five thousand shekels of bronze. He had greaves of bronze on his legs and a javelin of bronze slung between his shoulders. The shaft of his spear was like a weaver's beam, and his spear's head weighed six hundred shekels of iron; and his shield-bearer went before him."
>
> **The armor of Goliath, as described in**
> **1 Samuel 17.5–7**

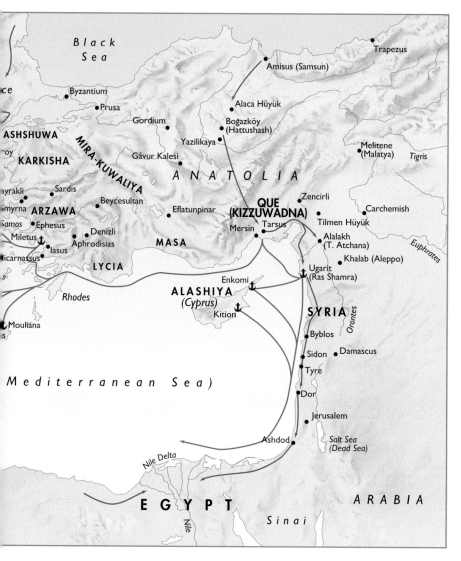

Trade routes of the 13th and 12th centuries BC, some utilized by the Mycenaeans and others followed by the Sea Peoples later (map left).

Route of the Exodus

The Exodus was the most important event in Israelite history. The captivity in Egypt, Yahweh's choice of Moses as deliverer, the plagues, escape, and the dangers of the journey to the Promised Land became a core part of the Israelites' oldest liturgy (*Deut 26.5–11*) and was celebrated in Passover - their most important festival.

Yet the dating of the event, and the route taken, is extremely difficult to confirm. Biblical chronology (*1 Kings 6.1*) places the Exodus about 1440 BC, 480 years before Solomon began to build the temple. Archaeological data, and information from elsewhere in the Bible, implies that this is too early. There is no reference to it in Egyptian records, but the background to the Exodus accords well with the 13th century BC, when the use of foreign labor is well attested, and the city of Ramesses (*Exod 1.11*) is often mentioned in Egyptian sources. The Merneptah stele shows that the Israelites had settled in Canaan by around 1208 BC, but how much earlier they arrived is impossible to say.

Some scholars doubt whether there was a single historical journey through the wilderness, but geographical study can seek to determine the route described in Numbers 33 and so discover how later generations of Israelites believed that their forefathers had traveled from Egypt to Canaan. However, Arabic names provide less help than usual in desert areas, and very few of the traditional locations are attested earlier than the 4th century AD. Research has to start with the limited number of places whose identification is relatively certain and choose between various routes linking them.

The route

The route of the Israelites through the wilderness is described in a series of itinerary notes in the books of Exodus, Numbers, and Judges (e.g. *Exod 12.37, 13.20; cf. 13.17–18*) and again more compactly in Numbers 33.1–49. Certain sections of the journey are described in other books of the Old Testament (*Deut 1.19–3.29; Judg 11.16–22*). The earliest accounts contain very little geographical information, only references to key points such as the Red Sea, Mount Sinai/Horeb, Kadesh, and the crossing of the river Jordan, and actually lay very little stress on movement from place to place at all. The notion of an Exodus route is due chiefly to Numbers 33.1–49, an itinerary composed on the pattern of similar documents known from other parts of the ancient Near East. It is probable that in Numbers 33 the references to Kadesh and Mount Hor originally preceded the mention of Ezion-geber, as is still the case with Kadesh in *Deut 1.2*. The idea that the Israelites passed through the wilderness east of Moab and Edom is not present in Numbers 33 (*Num 21.11–13; Deut 2.8; Judg 11.18*).

The spies

It is difficult to be precise about the route taken by the spies sent by Moses to report on the land to be occupied by the Israelite tribes. Two versions of the story of their mission appear (*Num 13.14; Deut 1.19–46*). Both list Kadesh, or the more general Wilderness of Zin, as the point of departure for their expedition. The Deuteronomy account implies that they explored the region of Hebron only. However, Numbers 13.21 tells of a journey through the land of Canaan from the Wilderness of Zin to Rehob of Lebo-hamath, used elsewhere (*1 Kings 8.65*) to define the northern part of the land.

Mount Sinai

The location of Mount Sinai (or Mount Horeb) is a particular problem, and over a dozen sites have been proposed for it. The clearest evidence is found in *Deut 1.2*: "It is eleven days' journey from Horeb by way of Mount Seir to Kadesh-barnea.". This points to the south of the Sinai peninsula, in the region that Christian, Jewish, and the oldest Arabic tradition favors, or, perhaps less likely, to a mountain east of the Gulf of 'Aqaba.

The "sea"

The "sea" where the Israelites were saved from the pursuing Egyptians (*Exod 14–15*) is traditionally equated

> "When Pharaoh let the people go, God did not lead them by way of the land of the Philistines, although that was nearer... So God led the people by the roundabout way of the wilderness toward the Red Sea. The Israelites went up out of the land of Egypt prepared for battle."
>
> *(Exod 13.17–18)*

with the Red Sea (or, more exactly, the Gulf of Suez). The Hebrew term *yam suf* (the sea of reeds) has led some scholars to argue for a freshwater lake in northeastern Egypt. But elsewhere in the Bible, *yam suf* refers to the Red Sea (in fact the Gulf of 'Aqaba). So the texts probably refer to the Gulf of Suez (which may have extended further to the north in antiquity). This weakens the case for a "northern route" that places Migdol and Baal-zephon (*Exod 14.2*) near the Mediterranean coast and locates the "sea" at Lake Bardawil, where catastrophes of a comparable kind have occurred.

Exodus 13.17 states explicitly that the Israelites did not leave by the coast road, "the way of the land of the Philistines." A southerly direction is therefore more likely. The route suggested is a plausible one for traders and mining expeditions; there is evidence of a connection between southern Sinai and Arad already in the Early Bronze Age, and discoveries at Kuntillet 'Ajrud attest the use of "the way of the Red Sea" in the period of the Israelite kingdoms. A considerable deviation from the most direct route is indicated in the Bible accounts that the Israelites were kept in the wilderness as a punishment for their disobedience and lack of faith (*Num 13.14; Deut 1.2*).

The Exodus according to the Old Testament

— main lines of communication

━ probable route described in *Num 33.1–49* (with Qadesh and Mount Hor [unidentified] placed earlier in the wanderings), Deut. 1-2

--- uncertain

— route described in Numbers 33.1–49

— probable route of the spies

— circuit of Transjordan referred to in Numbers 21.11–13, etc.

— proposed nothern route

FOUR

CONQUEST AND OCCUPATION

Tel Hazor, Israel.
Strategically positioned at the convergence of trade routes
into northern Canaan, Hazor was inhabited for some
3000 years. At its peak, between 1700 and 1200 BC, the city
occupied 190 acres. It was the only city burnt by the Israelites.

The conquests of Joshua in Canaan

According to the book of Joshua, the Israelites, under the leadership of Joshua, the successor to Moses, invaded Canaan from Transjordan. After crossing the Jordan, the 12 tribes quickly took the whole country, which had been promised to them, in three campaigns.

The most spectacular battles were those at Jericho, Ai, and Gibeon, cities located in the central part of the land (*Josh 6–9*); other campaigns were in the south (*Josh 10.16–42*); and in north Canaan (*Josh 11.1–15*). Joshua defeated the five Amorite kings and proceeded southward to "utterly destroy all that breathed." After a thrust northward there appears the tally: 31 kings were slain (*Josh 12.24*).

The conquest is summarized succinctly in Joshua 10.40: "So Joshua defeated the whole land, the hill country and the Negeb and the lowland and the slopes, and all their kings; he left no one remaining, but utterly destroyed all that breathed, as the LORD God of Israel commanded." Later he assigned the tribes to their inheritances and set borders for each.

Unconquered cities

Yet, the Israelites did not, in fact, drive out all of the inhabitants of the land. The vivid accounts of victories found in the first half of the book of Joshua - stories filled with details about spies, the collapse of a city wall at a shout, and the sun standing still - related to the conquest of Benjamin, a relatively small part of Canaan. Judges

1.27–30 (as well as scattered references in Joshua) lists cities not taken in the conquest: Beth-shean, Taanach, Dor, Ibleam, Megiddo, Gezer, Acco, Achzib, Aphek, and Beth-shemesh. According to this report, the major cities were not taken. The Canaanites were not driven out, but the Israelites are said to have dwelt in peace with them. This information concurs with the fact that, long after Solomon, many Canaanites still lived unhindered in the land. Apparently, the original inhabitants were later incorporated into Israel.

The problems arising from the very complex picture of the Israelite conquest presented in biblical traditions have prompted theories about how the land was actually

Having been defeated at Ai, Joshua decided to launch a full-scale attack on the city (*map right*). This battle is described in great detail in Joshua 8.10–29. This large-scale map shows the remains of Ai, located in the hill country 10 miles north of Jerusalem. Excavation of the remains has thrown up some conflicting evidence. For example, the town may have covered an area of about six acres and thus could have held a maximum of 1000 people. Joshua 8, however, speaks of 12,000 inhabitants defeated by 30,000 Israelites.

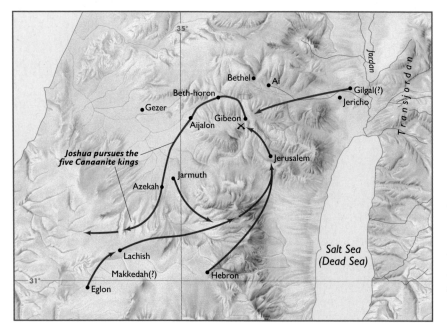

In Joshua 10.1–13, a league of Canaanite kings attacked Gibeon. In answer to the Gibeonites' plea for help, Joshua came up from Gilgal and defeated the Canaanites (*map left*).

The battle of Gibeon

⟶ Canaanite forces
➤ Israelite forces
✕ site of battle

1 main Israelite force arrives from Jericho

main force 6
turns on pursuers

2 Israelites feign
retreat

3 defending force
pursues the Israelites

2nd force pursues 7
the men of Ai

Ai

5 2nd Israelite force destroys
the undefended town

The battle of Ai

Canaanite forces

Israelite forces

4 about 5000 Israelite warriors
placed in ambush between
Bethel and Ai

to Bethel

occupied. Some scholars argue that the account in Joshua reflects an actual military campaign. Others argue that the account is a literary creation from a later period, albeit one that might incorporate historical events. The Late Bronze Age settlement at Jericho seems to have been followed by a gap in occupation in Iron Age I. Assuming Ai to be the mound of et-Tell near Deir Dibwan, the Early Bronze Age city was uninhabited until the 12th and 11th centuries BC - evidence that does not accord with the biblical account. At Hazor, the "head of all those kingdoms" (*Josh 11.10*), however, there is evidence of destruction during the 13th century BC.

Gradual infiltration

One theory is that Israel's settlement in Canaan occurred through the gradual infiltration of seminomads from desert areas into the less-populated regions of Palestine. This process could have extended over a long period of time. Certainly there are references in the Old Testament to groups of people coming to Canaan from elsewhere and in all probability from two different directions: one group from Kadesh-barnea towards the south and one via Transjordan moving toward the center of the land and perhaps northwards. No evidence, according to this view, points toward a violent invasion on a large scale. More probably, apart from the two groups just mentioned, other groups entered Canaan from time to time, but it is impossible to say from the preserved record how the

process of settlement was actually accomplished. With the exception of some local conflicts, the process seems to have been fairly pacific. In the era of the patriarchs, the Israelites lived mostly in harmony with the local populations. In the family of Judah there was marriage with Canaanite women (*cf. Gen 38*). Furthermore, references to attacks on Canaanite cities are very limited, while the city-states continued to exist for a considerable period of time - indeed, throughout the patriarchal period. In Joshua 24 there are also references to an agreement between the different tribes, some of whom had always lived in Canaan or had been settled there for so long that those coming later considered them to be indigenous.

Peasant uprising

Another proposed explanation of the settlement is the so-called peasant uprising. According to this theory, the group that later became known as Israel was not composed entirely of immigrants but was created out of a variety of elements. Among them were Canaanites who had rebelled against their overlords. These were joined by the 'apiru and by a group of Israelites who came into Canaan from Egypt. The emphasis this latter group placed upon liberation from slavery and the exodus from Egypt made a deep impression upon the other two groups. The "conquest" was a sociopolitical revolution of the oppressed against exploitation. The struggle mentioned in the Old Testament

The conquest of the Shephelah

→ Canaanite auxilliary force under Horam
→ Israelite forces

After the battle of Gibeon, Joshua pursued the five Canaanite kings into southern Canaan (*Josh 10.16–39*). The decline of the Egyptian 19th dynasty had left this area unprotected, and it fell easily to Israelite conquest (*map right*). This was probably the final phase of the occupation of Canaan. Shephelah means "lowland" and describes the low hills between the central mountain range and the coastal plains.

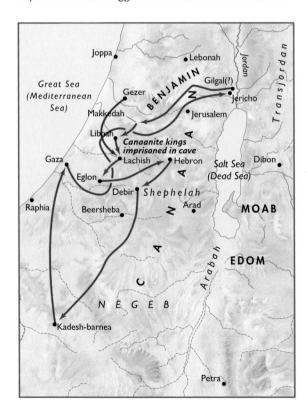

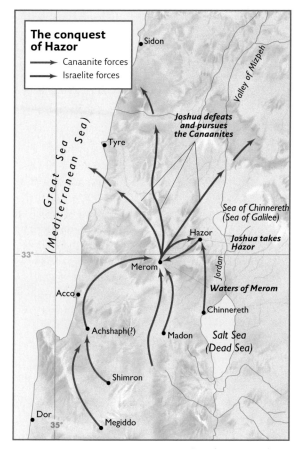

The conquest
of Hazor
→ Canaanite forces
→ Israelite forces

Sidon

Valley of Mizpeh

Great Sea
(Mediterranean Sea)

*Joshua defeats
and pursues
the Canaanites*

Tyre

Sea of Chinnereth
(Sea of Galilee)

*Joshua takes
Hazor*

33°

Hazor

Merom

Jordan

Waters of Merom

Acco

Chinnereth

Achshaph(?)

Madon

*Salt Sea
(Dead Sea)*

Shimron

Dor

35°

Megiddo

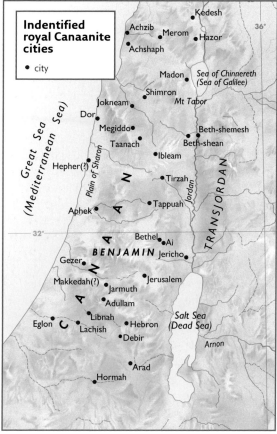

Indentified
royal Canaanite
cities

• city

36°

Kedesh

Achzib Merom Hazor

Achshaph

Madon Sea of Chinnereth
(Sea of Galilee)

Shimron Mt Tabor

Jokneam

Great Sea
(Mediterranean Sea)

Dor

Megiddo

Beth-shemesh

Taanach Beth-shean

Ibleam

Hepher(?)

Plain of Sharon

Tirzah

Jordan

TRANSJORDAN

Aphek

Tappuah

32°

Bethel Ai

BENJAMIN Jericho

Gezer

Makkedah(?) Jarmuth

Jerusalem

Adullam

Libnah

Eglon Lachish Hebron

Salt Sea
(Dead Sea)

Debir

Arnon

Arad

Hormah

concerns local battles in which only the rulers in a particular area were driven out. Obviously, this theory has certain elements in common with the other theories: there are references to a conquest and gradual penetration, but, according to this view, they take place harmoniously, and with a certain amount of cooperation from a section of the Canaanite people.

These settlement theories show that, from the partial record of this crucial event in Israel's history, it is impossible to determine exactly what is meant by the term "conquest." As we have seen, even within the book of Joshua itself, the picture is unclear. Although edited together to portray an invasion of all Canaan by a unified Israelite force, the conquest stories only account for a part of the land. Historically, it seems that Israel's movement into Canaan was a much more complex, gradual settlement over a long period. This settlement may well have resulted in localized military conflict with the native population, but this would be the exception, rather than the rule; elsewhere, the picture consists of immigrants reaching accommodation with the Canaanite people and even beginning to approximate their way of life. It was, therefore, more settlement than conquest, more a migration than an invasion.

Joshua defeated the Canaanite kings of the North at Merom and then destroyed their stronghold at Hazor (*Josh 11.1–15*) (*map above left*).

Joshua 12.9–24 lists 31 royal Canaanite cities west of the Jordan Israelites. Not all the sites can be identified (*map above right*).

"I gave you a land on which you had not labored, and towns that you had not built, and you live in them; you eat the fruit of vineyards and oliveyards that you did not plant. Now therefore revere the LORD, and serve him in sincerity and in faithfulness; put away the gods that your ancestors served beyond the River and in Egypt, and serve the LORD."

(Josh 24.13–14)

Occupation of the land

Once Canaan was conquered, it had to be occupied. Joshua 13–19 describes the assignation of territories to the tribes, territories with clearly defined borders and cities within them.

However, settlement of the land may not have been as immediate as the Bible implies. In Joshua 13–17 (and *Judg 1* and *3*) over 20 unconquered cities are named, including some of the oldest and most important population centers: they lay in the area west of the Jordan, in the northern Shephelah, in the north of the Plain of Sharon, in the Plain of Jezreel, in the northern coastal plain, in Upper Galilee, and one (Jerusalem) in the central hills.

The impression of a gradual, partial settlement is reinforced by the evidence for new settlements in the hill regions. Until the beginning of the Iron Age I, these areas had been uninhabited and uncultivated. Joshua 17.16–18 reports that the tribes of Manasseh and Ephraim were instructed to fell forests in the hill country in order to establish new settlements. Most of these Israelite settlements were small in the beginning and more like unfortified villages. Only in a few cases, with the larger settlements, is it possible to locate any of them with more precision.

Four-room house

A characteristic feature of Early Iron Age settlements is the distinctive architectural plan of the four-room house, which appears in a fully developed form at the very beginning of the Iron Age without any apparent antecedents. (It does not follow the Canaanite architectural tradition of a central courtyard surrounded by rooms on all sides.) It has been suggested that the four-room house plan developed out of a more simple type, which, in turn, was derived from a nomadic tent used by the Israelites. It is generally agreed that the homeland of the four-room pillared house and its variants was in the central hill country. Those who adhere to this view maintain that the pillared four-room house plan was a local invention, around 1200 BC, which was the result of rapid Israelite adaptation to the available resources and to a new rural way of life in the hilly regions. Examples of this plan dating to the Early Iron Age have been found in the central hill country at Ai, Shiloh, Khirbet Raddanah, and Giloth.

Unconquered cities in Joshua 13–17, Judges 1 and 3

● unconquered city

A number of cities in Joshua 13, 15, 16, and 17 and Judges 1 and 3 are listed as unconquered, and the Bible states that God deliberately denied the Israelites a complete victory (*map first right*). In the Iron Age I period, some cities were clearly newly built by settlers of that period, while others were built either on the remains of Late Bronze Age cities (implying possible military conquest) or of even older settlements (*map second right*).

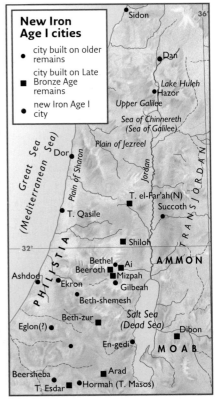

Whatever the case, during the course of the 11th century BC, the four-room house plan rapidly spread to other regions of the country, such as Philistia (T. Qasile Strata X–IX and T. Sera Stratum VIII), the Jezreel Valley (T. Megiddo Stratum VIB), Transjordan (Sahab near Amman and Khirbet el-Medeiyineh), and even at Israelite settlements in the Negeb desert.

Evidence for an occupation of a site by a new people is a change in the material culture. Discontinuity between the material culture of the Late Bronze Age and that of the Early Iron Age is slight, but the change in architectural style from the courtyard plan to the four-room house seems to have occurred at about the time of Israel's gradual settlement in the land as it is described in the second half of Joshua and chapters 1 and 3 of Judges.

> "Then Joshua said to the house of Joseph, to Ephraim and Manasseh, 'You are indeed a numerous people, and have great power; you shall not have one lot only, but the hill country shall be yours, for though it is a forest, you shall clear it and possess it to its farthest borders; for you shall drive out the Canaanites, though they have chariots of iron, and though they are strong.'"
>
> *(Josh 17.17–18)*

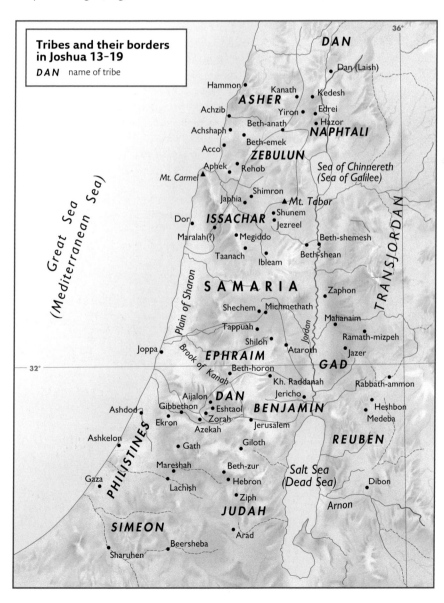

Tribes and their borders in Joshua 13–19

DAN   name of tribe

The way in which the 12 tribes of Israel were to apportion the Promised Land is superimposed on a modern map (*map left*). However, this does not give a reliable picture of the country at that time (e.g., the Song of Deborah lists only 10 and not 12 tribes).

The Philistines

Shortly after Israel's entry into Canaan, the Philistines became a major threat. Samson, the hero of the tribe of Dan, engaged in skirmishes with the Philistines, and eventually the entire tribe was forced to migrate to a new home in the north. The major battles with the Philistines were those fought by Saul and David for the possession of strategic and fertile areas, yet the Philistines never exercised permanent control over more than the limited area occupied by their five-city league of Gaza, Ashkelon, Ashdod, Ekron, and Gath.

In the book of Samuel, there are Egyptian accounts of an invasion in the 12th century BC of "Sea Peoples", one of which was the Philistines (Peleset). The 12th century BC reliefs and inscriptions of the mortuary temple of Ramesses III, at Medinet Habu in Upper Egypt, record the destruction of the Hittite empire and the attempts by the Sea Peoples to invade Egypt. The reliefs depict and describe two great battles with the Sea Peoples, one on land, fought in Phoenicia or Syria, and the other on the sea, probably fought in the Nile Delta. It is clear that one group of Sea Peoples fought the Egyptians in a great land battle but were not decisively defeated. They were strong enough to attempt to invade Egypt by sea, this time in alliance with another of the Sea Peoples, the Sherden, when they were defeated and eventually settled permanently in Palestine. This group included the Philistines.

Mainly, they settled in the southern part of the Canaanite coastal plain. In the course of time, they established five strong city-states, three of which, Ashkelon, Ashdod, and Gaza, were beside the coastal road.

Their arrival was reflected in new styles of architecture, burial customs, and religious cults. At Tel Qasile, the first unmistakable Philistine temples were found, often containing cult vessels and even a socketed bronze double axe, which has Aegean connections. No exact parallels for the temples' architecture has been found in Palestine, though some features show Canaanite influence. It is not known what gods the Philistines worshipped when they arrived in Canaan, but their deities of later times, Dagon, Ashtoreth, and Beelzebub, are of Canaanite origin.

Iron and metalwork

It has been generally accepted that the Philistines introduced iron into Palestine and that their control of the metal industry was one of the factors that enabled them to achieve military superiority over the rest of the population (1 Sam 13.19–21). Most iron tools and weapons of the Iron Age I come from sites, showing Philistine occupation or influence. Very few iron products, and even fewer bronze objects, have been found at Canaanite or Israelite sites.

Although the Philistines ceased to be a threat to Israel after the time of David, they maintained their identity for centuries in their traditional homeland. Assyria extracted tribute, and Philistine cities often played a role in the political conflicts involving Assyria, Egypt, and Judah, until the time of the Babylonian exile. The Greeks and the Romans, who approached the Levant from the west, made use of the term "land of the Philistines" (Palaestina) as a designation for the entire land extending as far east as the river Jordan. It is ironic that Israel's land should for centuries be called by the name of its most bitter and persistent enemy.

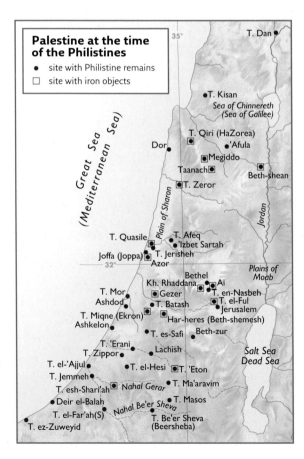

Palestine at the time of the Philistines

- site with Philistine remains
- □ site with iron objects

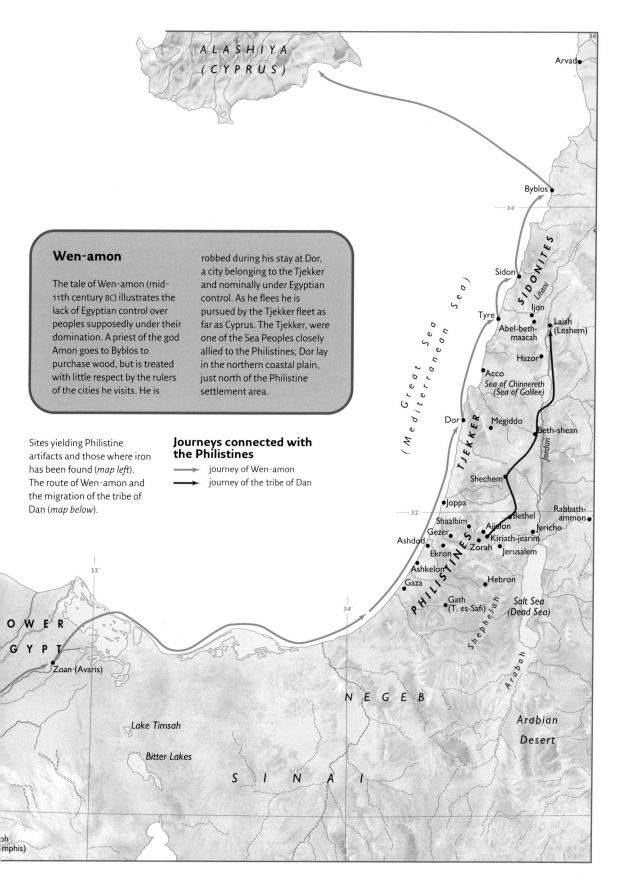

Wen-amon

The tale of Wen-amon (mid-11th century BC) illustrates the lack of Egyptian control over peoples supposedly under their domination. A priest of the god Amon goes to Byblos to purchase wood, but is treated with little respect by the rulers of the cities he visits. He is robbed during his stay at Dor, a city belonging to the Tjekker and nominally under Egyptian control. As he flees he is pursued by the Tjekker fleet as far as Cyprus. The Tjekker, were one of the Sea Peoples closely allied to the Philistines; Dor lay in the northern coastal plain, just north of the Philistine settlement area.

Sites yielding Philistine artifacts and those where iron has been found (*map left*). The route of Wen-amon and the migration of the tribe of Dan (*map below*).

Journeys connected with the Philistines

→ journey of Wen-amon
→ journey of the tribe of Dan

The age of the judges

The heroes who emerged among the individual tribes, who became known as "judges," were very different from the national figures of Moses and Joshua. They were chosen to lead in times of emergency, sometimes obtained the help of other tribes, and when the crisis was over seemed to lapse into obscurity.

These tribal figures, such as Jephthah, Barak, Gideon, Ehud, and Samson, distinguished themselves by bravery, cleverness, and physical strength as they repulsed assaults upon the individual tribes by Ammonites, Canaanites from the north, Midianites, Moabites, and Philistines. The stories are difficult to date, but they do show us something of premonarchical Israel.

Most notably, the tribes and clans rarely acted together. Ehud's battle against the Moabites involved the tribes of Benjamin and Ephraim. Gideon's repulsion of the Midianites probably involved his own clan of Abiezrites, together with the tribe of Ephraim. Jephthah led Gilead to victory over the Ammonites. Samson was a local hero of the tribe of Dan. Only Judges 4 records a significant victory of a relatively wide tribal alliance led by Deborah and Barak over the Canaanites; however, even there, several tribes stayed away (*Judg 5.16–17*).

Tribe, clan, and family

The society of the Canaanite city-states was characterized by a sharp distinction between ruler and ruled, rich and poor, and by the separation of workers into guilds, such as weavers, masons, chariot makers, and others. In contrast, the Israelite tribes, as described in Judges, were egalitarian societies, based on a pastoral-agricultural economy. The growing of wheat and barley; the tending of sheep, goats, and cattle; and the cultivation and pruning of vineyards were fundamental to tribal life. The Gideon story tells of Midianite raids on Israel's fields, their destruction, and the looting of crops and animals (*Judg 6.1–6*). Judges occasionally mentions cities, but these may just have been unfortified settlements inhabited by agricultural workers.

The fundamental social and economic unit was the extended family. This was a largely self-sufficient unit, owning property and having few occupations apart from the tending of livestock and the growing of crops. The family belonged to the clan, which functioned as the social context within which the families intermarried and found aid and protection. The tribe, however, was a much more fluid entity. It was both a social and a territorial unit, subject to continual change in the international clan membership and indeed in its very existence. It was the clan or family, rather than Israel, that was of primary importance to the Israelites.

Occasional unified leadership was afforded in times of emergency by charismatic leaders who came forward to deal with just those situations. The elders exercised a representative function but with no real power; effective decision making was done by general assemblies of the

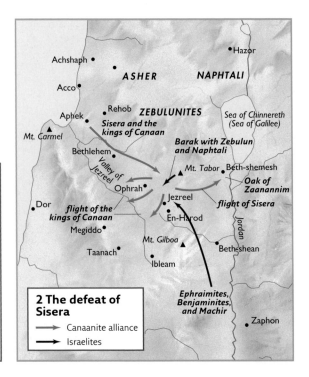

1 Jephthah and the Ammonites

→ Jephthah
→ Ammonites

Jabesh-gilead • Zaphon • Succoth • GILEADITES • Jabbok • Mahanaim • EPHRAIMITES • Jordan • Mizpeh-gilead • Ataroth • Jazer • Fords of the Jordan • AMMONITES • Rabbath-ammon • Jericho • Abel-keramim

2 The defeat of Sisera

→ Canaanite alliance
→ Israelites

Hazor • Achshaph • ASHER • NAPHTALI • Acco • Rehob • ZEBULUNITES • Aphek • Sisera and the kings of Canaan • Sea of Chinnereth (Sea of Galilee) • Mt. Carmel • Barak with Zebulun and Naphtali • Bethlehem • Valley of Jezreel • Mt. Tabor • Beth-shemesh • Ophrah • Oak of Zaanannim • Jezreel • flight of Sisera • Dor • flight of the kings of Canaan • En-Harod • Jordan • Megiddo • Mt. Gilboa • Beth-shean • Taanach • Ibleam • Ephraimites, Benjaminites, and Machir • Zaphon

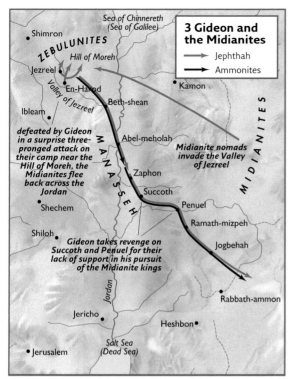

3 Gideon and the Midianites
→ Jephthah
→ Ammonites

Sea of Chinnereth (Sea of Galilee)
Shimron
ZEBULUNITES
Hill of Moreh
Jezreel
Valley of Jezreel
En-Harod
Beth-shean
Kamon
Ibleam
MANASSEH
Abel-meholah
Midianite nomads invade the Valley of Jezreel
defeated by Gideon in a surprise three-pronged attack on their camp near the Hill of Moreh, the Midianites flee back across the Jordan
Zaphon
MIDIANITES
Shechem
Succoth
Penuel
Shechem
Ramath-mizpeh
Shiloh
Gideon takes revenge on Succoth and Penuel for their lack of support in his pursuit of the Midianite kings
Jogbehah
Jordan
Rabbath-ammon
Jericho
Heshbon
Jerusalem
Salt Sea (Dead Sea)

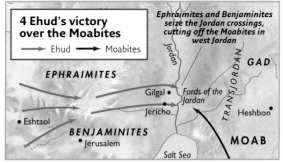

4 Ehud's victory over the Moabites
→ Ehud → Moabites

Ephraimites and Benjaminites seize the Jordan crossings, cutting off the Moabites in west Jordan
GAD
EPHRAIMITES
Jordan
Gilgal
Fords of the Jordan
TRANSJORDAN
Jericho
Heshbon
Eshtaol
BENJAMINITES
Jerusalem
Salt Sea
MOAB

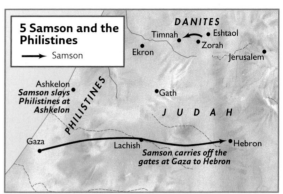

5 Samson and the Philistines
→ Samson

DANITES
Timnah
Eshtaol
Zorah
Ekron
Jerusalem
Ashkelon
Samson slays Philistines at Ashkelon
PHILISTINES
Gath
JUDAH
Gaza
Lachish
Hebron
Samson carries off the gates at Gaza to Hebron

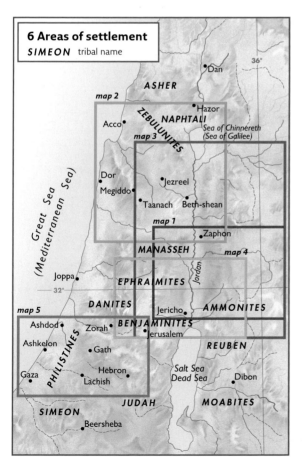

6 Areas of settlement
SIMEON tribal name

Dan
36°
ASHER
map 2
Hazor
ZEBULUNITES
NAPHTALI
Acco
Sea of Chinnereth (Sea of Galilee)
map 3
Great Sea (Mediterranean Sea)
Dor
Jezreel
Megiddo
Taanach
Beth-shean
map 1
Zaphon
MANASSEH
map 4
Joppa
Jordan
32°
EPHRAIMITES
map 5
DANITES
Jericho
AMMONITES
Ashdod
Zorah
BENJAMINITES
Jerusalem
Ashkelon
Jerusalem
REUBEN
Gath
Salt Sea
Gaza
Hebron
Dead Sea
Dibon
PHILISTINES
Lachish
JUDAH
MOABITES
SIMEON
Beersheba

"men of the city." Defense was the responsibility of all those capable of bearing arms rather than of a professional army. Disputes were settled either by the elders or by judges.

Israelite tribalism emerged primarily in the mountain areas of Palestine, while the Canaanite city-state system continued to dominate the plains (*Judg 1.27–35*). The events of the period of the judges took place in those less-accessible districts lying largely outside the city-state range of control. The victory of Sisera (*Judg 4*) marks the first appearance of Israelite tribes in the plains and a significant stage in the development by which Israel under the monarchy came to dominate Palestine.

Map 1 Jephthah leads the Gileadites in resisting the Ammonite expansion (*Judg 11.1–12.7*).
Map 2 Sisera is defeated by forces of Barek and Deborah in a decisive battle at Taanach (*Judg 5.19*). Sisera is slain by Jael at the "Oak of Zaanannim" (*Judg 4–5*).
Map 3 Gideon and his clan of Abiezrites mount a surprise attack on Midianite raiders and expel them from Israelite territory (*Judg 6–8*).

Map 4 Ehud of Benjamin kills Eglon the Moabite king and inflicts a decisive defeat on the Moabites (*Judg 3.12–30*).
Map 5 Samson of Dan kills Philistines with his own strength and destroys their fields until, betrayed by Delilah, he meets his death at the Philistine temple at Gaza (*Judg 13–16*).
Map 6 Background map showing the tribal areas of settlement.

FIVE

THE UNITED KINGDOM

**Solomon greets the Queen of Sheba in Jerusalem,
Lorenzo Ghiberti.**
A detail from the "Gates of Paradise"; the east doors of the
Baptistry of the Duomo in Florence. Solomon greets the
Queen of Sheba at the portal to his temple.

Saul's kingdom

Saul emerged as a local military hero who led the Benjaminite–Ephraimite resistance against surrounding enemies, especially the Philistines. Proclaimed king by his countrymen in response to his early victories, Saul spent the remainder of his career defending the fledgling kingdom of Israel.

Saul lived around 1000 BC and belonged to the small Israelite tribe of Benjamin, which was overshadowed by the neighboring tribe of Ephraim. Both tribes were settled in the hill country north of Jerusalem, along with various other population elements, such as Hivites and Arkites.

Saul accomplished two major victories early in his career. One was against the Philistines in his own Benjaminite neighborhood, at the strategic crossing of a steep valley that separated Gibeah and Michmash (1 Sam 13.2–14.46). The Philistines were camped on the opposite (northern) side of the crossing and began to raid the countryside (1 Sam 13.16–18). The turning point in the struggle occurred, according to the biblical narrative, when Saul's son Jonathan made a surprise raid on the Philistine camp. The Philistines were routed and fled the hill country, leaving Saul to establish his residence at Gibeah.

The other battle was against the Ammonites who were attacking the city of Jabesh in Gilead (1 Sam 11). When the Jabeshites appealed for a peace settlement, the Ammonite king offered impossible terms. "On this condition I will make a treaty with you, namely that I gouge out everyone's right eye, and thus put disgrace upon all Israel." (1 Sam 11.2). Thereupon the Jabeshites sent to Saul for help. Saul hurriedly mustered an army, marched to Jabesh, and saved the day.

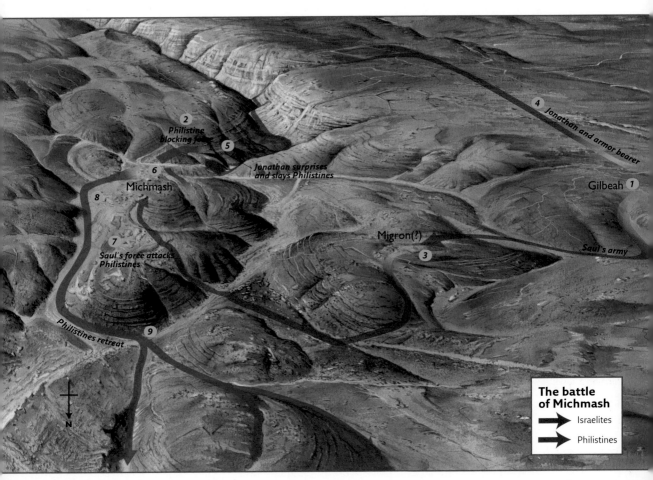

2 Philistine blocking force
5
6
Michmash
8
7 Saul's force attacks Philistines
Jonathan surprises and slays Philistines
4 Jonathan and armor bearer
Gilbeah 1
Migron(?)
3
Saul's army
9
Philistines retreat

N

The battle of Michmash
→ Israelites
→ Philistines

Saul's kingdom did not have a highly organized administration of precisely defined boundaries. In peripheral areas, the degree of Saul's authority may have varied from time to time, depending on whether his troops were present or whether the local people needed his protection against other threats. Even in the Benjamin-Ephraim-Gilead zone, the core of his territorial domain, some cities may have remained independent. Certainly Jerusalem was never incorporated into his kingdom (2 Sam 5.6–8).

Few details are known about Saul's reign, other than his military actions and his dealings with David. David, from the tribe of Judah and the village of Bethlehem, gained a reputation as a daring and successful Philistine fighter, became close friends with Jonathan, and married Michal, Saul's daughter. Saul began to regard David as a threat and sought to kill him, but he escaped to the vicinity of Adullam, southwest of Jerusalem. When Saul learned of David's whereabouts in the Adullam vicinity, David and his men moved to the "wilderness" area southeast of Hebron, where Saul continued to search and pursue. Finally, still on the run from Saul, David allied

himself with the Philistines, specifically with Achish, the Philistine ruler of Gath, who, as a mark of favor, assigned to David the city of Ziklag.

David and his men were thus allies with the Philistines at the time of the battle and actually marched with the Philistines to Aphek on the eve of the battle. The Philistines, however, fearing that David might switch sides during the fighting, sent him and his troops back to Ziklag (1 Sam 29).

Saul met the Philistines beside Mount Gilboa, overlooking the Plain of Jezreel. The battle was a catastrophe for Israel. Saul and three of his sons (including Jonathan) were killed by the Philistines, who subsequently reoccupied much of the country. Saul's kingdom was in tatters (1 Sam 31.1–7).

Saul's decapitated body was taken to the Philistine city of Beth-shan, where it was nailed to the city wall. In a moving epilogue to this tragedy, a group of Jabeshite warriors risked their lives to retrieve the body. They took it back to Jabesh-gilead and buried it "under the tamarisk tree" as a mark of respect for the man who had rescued them early in his reign (1 Sam 31.11–13).

1 Samuel 14 describes a battle between the Israelites (led by Saul and Jonathan) and the Philistines at Michmash (*map left*).
1 Saul is at Gibeah-Geba with 600 men.
2 The Philistines had blocked the passage of Michmash.
3 Saul moves to Migron.
4 Jonathan and his armor bearer carry out a raid.
5 In a surprise attack Jonathan kills some Philistines.
6 There is panic at the Philistine camp at Michmash.
7 A frontal assault by Saul's force adds to the Philistine confusion.
8 The Philistines are defeated.
9 They retreat north and west.

According to Samuel 11, Saul was sent for by the Jabeshites when they were attacked by Ammonites. He came up from Gibeah and scattered the Ammonite army (*map right*).

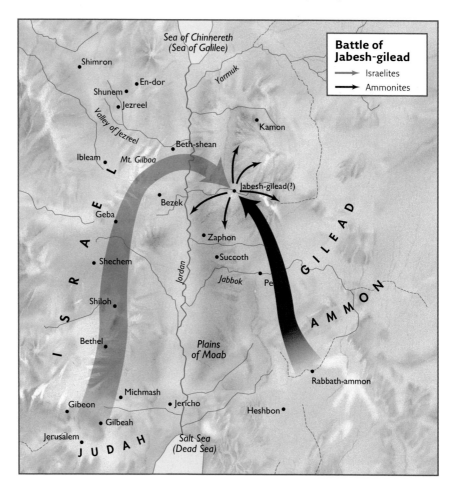

Battle of Jabesh-gilead
→ Israelites
→ Ammonites

Sea of Chinnereth (Sea of Galilee)
Shimron
En-dor
Shunem
Jezreel
Valley of Jezreel
Yarmuk
Kamon
Beth-shean
Ibleam
Mt. Gilboa
Jabesh-gilead(?)
Bezek
Geba
GILEAD
Zaphon
Succoth
AMMON
Shechem
Jordan
Jabbok
Pe
Shiloh
Bethel
Plains of Moab
Rabbath-ammon
ISRAEL
Michmash
Gibeon
Jericho
Heshbon
Gilbeah
Jerusalem
JUDAH
Salt Sea (Dead Sea)

David's rise to power

Saul's son Ishbosheth (or Eshbaal) was recognized as his successor, without opposition but without much enthusiastic support either. Ishbosheth turned out to be a weak king who attempted to rule from the safety of a Transjordanian city, Mahanaim. David, in the meantime, occupied Hebron with his soldiers and was crowned king there by the elders of the tribe of Judah.

Three military incidents illustrating his expanding influence are reported for the next stage of David's career.

The pool of Gibeon

A skirmish erupted between David's and Ishbosheth's soldiers "by the pool" at Gibeon and ended with David's men victorious (2 Sam 2.12-32). Gibeon (modern el-Jib) was eight miles northwest of Jerusalem, bordering Benjaminite territory. Saul seems to have offended the people of the city in some way (2 Sam 21.1-6). The fact that David's and Ishbosheth's men met at Gibeon may suggest that David was encroaching on the edge of Benjaminite territory.

The conquest of Jerusalem

Perhaps the most important event of David's career was his conquest of Jerusalem (2 Sam 5.6-10), by the Jebusites. At the time, it was a small, relatively unimportant place; yet, for David's purposes, Jerusalem was an ideal capital. Besides offering a defendable position with a good spring for water, it had no strong tribal or family ties with either the Israelite tribes to the north or the surrounding tribes of Judah. As David's kingdom expanded beyond the hill country into the lowlands and Transjordan, Jerusalem's central position served him well for administrative purposes. Probably the city that David conquered was confined to Ophel, the knoll immediately south of what is known today as Temple Mount or Haram al-Sharif. Ongoing excavations have revealed a substantial monumental building, provisionally dated to the very late Iron Age I, or early Iron Age IIA (around 1000 BC), and built outside the walls of the Jebusite city. Whether or not this proves to be, as it is claimed, King David's palace, it may be evidence of substantial public building work during the time that David was creating his new capital.

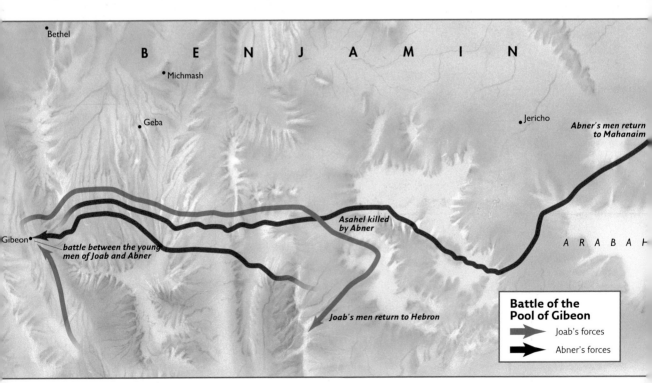

Bethel

B E N J A M I N

Michmash

Geba

Jericho

Abner's men return
to Mahanaim

Gibeon

battle between the young
men of Joab and Abner

Asahel killed
by Abner

ARABAH

Joab's men return to Hebron

**Battle of the
Pool of Gibeon**

→ Joab's forces
→ Abner's forces

Philistine aggression

As David assumed his role of king and protector of the Israelite and Judean villages, the relationship between him and the Philistines turned to enmity. After all, it was primarily the Philistines against whom the hill country villages needed protection. Thus, "when the Philistines heard that David had been anointed king over Israel, all the Philistines went up in search of David" (2 Sam 5.17). The following verses (17b–25) report two Philistine raids, both of which were defeated by David.

David's monarchy is understood to have been a direct continuation of Saul's Israelite kingdom. David may have emphasized the continuity - by bringing the ark to Jerusalem, for example, and by using the name "Israel" for his realm. Yet the biblical materials indicate that the Israelites and Judeans were distinct groups, neither of which had prior connections with Jerusalem. Moreover, once David established himself in Jerusalem, it became the real administrative, military, and cultural center of a state that eventually extended well beyond the range of Israelite and Judean settlement and depended heavily on foreign mercenaries (including Philistines) for internal and external security. Thus David's kingdom was essentially a Jerusalem-based monarchy with a far more pluralistic constituency than Saul's Israel.

David's name is associated with "The Psalms of David." The superscriptions of 73 psalms carry his name, and 13 of these connect the poem with particular incidents in his career. Also, Jerusalem, the small city that he made his capital, has endured for three millennia as the "City of David" (2 Sam 5.7).

2 Samuel 2.12–32 describes the battle between the 12 men of Joab and the 12 men of Abner at the pool of Gibeon. The map shows the pursuit of Abner's men by Joab's force and the death of Asahel at the hand of Abner (map left). David's capture of Jerusalem from the Jebusites gave him the capital city he needed. He twice defended it from Philistine attacks in the Valley of Rephaim (2 Sam 5.17–25). After the second attack, he pursued the Philistines as far as Gezer (map right).

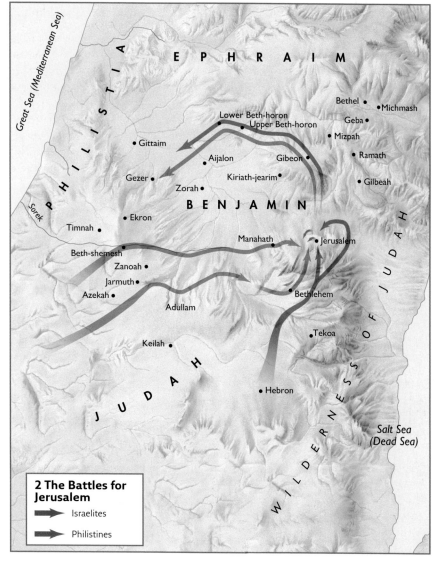

2 The Battles for Jerusalem

→ Israelites
→ Philistines

David's kingdom

David's kingdom expanded to include most of western Palestine (excluding Philistia and some Phoenician presence along the coast north of Mount Carmel) and a large portion of Transjordan extending from the river Arnon to Damascus.

The battle against Hadadezer

Early in his reign, David formed an alliance with Nahash, king of the Ammonites. When Nahash died, the alliance collapsed, and David sent troops commanded by Joab to attack Rabbah, the chief Ammonite city. The Ammonites appealed to Hadadezer, the Aramaean king of Zobah, who represented a major power in southern Aram. Hadadezer responded with troops from various Aramaean cities under his influence but was defeated by David's army at Rabbah and at Helam, somewhere in Transjordan. David therefore expanded his domain to include some of the area between Damascus and Gilead. Toi of Hamath, an enemy of Hadadezer, sent his son to David with congratulations and gifts (2 Sam 8.9–10). Whether David invaded the heartland of Hadadezer's realm depends on the interpretation of 2 Samuel 8.7–8.

Conflict with the Moabites and Edomites

David is reported to have defeated the Moabites and to have executed two-thirds of the prisoners taken (2 Sam 8.2). Even if David conducted military campaigns into Moab proper, the geographical isolation of that region would have made any sort of permanent rule from Jerusalem impractical. David also made war with the Edomites; the one battle recorded took place "in the Valley of Salt," probably between the Dead Sea and Beersheba. Presumably, it was Edomite-related tribal groups along the southern frontier that David defeated and garrisoned. David may also have brought under control the "unconquered cities" listed in Judges (Judg 1.21, 27–36).

Later events of David's reign

At some point after establishing himself in Jerusalem, David had to crush two rebellions.

The first was led by his son, Absalom, apparently the crown prince. Appealing to popular grievances, and drawing support from both Israelites and Judeans, Absalom had himself crowned king in Hebron and then marched on Jerusalem. David and a core of loyalists fled to Mahanaim in Transjordan, leaving Absalom to rule in Jerusalem for a short time. Had Absalom moved quickly against David's fleeing army, the rebellion may have succeeded, but he delayed until he had lost the tactical advantage. When he did pursue, he was killed, when the long hair for which he was famous became entangled in the branches of a tree (2 Sam 18.9–15).

Upon receiving the news of the death of Absalom, David withdrew into seclusion and refused to take any responsibility for his army. It was only after the strong rebuke of Joab for this self-indulgent personal grief that he participated in the celebration of the victory (2 Sam 19.1–8). This emotional side of David's character may explain some of the failures in the latter part of his reign.

The second rebellion was initiated by Sheba, a Benjaminite, and seems to have received less-widespread support. It was quickly crushed, and Sheba was beheaded. Since Sheba was from the same tribe as Saul, and since he specifically exhorted the Israelites to reject David's rule, he may have hoped to place one of Saul's descendants on its throne. Immediately following the account of Sheba's rebellion appears the report of the execution of Saul's descendants at Gibeon (2 Sam 21.1–14), possibly an added precaution against future attempts to revive the dynasty of Saul.

> "David went out and was successful wherever Saul sent him; as a result, Saul set him over the army. And all the people, even the servants of Saul, approved. As they were coming home, when David returned from killing the Philistine, the women came out of all the towns of Israel, singing and dancing, to meet King Saul, with tambourines, with songs of joy, and with musical instruments. And the women sang to one another as they made merry, 'Saul has killed his thousands, and David his ten thousands.'"
>
> **(1 Sam 18.5–7)**

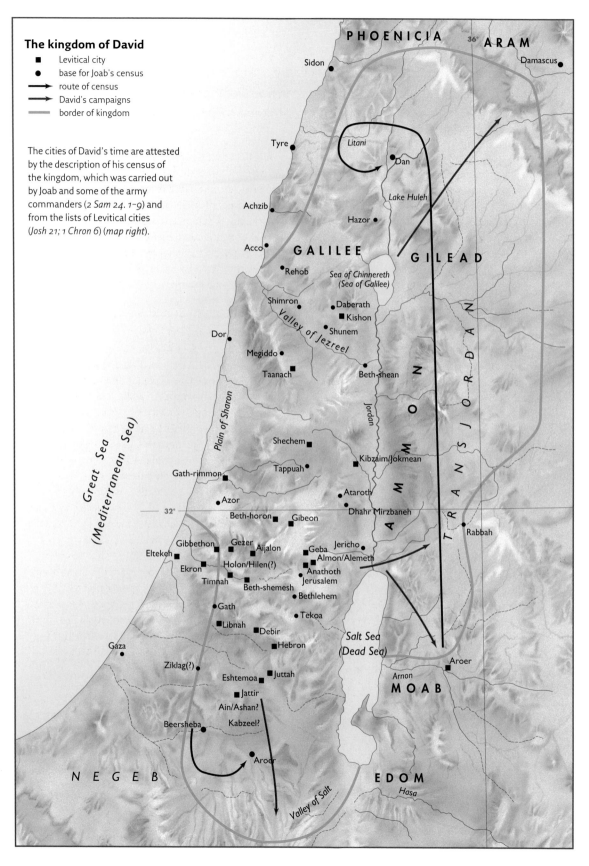

The kingdom of David

- ■ Levitical city
- ● base for Joab's census
- → route of census
- ➤ David's campaigns
- ━ border of kingdom

The cities of David's time are attested by the description of his census of the kingdom, which was carried out by Joab and some of the army commanders (*2 Sam 24. 1–9*) and from the lists of Levitical cities (*Josh 21; 1 Chron 6*) (*map right*).

PHOENICIA

ARAM

Sidon

Damascus

Tyre

Litani

Dan

Achzib

Lake Huleh

Acco

Hazor

GALILEE

GILEAD

Rehob

Sea of Chinnereth (Sea of Galilee)

Shimron

Daberath

Kishon

Shunem

Dor

Megiddo

Taanach

Valley of Jezreel

Beth-shean

Jordan

A M M O N

Plain of Sharon

Shechem

Tappuah

Kibzaim/Jokmean

T R A N S J O R D A N

Ataroth

Gath-rimmon

Dhahr Mirzbaneh

Azor

32°

Rabbah

Beth-horon

Gibeon

Great Sea (Mediterranean Sea)

Gibbethon

Gezer

Aijalon

Geba

Jericho

Almon/Alemeth

Eltekeh

Ekron

Holon/Hilen(?)

Anathoth

Timnah

Beth-shemesh

Jerusalem

Gath

Bethlehem

Libnah

Debir

Tekoa

Gaza

Hebron

Salt Sea (Dead Sea)

Ziklag(?)

Juttah

Eshtemoa

Aroer

Jattir

Arnon

Ain/Ashan?

Kabzeel?

MOAB

Beersheba

N E G E B

Aroer

EDOM

Hasa

Valley of Salt

36°

Solomon's kingdom

David's successor, Solomon, came to the throne around 965 BC. The reputation he enjoyed for wisdom (*1 Kings 4.30*) and the wealth and extravagance of his court were so firmly, rooted in folk memory that, centuries later, Jesus could still talk of "Solomon in all his glory" (*Matt 6.29*).

Allowing for the hyperbole that attaches itself to famous men, Solomon does seem to have been unusually successful in trade and commerce. Freed from the need to fight wars, Solomon was able to devote himself to building a strong economy and engaging in foreign trade to a degree never before seen in Israel's history. He brought Israel to its peak of prosperity at home and involvement in affairs abroad. Archaeology confirms a rise in the general standard of living and progress in technical matters, during the Solomonic period, although there are no sources for Solomon's prosperity apart from those within the Bible.

The Bible speaks of Solomon trading with Egypt, Africa, Arabia, Phoenicia, and Lebanon. Situated on the old north-south trade routes - the "Way of the Sea" and the Transjordanian King's Highway - Solomon's kingdom was ideally situated to benefit from trade passing between Egypt and Syria. He served as a middleman in the trade in horses and chariots between Asia Minor and Egypt, sourcing wooden chariots from Egypt and horses from Kue and selling them on to Syrian kingdoms beyond the Euphrates (*1 Kings 10.28-29*). Biblical sources also credit Solomon with maritime operations on the Red Sea and with expeditions of Phoenician-built ships sailing from Ezion-geber to Ophir (*1 Kings 9.26-28, 10.22-12*). Ophir - usually identified with the land of Punt along the eastern coast of Africa - was a major exporter of gold; an ostracon found at T. Qasila had a Hebrew inscription reading, "Gold of Ophir belonging to Beth Horon thirty shekels." Israel also traded at this time with Phoenicia and the Lebanese mountain communities for timber (*1 Kings 5.10-11*). According to the Bible, Hiram from Tyre gave Solomon timber of cedar and fir in exchange for large quantities of wheat and olive oil.

Two lists of provisions (*box right*): Solomon's requirements for one day (*1 Kings 4.22-23*) and a list of food and drink for a banquet given by King Ashurnasirpal II of Assyria for over 69,000 guests at the inauguration of the palace at Calah, in northern Mesopotamia. It is impossible, obviously, to compare the quantities of food needed by Solomon and his relatively small tribal household with those required by the Assyrian banquet. The two lists are, however, revealing for the variety of foodstuff mentioned.

Solomon's tax districts

The Bible lists tax collectors for each of the 12 districts of his kingdom. Each of the collectors (two of them were sons-in-law of Solomon) was responsible for the provisions needed for the king and his household for one month of the year. To judge from the list of provisions for one day, the tax liability for one month would have been quite considerable (*1 Kings 4.22-23*).

Solomon's Banquet
"Solomon's provision for one day was 30 cors of choice flour, and 60 cors of meal, 10 fat oxen, and 20 pasture-fed cattle, one hundred sheep, besides deer, gazelles, roebucks, and fatted fowl."
(*1 Kings 4.22-23*)

Ashurnasirpal's Banquet
"When Ashurnasirpal, king of Assyria, inaugurated the palace in Calah... [he prepared a banquet of] 1,000 fattened head of cattle, 1,000 calves, 10,000 stable sheep, 15,000 lambs - for my lady Ishtar [alone] 200 head of cattle and 1,000 sihhu-sheep - 1,000 spring lambs, 500 stags, 500 gazelles, 1,000 ducks, 500 geese, 500 kurkû-geese, 1,000 mesuku-birds, 1,000 qaribu-birds, 10,000 doves, 10,000 sukanunu-doves, 10,000 other [assorted] small birds, 10,000 [assorted] fish, 10,000 jerboa, 10,000 [assorted] eggs; 10,000 loaves of bread, 10,000 [jars of] beer, 10,000 skins with wine, 10,000 pointed bottom vessels with su'u-seeds in sesame oil, 10,000 small pots with sarhu-condiment, 1,000 wooden creates with vegetables, 300 [containers of] oil, 300 [containers of] salted seeds... 100 [containers of] fine mixed beer, 100 pomegranates, 100 bunches of grapes, 100 mixed zamru-fruits, 100 pistachio cones, 100 with the fruits of the susi-tree, 100 with garlic, 100 with onions, 100 with kuniphu [seeds], 100 with the ... of turnips, 100 with hinhinni-spice, 100 with budu-spice, 100 with honey, 100 with rendered butter, 100 with roasted barley, 100 with roasted su'u-seeds, 100 with karkartu-plants, 100 with fruits of the ti'atu-tree, 100 with Kasu-plants, 100 with milk, 100 with cheese..."
The banquet reportedly treated over 69,000 people with food and drink, all of whom were sent back, "healthy and happy, to their own countries."

From the Palace of Ashurnasirpal II at Calah

Trade with Phoenicia

The most significant factor in the panorama of Mediterranean trade - certainly from the 9th century BC, and possibly already in the 10th - was the maritime commerce of the Phoenician cities. Phoenician traders had access to Egyptian ports, which meant that items of Egyptian manufacture passed through Tyre and Byblos to the rest of the Near East, and, in addition, decorative and artistic motifs of Nilotic origin became familiar around the Mediterranean in Phoenician "guise." The most traveled routes for Phoenician merchantmen were those that led to Cyprus, the Aegean, North Africa, and the western Mediterranean. To all the communities alongside the Mediterranean shore these merchants traded timber, cloth, purple dye, metalwork, and grain, in return for the products of North Africa, the silver and iron of Spain, the slaves and manufactures of the Aegean, and possibly the opium of Cyprus.

The list of Solomon's 12 tax collectors responsible for providing food for the king and his household is given in 1 Kings 4.7–19, along with several cities to identify each of the 12 districts (*map right*). The area of Judah is conspicuously missing from the administrative districts, indicating the tacit recognition of the division between the two kingdoms. This omission of Judah from the list is perhaps a harbinger of the subsequent division of the United Kingdom into Israel and Judah upon the death of Solomon. Although the list of the 12 officials is complete, the areas are poorly designated. Some of the districts coincide with the old tribal areas, while others are defined only by the names of the cities found within them.

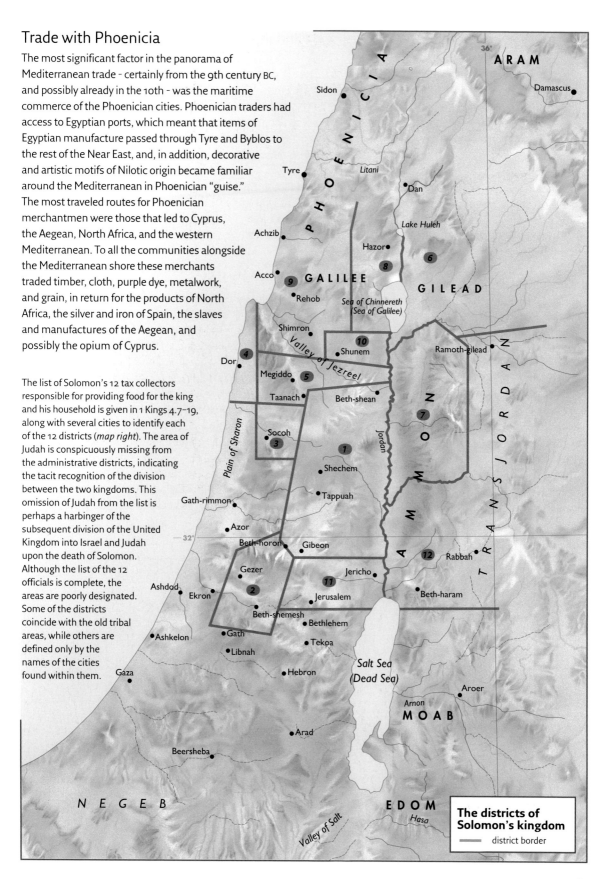

The districts of Solomon's kingdom

── district border

Temples and shrines in Palestine

The very first cult places were outside, perhaps by a sacred tree or spring. They were eventually enclosed, though much of the ritual continued to be conducted in the open air of a walled courtyard. The earliest Palestinian temples were based on a broad-room plan, but later other designs developed.

In ancient Canaan, the temple was viewed as the home of the god or goddess; the need to feed them required areas set aside for sacrifice and offerings. The temple was usually part of a complex that included service buildings, storehouses, and courtyards. The earliest known temple in Palestine is at Jericho, dating from the Neolithic period. It consisted of a porch leading into a hall with an inner shrine behind it, a tripartite structure that was to be the norm for later Bronze and Iron Age temples.

Broad-room temples

One of the best-preserved early temples was found at En-gedi. Dating from the Chalcolithic period, it consists of a broad room entered from one of the long sides, together with an annex, a walled courtyard with a basin in the center, and a gatehouse as part of the enclosure wall. Similar temples from this period have been found at Ai, Tuleilat Ghassul, Megiddo, and Arad.

The distinctive Canaanite broad-room temple became popular in the Early Bronze Age. The well-preserved example at Megiddo has a broad room with a roof that was supported by two columns, an open porch, and a

court. Against the wall facing the entrance was an altar with four steps. Just south of the building was an open-air altar, 25 ft wide and 5 ft high with steps leading to the top, which, when excavated, was covered with soot from fires.

Bronze Age temples

In the Late Bronze Age, the broad-room plan developed into a tripartite structure, with a porch and main room with cult niche or holy of holies. There were two courtyards, an outer and an inner. The former was entered through a propylaeum, or gateway. Benches line the walls, and on both sides of the entrance were tables (*cf. Ezek 40.39–43*). In the main room of the latest temple at Hazor built on this general plan, several cult objects were found, as well as libation tables, incense altars, seals, and bronze figurines. In addition, two columns, one on each side of the temple entrance, are reminiscent of the position of the pillars Jachin and Boaz in the Temple of Jerusalem (*1 Kings 7.21; 2 Chron 4.17*). The temple was probably dedicated to the Canaanite god Baal.

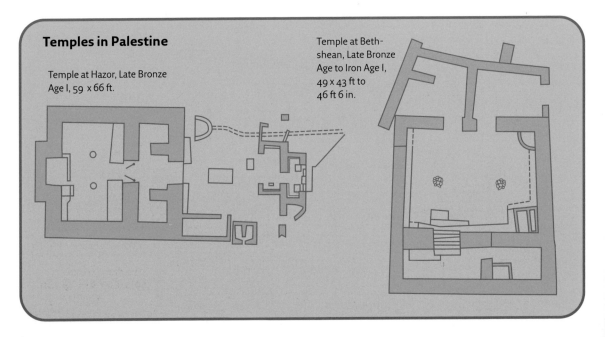

Temples in Palestine

Temple at Hazor, Late Bronze Age I, 59 x 66 ft.

Temple at Beth-shean, Late Bronze Age to Iron Age I, 49 x 43 ft to 46 ft 6 in.

The temple at Arad

At the end of the Bronze Age, many cities throughout Palestine were destroyed and their temples with them. The temple at Arad, which was in use from about 700–600 BC, is the earliest Israelite, as opposed to Canaanite, temple to be discovered in any excavation. Built in the northwest corner of the citadel, with an eastward orientation, it consisted of a main room with a raised cult niche and a courtyard. Benches lined the walls of the main room. In the cult room was found a *massebah* ("standing stone"). Two incense altars were found at the entrance to the debir. The courtyard was divided into two parts and in the large outer area was found an altar for burnt offerings, built of unworked stones and conforming to the regulations laid down in Exodus 20.25. Two column bases were found, one on each side of the entrance to the main room.

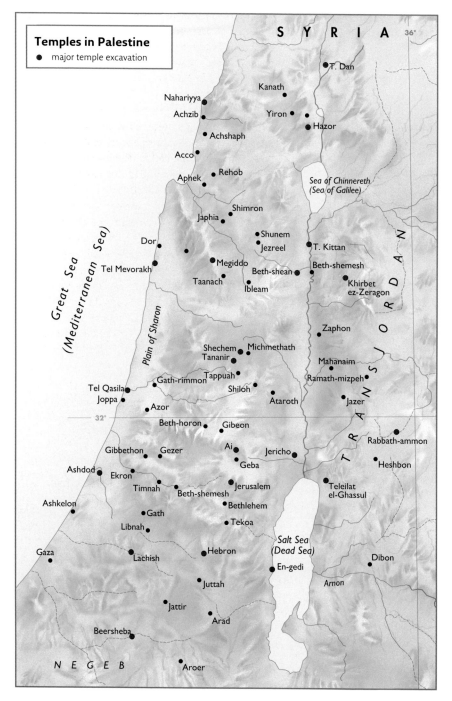

Temples in Palestine

● major temple excavation

S Y R I A — 36°

T. Dan
Kanath
Nahariyya
Achzib
Yiron
Achshaph
Hazor
Acco
Aphek — Rehob
Sea of Chinnereth (Sea of Galilee)
Shimron
Japhia
Shunem
Dor
Jezreel
T. Kittan
Tel Mevorakh
Megiddo
Beth-shean
Beth-shemesh
Taanach
Ibleam
Khirbet ez-Zeragon
Great Sea (Mediterranean Sea)
Plain of Sharon
Zaphon
Shechem — Michmethath
Tananir
Mahanaim
Tappuah
Gath-rimmon
Ramath-mizpeh
Shiloh
Tel Qasila
Joppa
Ataroth
Jazer
Azor
32°
Beth-horon
Gibeon
Rabbath-ammon
Gibbethon
Gezer
Ai
Jericho
Heshbon
Ashdod
Geba
Ekron
Timnah
Jerusalem
Teleilat el-Ghassul
Beth-shemesh
Ashkelon
Bethlehem
Gath
Tekoa
Libnah
Gaza
Salt Sea (Dead Sea)
Hebron
Dibon
Lachish
En-gedi
Juttah
Arnon
Jattir
Arad
Beersheba
N E G E B
Aroer
T R A N S J O R D A N

Major temple excavations in Palestine (*map left*). Although the redactors of the Hebrew Bible saw the temple in Jerusalem as "the" temple, archaeology has revealed many more Canaanite, Philistine, and Israelite temples and shrines. There is no precise word in the Hebrew Bible for temple or sanctuary. *Beit* ("house") is commonly used for a temple dedicated to a particular deity (e.g. the House of Dagon at Ashdod). The term "high place" usually refers to a Canaanite shrine.

Solomon's Jerusalem

The development of international trade and the establishment of a strong central government by Solomon made possible the first public building program in Israel's history.

Solomon converted Jerusalem into a royal capital by adding the Temple Mount and turning it into a monumental acropolis. Archaeologists have discovered a massive sloping "stepped structure" about 55 ft high, which is thought to have served as a retaining wall for the southern end of the raised platform on which Solomon's royal city was built. If this structure is to be identified with the Millo ("the fill"), then the building activities in 1 Kings 9.15 proceeded in geographical order from north to south: the house of the Lord, the house of the King, the Millo, and the city wall.

The Millo ensured a sharp distinction between the lower city and the upper precinct, and at the same time served to expand the area devoted to public buildings from about 10–12 to 20–35 acres (partially at the expense of the area for private houses). However, the total population is unlikely to have exceeded 1500 during Solomon's reign.

The temple and its courtyards covered a considerable area, most probably at the highest and northernmost end of the city. The plan of the king's palace is not clear. It is likely that there was a cluster of palaces, possibly arranged around a common courtyard, similar to the plan of the acropolis at Zinjirli (ancient Sam'al) of the 9th–8th centuries BC.

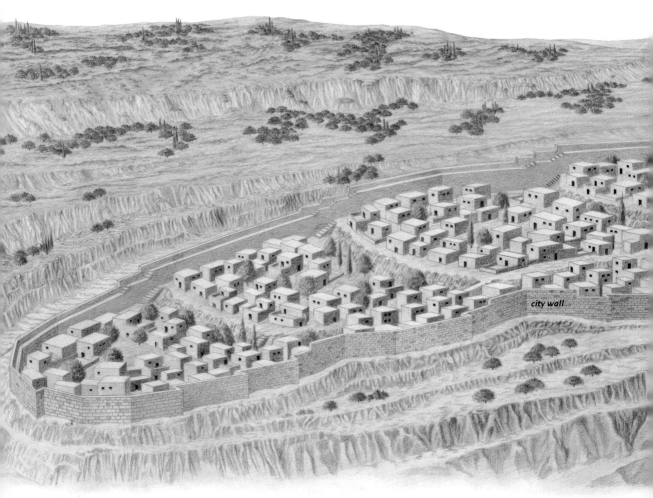

city wall

Solomon's temple

The description of the temple appears in 2 Kings 6-8, 2 Chronicles 3-5, and in Ezekiel's vision in Ezekiel 40-42. These passages have been subject to detailed scrutiny, since no actual remains of Solomon's temple have ever been discovered from archaeological work. The plan follows the tradition of the long-room temple type excavated at several Middle and Late Bronze Age sites in northern Syria. The temple was a tripartite structure with an *ulam* (porch or vestibule), *hekal* (nave or temple), and *debir* (inner sanctuary) - although it has been suggested that the terms apply more to the ceremonial significance of these units than to their structural arrangement. The *debir* was most probably a large cabinet made of cedar beams at the rear of the *hekal*, while the *ulam* was evidently an unroofed passage open at the front and protected by two side walls.

The term used for the main unit, which includes the *hekal* and *debir*, is the "house" (*1 Kings 6.2-3, 17*, etc.). The house measured 60 x 20 cubits (about 90 x 30 ft), surrounded by lower storerooms on three sides. Two ceremonial pillars, called Jachin and Boaz, stood before the temple. Light was provided through windows that were wide on the outside and narrow within. The sacrificial altar, the bronze basin, and the 10 stands for lavers of bronze stood in the courtyard in front of the temple (*1 Kings 7.23-39*). The 10 lampstands of pure gold, golden altar, table, and utensils (*1 Kings 7.48-49*) were inside the *hekal*. The cherubim of olive wood overlaid with gold (*1 Kings 6.23-28*) were in the *debir* alongside the Ark of the Covenant with the two tables of stone (*1 Kings 8.9*). The entire Temple was paneled with precious cedar wood and inlaid with gold.

Reconstruction of Solomon's Jerusalem based on surveys made since 1864 and from excavations. Details of walls, gates, houses, and palace buildings have been inferred from excavated sites of the period.

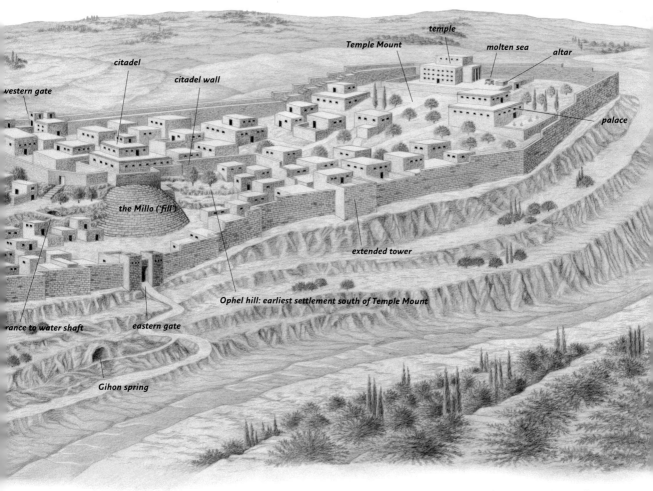

Israel's relationship with Phoenicia

When the Levant recovered from the events that caused the collapse of the Bronze Age empires in the 11th century BC, both Israel and its Phoenician neighbors developed into important regional entities.

Israel and Phoenicia inherited much from their Canaanite past, including closely related languages, but while the Israelite kingdom was mainly agricultural, the narrow coastal plain encouraged the Phoenicians to look outwards. The Phoenicians were sailors, traders, and craftsmen, producing and selling luxury goods, especially in bronze, ivory, precious metals, and textiles.

They exploited their own natural resources, such as timber (especially cedar), fish, and the murex shell (from which a highly prized purple dye was extracted), but they also developed markets and acquired raw materials from far-off places. Their ships (the biblical "ships of Tarshish") sailed as far as the Straits of Gibraltar and beyond into the Atlantic. Gold, ivory, and slaves, along with other exotic goods, came from Africa; metals, especially silver and tin, came from Spain, and copper from Cyprus. Foreign products such as faïence and glass were imported and redistributed abroad and were later imitated and produced locally.

By the 8th century BC, Phoenician settlements flourished in many places. Traders were active in Spain, particularly in the south and around the Guadalquivir basin (known as Tartessos to the Greeks and sometimes proposed as the biblical Tarshish) where there were rich metal deposits. In Cyprus, Phoenician influence is discernible from the 11th century BC, and by the 9th century the Tyrians had established a large settlement at Kition (Larnaca).

The riches that flowed into the Phoenician city-states - of which Sidon and Tyre were the most powerful - made them welcome partners in political and commercial alliances. Phoenician deities were often worshipped abroad - the ruler of Damascus set up a stela to the Tyrian god Melqart, the same deity worshipped by Jezebel, the Sidonian wife of king Ahab, in Israel.

Perhaps the most important legacy of the Phoenicians was the alphabet, which was generally adopted and passed on by the Greeks to the Western world.

Israel and Phoenicia

Collaboration between the Phoenicians and Israel made economic sense: Israel controlled important international trade routes and could supply agricultural products such as corn, wine, oil, and balsam (*Ezek 27.17*). In return, the Phoenicians provided craftsmen of great skill, and fine luxury goods. They were closely involved with Solomon's building program (*2 Chron 2*) and a joint venture to Ophir along the Red Sea coast.

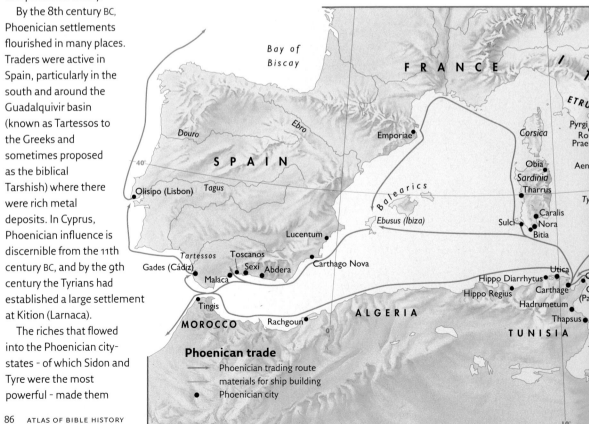

Phoenican trade

→ Phoenician trading route
— materials for ship building
• Phoenician city

Alliances established by David and Solomon and renewed by the House of Omri were strengthened by the dynastic marriages of Jezebel and Athaliah into the royal families of Israel and Judah.

Inscriptions show that the Phoenicians were widely present in Israel and Judah, not only in Galilee and the coastal plain but also inland, even as far as Kuntillet Ajrud, in the Negeb. Phoenician carved ivory has been found at Samaria, and Phoenician-style metal bowls have been found at Nimrud in Mesopotamia.

The relationship of peace and economic cooperation that prevailed between the Phoenician city-states and Israel was unique. Even though the religious practices of Tyre and Sidon were a threat at times to the monotheistic faith of Israel (*1 Kings 18.16–40*), there was never armed conflict between these two adjacent powers.

The map shows the routes by which the Phoenicians were able to trade throughout the whole Mediterranean area and beyond (*map below*). Phoenician influence in Palestine is attested by finds of inscriptions and high-quality luxury goods typical of Phoenician workmanship (*map right*).

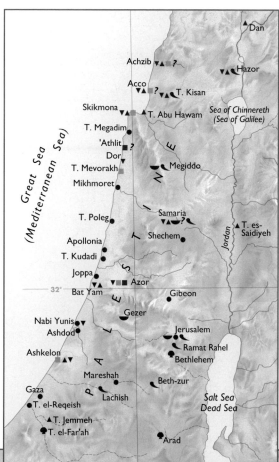

Phoenician influence in Palestine
- ●   site with Phoenician links
- ■ (grey)   Tyrian influence
- ■   Sidonian influence

Phoenician finds
- ▲   Pre-Exilic inscription
- ▼   Post-Exilic inscription
- ◟   ivory carving
- ◡   metal vessel
- ♣   tridacna shell palette

SIX

THE DIVIDED KINGDOM

Ishtar Gates, Babylon.
A reconstruction of one of the eight gates of the inner city of
Babylon. The original, built during the reign of Nebuchadnezzar II
(604–562 BC), was covered with glazed blue tiles, and decorated
with reliefs of lions, dragons, and bulls.

The kingdom divided

The catalyst for the separation of Israel from Judah was the accession of Solomon's son Rehoboam to the throne. Confronted at Shechem by an assembly that was critical of his father's policies, Rehoboam chose a hard line: "My father disciplined you with whips," he told them, "but I will discipline you with scorpions" (1 *Kings 12.14*). This decision was to lead to a split that would last for more than three centuries.

Rehoboam's accession to the throne in Jerusalem was automatic; the dynastic principle was favored in the south, and his acceptance as Solomon's heir was unquestioned. In the north, however, the choice of Rehoboam was not a foregone conclusion. The rift between north and south had widened since Saul's death. His son Ishbaal (or Ish-bosheth) had been murdered by David's supporters (2 *Sam 4.5–8*) - obviously to insure David the Judean kingship - and further northern resentment had been engendered when David took the re-captured ark of the covenant to Jerusalem (1 *Chron 15.25 ff*). The northern tribes had been bound into the United Kingdom by treaty rather than by any inherent concept of unity. Thus, following his accession in Jerusalem, it was necessary for Rehoboam to travel to Shechem to renew the covenant.

Solomon had built the temple and his palaces using not only forced labor from Canaanite tribes, but also a corvée of workers from Israelite tribes (1 *Kings 5.29–31*). Jeroboam ben-Nebat was an overseer of one of those corvées, where his leadership skills had brought him to Solomon's attention. However, in Solomon's eyes, Jeroboam's influence grew too strong, so the king sought to have him eliminated (1 *Kings 11.4*). Jeroboam escaped to Egypt, where he took refuge with Pharaoh Shoshenq I (known in the Bible as Shishak) (1 *Kings 11.26–40*).

Jeroboam returned after Solomon's death, and was present at the meeting at Shechem. At the assembly the northerners appeared willing to accept Rehoboam's kingship, but only under certain conditions; chiefly a reduction in taxation and the forced labor that had been imposed by Solomon. Rehoboam requested three days to consult his advisers; then he refused. The reaction was swift: Rehoboam's chief of forced labor was murdered and Jeroboam was proclaimed king of Israel. Rehoboam returned to Jerusalem and launched a campaign against the north (1 *Kings 12*). The unity of Solomon's kingdom was short-lived.

Conflict over territory

After the assembly at Shechem, there would seem to have been continuous conflict between Israel and Judah. Most disputed was the territory of Benjamin, and the border between the two kingdoms was not fixed for several generations. Initially it seems to have run south of Bethel, and on the west and east it ran north of Aijalon and south of Jericho respectively. The period of conflict between the rival states allowed the areas conquered under the United Monarchy to break away. The situation in Transjordan is unclear but, since, according to the Mesha stela, Omri re-conquered Moab, it must be assumed that it had gained independence. That Israel maintained control over at least part of Ammon is clear from Jeroboam's claim to have "built" Penuel, a site on the Wadi Zerqa. This may have been one of Jeroboam's capitals in the new state. He also enlarged Shechem (T. Balatah) and Tirzah (T. el-Far'ah [N]) for use as royal residences.

Rehoboam's 18-year reign was not a happy one. At the beginning, the northern tribes were lost; in the fifth year of his reign Pharaoh Shishak invaded; and insecurity within may have necessitated the building of a string of "cities of defense" (2 *Chron 11.5–12*). According to the Bible "The war begun between Rehoboam and Jeroboam continued all the days of his life" (1 *Kings 15.6*).

And beyond: Rehoboam's successor, Abijah or Abijam continued the conflict. According to the book of Chronicles he attacked Jeroboam, capturing the cities of Bethel, Jeshanah and Ephron and their surrounding districts (2 *Chr 13.19*). Outright hostility continued for at least four decades; it set the tone for an uneasy relationship which was to continue for the next two hundred years.

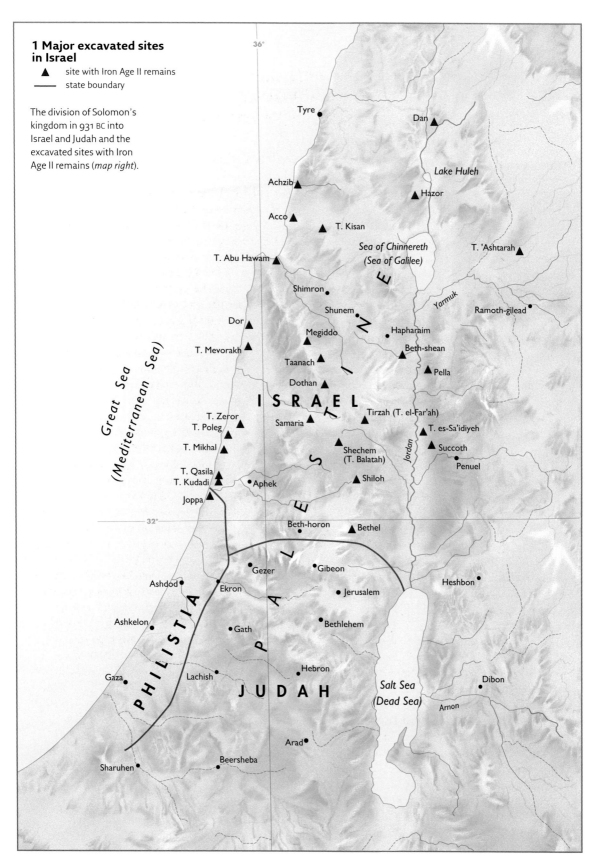

1 Major excavated sites in Israel

▲ site with Iron Age II remains

── state boundary

The division of Solomon's kingdom in 931 BC into Israel and Judah and the excavated sites with Iron Age II remains (*map right*).

36°

Tyre

Dan ▲

Lake Huleh

Achzib ▲

Hazor ▲

Acco ▲

T. Kisan ▲

Sea of Chinnereth (Sea of Galilee)

T. 'Ashtarah ▲

T. Abu Hawam ▲

Shimron

Shunem

Yarmuk

Ramoth-gilead

Dor ▲

Megiddo ▲

Hapharaim

T. Mevorakh ▲

Taanach ▲

Beth-shean ▲

Pella ▲

Dothan ▲

I S R A E L

T. Zeror ▲
T. Poleg ▲

Samaria ▲

Tirzah (T. el-Far'ah) ▲

T. es-Sa'idiyeh ▲

T. Mikhal ▲

Shechem (T. Balatah) ▲

Succoth ▲

Jordan

Penuel

T. Qasila ▲
T. Kudadi ▲

Aphek

Shiloh ▲

Joppa ▲

P A L E S T I N E

Great Sea (Mediterranean Sea)

32°

Beth-horon

Bethel ▲

Gezer

Gibeon

Ashdod

Ekron

Jerusalem

Heshbon

Ashkelon

Gath

Bethlehem

P H I L I S T I A

Hebron

Gaza

Lachish

J U D A H

Salt Sea (Dead Sea)

Dibon

Arnon

Arad

Sharuhen

Beersheba

Shishak's invasion

During Solomon's reign, Shishak, founder of the 22nd (Libyan) dynasty, became pharaoh of Egypt. Although Shishak offered asylum to Jeroboam, Solomon's enemy, relations between Egypt and Israel were probably peaceful. With the division of the kingdom, however, all that changed.

The identification of Shoshenq I with the biblical Shishak is widely accepted, despite recent challenges by champions of the "new chronology." He came to power about 945 BC having previously been the chief advisor to his predecessor Psusennes II and commander of the Egyptian army.

Rehoboam, fearing, perhaps, a "special relationship" between Shishak and Jeroboam, seems to have prepared for an Egyptian invasion by building fortified cities in the Judean hills extending south and west from Jerusalem. In 925 BC, his fears were realized, as Shishak struck in a blitzkrieg-style lightning raid, completely overrunning the central highlands of the Negeb as well as many coastal towns and the city of Megiddo. Any ideas of a special relationship proved illusory, however, since Shishak attacked Israel as well as Judah. The degree of devastation is difficult to assess; Shishak's own account (see below) lists over 150 cities but does not indicate whether they were destroyed or whether they surrendered.

The biblical description records only Shishak's plunder of the Jerusalem temple and the royal palace in the fifth year of Rehoboam (1 Kings 14.25–26). A longer account (2 Chron 12.2–9) contains essentially the same information, but adds that Shishak "took the fortified cities of Judah." It also adds an explanation for the disaster spoken by the prophet Shemaiah: Rehoboam and the princes had been unfaithful to the Lord. It was only the repentance of the king and the princes that had spared the city of Jerusalem from attack.

Evidence from Egypt

The main evidence for the campaign comes from the pharaoh himself. On a wall of the Amon temple at Karnak is a topographical list of cities conquered by Shishak. As it stands, the order of the list seems haphazard, but in 1957 Benjamin Mazar suggested that the text was written in boustrophedon order (like oxen ploughing) - that is, one line from left to right and the following from right to left, and so on. According to this, it is possible to establish a line of advance from one city to another. Shishak's campaigns would appear to have been principally in Israel to the north and in the Negeb; the territory of Judah would seem to have escaped.

A third piece of evidence for Shishak's campaign is a fragment of a stela of victory found at Megiddo, a city that appears in the Karnak list. The absence of Jerusalem in the Shishak list presents a problem in the light of the explicit statement in 1 Kings 14.25 about the pharaoh's visit to Jerusalem. One suggestion for resolving this discrepancy is that Rehoboam negotiated for the payment of gold shields (1 Kings 14.26) at some nearby city, possibly Gibeon, and that Shishak agreed to bypass Jerusalem and then proceeded northward to attack the cities of Israel.

The main force probably followed a line through Gaza in Philistia to Gezer and the Judean hills. Having received the tribute of Rehoboam, the army advanced into Israel, probably taking Shechem and then Tirzah. The Egyptians appear to have turned southeastward, crossing the Jordan opposite Adam (T. ed-Damiyeh). This foray into Transjordan may have been to capture Succoth (T. Dair Alia) and Zaphon (possibly T. es-Saidiyeh). Afterwards, Shishak recrossed the river and went to Beth-shean and the Plain of Esdraelon. The Egyptians may have set up a base at Megiddo and then returned home via the Plain of Sharon and the Via Maris; the exact itinerary cannot be reconstructed further, as the Karnak inscription breaks off here.

Despite this evidence about the invasion of Palestine by Shishak in 925 BC, much remains obscure and uncertain. There seems to have been no intention to establish permanent control over Israel; it may be that the campaign was simply a show of Egyptian strength occasioned by the division of the kingdom of David and Solomon. Nevertheless, the list of cities conquered provides a unique source of topographical information about the occupation of the land at the end of the 10th century BC.

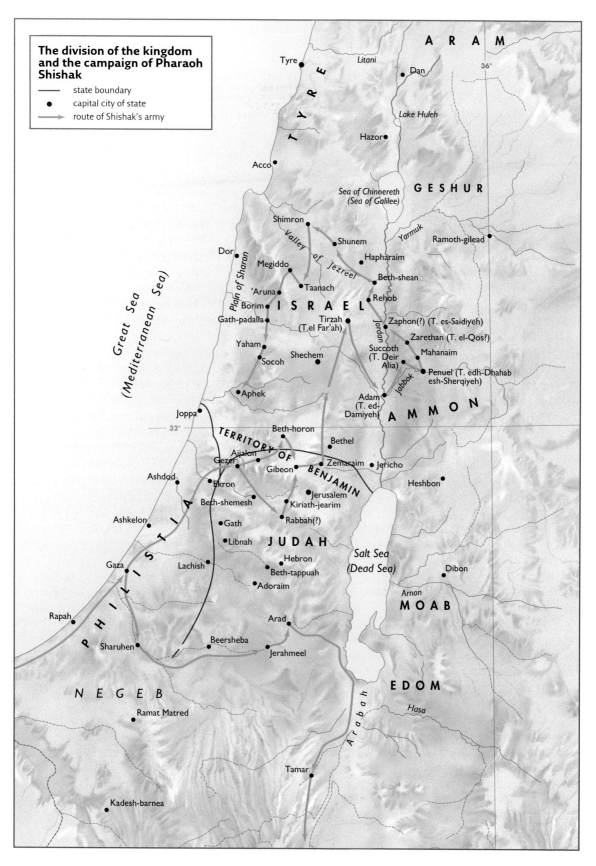

The division of the kingdom and the campaign of Pharaoh Shishak

—— state boundary

● capital city of state

→ route of Shishak's army

A R A M

Tyre

Litani

Dan

Lake Huleh

Hazor

T
Y
R
E

Acco

*Sea of Chinnereth
(Sea of Galilee)*

G E S H U R

Shimron

Shunem

Yarmuk

Ramoth-gilead

Dor

Valley of Jezreel

Megiddo

Hapharaim

'Aruna

Taanach

Beth-shean

Borim

Rehob

I S R A E L

Gath-padalla

Zaphon(?) (T. es-Saidiyeh)

Tirzah
(T.el Far'ah)

Zarethan (T. el-Qos?)

Yaham

Jordan

Succoth
(T. Deir
Alia)

Mahanaim

Socoh

Shechem

Penuel (T. edh-Dhahab
esh-Sherqiyeh)

Aphek

Jabbok

Adam
(T. ed-
Damiyeh)

A M M O N

Joppa

32°

T E R R I T O R Y   O F

Beth-horon

Bethel

Gezer

Aijalon

Zemaraim

Jericho

Gibeon

B E N J A M I N

Ashdod

Ekron

Jerusalem

Heshbon

Beth-shemesh

Kiriath-jearim

Ashkelon

Gath

Rabbah(?)

Libnah

J U D A H

*Salt Sea
(Dead Sea)*

Gaza

Lachish

Hebron

Dibon

Beth-tappuah

Adoraim

Arnon

M O A B

P
H
I
L
I
S
T
I
A

Rapah

Arad

Sharuhen

Beersheba

E D O M

Jerahmeel

Hasa

N E G E B

Arabah

Ramat Matred

Tamar

Kadesh-barnea

*Great Sea
(Mediterranean Sea)*

Plain of Sharon

36°

Omri, Ahab, and Elijah

Omri (885–874 BC) did not acquire the kingship easily. Yet he not only founded a dynasty that ruled over Israel for 40 years, he also founded a new capital, Samaria, that was to become both religiously significant and internationally important.

Omri first appears as commander-in-chief of the army at Gibbethon during a campaign against the Philistines in 885 BC (1 Kings 16.15–18). Another army commander, Zimri, murdered King Elah of Israel (886–885 BC) at Tirzah, the capital city, and made himself king. Omri was proclaimed king by his own army and marched against his rival. After a siege of seven days, Zimri burnt the royal palace and perished in the flames. Omri did not gain immediate control; another group supported an alternative ruler, Tibni, a support that ended only with Tibni's death in 880 BC.

Omri planned a new capital city and purchased a suitable site from a private citizen named Shemer for two talents of silver. Omri named his new capital Samaria after its former owner (1 Kings 16.23–24). However, Omri only lived for six years after moving to Samaria; his building projects were completed by his son Ahab.

Ahab

The move to Samaria, with its westward orientation, may reflect a growing association with Solomon's old ally, Phoenicia, ruled at this time by Ethbaal I of Tyre (1 Kings 16.31). Omri's son Ahab (874–853 BC) married Ethbaal's daughter Jezebel, who brought her cult to the Israelite kingdom. The style of the masonry of Samaria suggests that Omri and Ahab may have enlisted the aid of Phoenician craftsmen for this work.

Under Ahab, Israel joined a coalition of states in an attempt to halt the advance of the Assyrian king Shalmaneser III (825–824 BC). The coalition included forces from Hamath, Damascus, and Israel, with support from Egypt, as well as an Arab contingent mounted on camels. They fought at Qarqar and, although Shalmaneser was not defeated, the Assyrian advance was checked.

Soon after, Ahab was killed during a battle against the Aramaeans at Ramoth-gilead. He was succeeded by his son Ahaziah (852–852 BC) and then by another of his sons, Jehoram (or Joram) (852–841 BC). During the short reign of Ahaziah and Joram, increasingly close links developed with the kingdom of Judah.

The prophets

In these times, the *nabi* ("prophet"), appeared in wandering bands, and made use of music that on occasion aroused ecstatic states of behavior. A prophet could also anoint a king, as well as depose him (1 Sam 10.1, 15.26). Elijah and Elisha were zealous for the God of Israel - Elijah's zeal extended even to the slaying of 450 prophets of Baal (2 Kings 18.40) - spoke out against royalty, and were remembered for miracles.

Elijah and Elisha constantly inveighed against the rulers of Israel for allowing the worship of foreign deities. The climax of the unrest came with the revolt of Jehu, who seized control of the kingdom; murdered both Jehoram and Ahaziah, the Judean king and completely wiped out the family of Ahab, including Jezebel and much of the royal family of Judah. In this bloodthirsty fashion, the dynasty of Omri came to an end. For more than a century, however, the name of its founder lived on in Assyria as the name of the Israelite kingdom. For Shalmaneser III and Sargon II, Israel was "Omri-land" or the "house of Omri."

The reign of Omri and the lives of the Prophets

→ route of Omri
12 events in the lives of Elijah and Elisha

Activities of Elijah
1 Elijah originated from Tishbe in Gilead (1 Kings 17.1)
2 During the drought sent to punish the Israelites, Elijah finds refuge at the brook of Cherith (1 Kings 17.3–5). Here he is fed by the ravens.
3 The brook runs dry and Elijah flees to Zarephath (1 Kings 17.9), where he is cared for by a widow. Later he intervenes with the Lord to restore her dead son to life (1 Kings 17.17–24).
4 At Mount Carmel, Elijah discredits and then executes the prophets of Baal (1 Kings 18.30–40).
5 Ahab, with Elijah running before his chariot, goes to Jezreel (1 Kings 18.41–6).
6 Threatened by Jezebel, Elijah flees to Beersheba (1 Kings 19.1–3).
7 Elijah meets the Lord in the wilderness (1 Kings 19.4–18)
8 Elijah ascends to heaven (2 Kings 2.1–11)

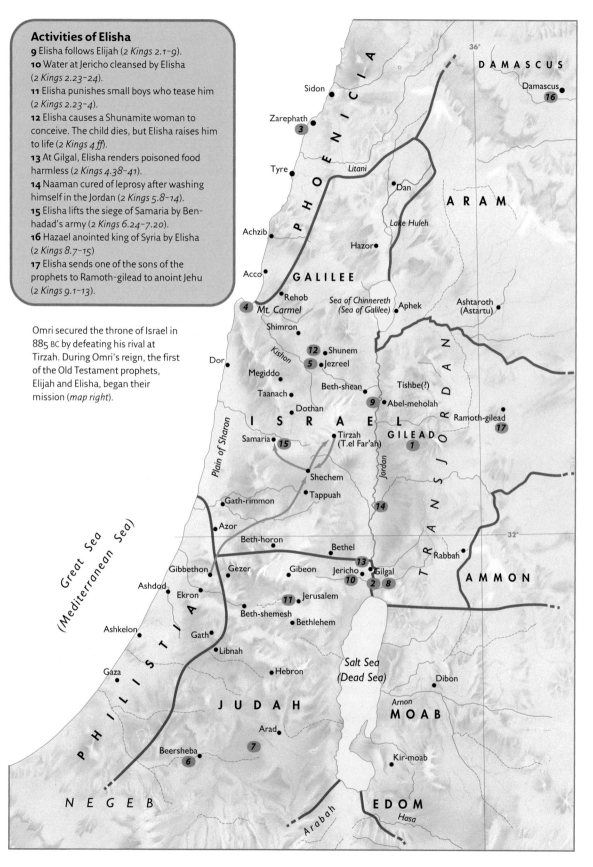

Activities of Elisha

9 Elisha follows Elijah (2 Kings 2.1–9).

10 Water at Jericho cleansed by Elisha (2 Kings 2.23–24).

11 Elisha punishes small boys who tease him (2 Kings 2.23–4).

12 Elisha causes a Shunamite woman to conceive. The child dies, but Elisha raises him to life (2 Kings 4 ff).

13 At Gilgal, Elisha renders poisoned food harmless (2 Kings 4.38–41).

14 Naaman cured of leprosy after washing himself in the Jordan (2 Kings 5.8–14).

15 Elisha lifts the siege of Samaria by Ben-hadad's army (2 Kings 6.24–7.20).

16 Hazael anointed king of Syria by Elisha (2 Kings 8.7–15)

17 Elisha sends one of the sons of the prophets to Ramoth-gilead to anoint Jehu (2 Kings 9.1–13).

Omri secured the throne of Israel in 885 BC by defeating his rival at Tirzah. During Omri's reign, the first of the Old Testament prophets, Elijah and Elisha, began their mission (*map right*).

DAMASCUS

Damascus **16**

Sidon

Zarephath **3**

PHOENICIA

ARAM

Tyre

Litani

Dan

Lake Huleh

Achzib

Hazor

Acco

GALILEE

Rehob

Sea of Chinnereth (Sea of Galilee)

Aphek

Ashtaroth (Astartu)

4 Mt. Carmel

Shimron

Dor

12 Shunem

Kishon

5 Jezreel

Megiddo

Taanach

Beth-shean

Tishbe(?)

Dothan

9 Abel-meholah

ISRAEL

Samaria **15**

Tirzah (T.el Far'ah)

GILEAD

Ramoth-gilead **17**

1

Jordan

Shechem

Tappuah

Plain of Sharon

Gath-rimmon

14

Azor

TRANSJORDAN

Beth-horon

Bethel

Rabbah

Gibbethon

Gezer

Gibeon

Jericho **13** Gilgal

AMMON

Ashdod

10 **2** **8**

Ekron

11 Jerusalem

Beth-shemesh

Bethlehem

Ashkelon

Gath

Libnah

Great Sea (Mediterranean Sea)

PHILISTIA

Gaza

Hebron

Salt Sea (Dead Sea)

Dibon

Arnon

JUDAH

Arad

MOAB

Kir-moab

7

Beersheba

6

NEGEB

EDOM

Arabah

Hasa

36°

32°

Israel and Moab

The land of Moab was a strip of arable land lying between the Dead Sea and the desert to the east. Moab and Israel shared a common material culture and spoke closely-related languages, but they had distinctive religions.

The book of Ruth, set shortly before the time of the monarchy, describes a family of Bethlehem that went to live in Moab during a time of famine (*Ruth 1.1-2*). Ruth distinguished herself by her loyalty to Naomi, her widowed mother-in-law. They returned to her native Bethlehem, where Ruth married Boaz and eventually became the great-grandmother of King David.

The northern region of Moab, separated from Moab proper by the river Arnon (Wadi el-Mujib), was disputed territory between the Israelites, Ammonites, and Moabites for centuries. The book of Joshua (*Josh 13*) claims for Israel the cities north of the Arnon; David, Solomon, and Omri dominated that area but were probably unable to exercise any permanent control over the more isolated cities lying between the Wadi el-Mujib and the Wadi Hasa at the southern end of the Dead Sea.

The relations between Israel and Moab are more fully documented during the reign of King Mesha over Moab. In addition to biblical information (*2 Kings 1.1, 3.4-27*) there is a detailed account of Mesha's wars and building accomplishments engraved on the "Moabite Stone," a stela discovered near Dibon in 1868. This inscription mentions Omri, King of Israel; Yahweh, god of Israel; Moab's national god Ashtar-Chemosh (*1 Kings 11.7*), and some 10 of the Moabite cities found in the Old Testament text.

Under Omri and his son Ahab, Israel extended its control over northern Moab and extracted payments of tribute from its cities. Mesha probably did not challenge Israel's authority in Moab until Ahab died (*1 Kings 1.1, 3.4*), refusing to deliver the annual tribute, seizing control of northern Moab, and making preparations to defend his country against Israel's retaliatory attack, which he

The Moabite Stone

This important inscription was discovered intact in 1868; it was subsequently broken, presumably by local Bedouin tribesmen, and in 1873 it was taken to the Louvre.

The date of the Mesha Stela is roughly fixed by the reference to Mesha, king of Moab in 2 Kings 3.4 as about the mid-9th century BC.

The following is a translation of the stela:

I [am] Mesha, son of Chemosh [...], king of Moab, the Dibonite - my father [had] reigned over Moab thirty years, and I reigned after my father, - [who] made this high place for Chemosh in Qarhoh [...] because he saved me from all the kings and caused me to triumph over all my adversaries. As for Omri king of Israel, he mubled Moab many year [lit., days], for Chemosh was angry at his land. And his son followed him and he also said, "I will humble Moab." In my time he spoke [thus], but I have triumphed over him and over his house, while Israel hath perished for ever! [Now] Omri had occupied the land of Medeba, and [Israel] had dwelt there in his time and half the time of his son [Ahab], 40 years; but Chemosh dwelt there in my time.

And I built Baal-meon, making a reservoir in it, and I built Qaryaten. Now the men of Gad had always dwelt in the land of Ataroth, and the king of Israel had built Ataroth for them; but I fought against the twon and took it and slew all the people of the town as satiation [intoxication] for Chemosh and Moab. And I brought back from there Arel [or Oriel], its chieftain, dragging him before Chemosh in Kerioth, and I settled there

men of Sharon and men of Maharith. And Chemosh said to me, "Go, take Nebo from Israel!" So I went by night and fought against it from the break of dawn until noon, taking it and slaying all, seven thousand men, boys, women, girls, and maid-servants, for I had devoted them to destruction for [the god] Ashtar-Chemosh. And I took from there the [...] of the Lord, dragging them before Chemosh. And the king of Israel had built Jahaz, and he dwelt there while he was fighting against me, but Chemosh drove him out before me. And I took from Moab two hundred men, all first-class [warriors], and set them against Jahaz and took it in order to attach it to [the district of] Dibon.

It was I [who] built Qarhoh, the wall of the forests and the wall of the citadel; I also built its gates and I built its towers and I built the king's house, and I made both of its reservoirs for water inside the town. And there was no cistern inside the town at Qarhoh, so I said to all the people, "Let each of you make a cistern for himself in his house!" And I cut beams for Qarhoh with Israelite captives. I built Aroer, and I made the highway in the Arnon [valley]; I built Beth-bamoth, for it had been destroyed; I built Bezer - for it lay in ruins - with 50 men of Dibon, for all Dibon is [my] loyal dependency.

And I reigned [in peace] over the hundred towns that I had added to the land. And I built [...] Medeba and Beth-diblathen and Beth-baal-meon, and I set there the [...] of the land. And as for Hauronen, there dwelt in it [...And] Chemosh said to me, "Go down, fight against Hauronen." And I went down [and I fought against the town and I took it], and Chemosh dwelt there in my time.

assumed would occur as soon as a new king was established in Samaria. The expected attack only came after Ahaziah had died and was succeeded by Joram (Jehoram). After collecting the king of Judah in Jerusalem, Jehoram marched "by the way of the wilderness to Edom," approaching Moab from the southwest, where the terrain is extremely rugged. This surprise approach by a route that led up the steep north bank of the Wadi Hasa proved successful. The invaders devastated Moab until only Kir-hareseth was left standing and the King of Moab had taken refuge behind its walls (2Kings 3.25).

The Moabite Stone was probably erected in connection with the dedication of a sanctuary to Chemosh at a place called Qarhoh. Lines 9–21 of the inscription recount Mesha's key moves in his recovery of the land of Medeba from Israel. Specifically, he attacked, massacred, and looted two Israelite settlements in northern Moab (Ataroth and Nebo); fortified two other sites, Beth-baal-meon and Qaryaten (probably biblical Kiriathaim), and placed his own loyalists in Jahaz which had been built (or fortified) by the Israelites to serve as a military and administrative base during their occupation of northern Moab.

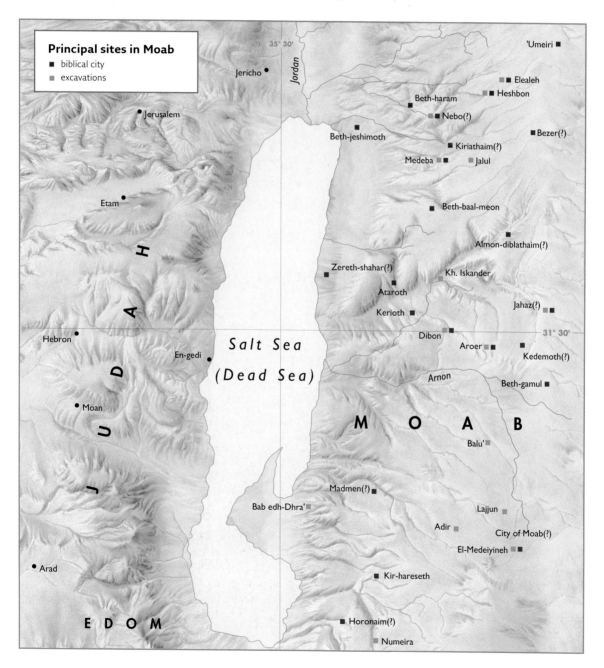

Principal sites in Moab
- ■ biblical city
- ■ excavations

Israel's relations with Aram

During the 9th and 8th centuries BC, Israel and Judah were involved with their northern neighbor Aram. Relations varied between rivalry for territory and trade, occasional treaties, payment of tribute to Aram, as well as open warfare.

Ben-Hadad I

Ben-Hadad I, king of Aram (c. 900–c. 860 BC), invaded Israelite territory on call from Asa of Judah, with whom he had a treaty and who was militarily threatened by Baasha of Israel. Although Ben-Hadad also had a treaty with Baasha, a payment of treasure from Asa led him to take Asa's side. Ben-Hadad I advanced from the north and took important Israelite cities.

Hazael

Hazael (c. 843–780 BC), who had killed Ben-Hadad II and usurped the throne, extended Aram's control east of the Jordan as far south as Aroer in Moab, becoming a significant threat to the kingdoms of Israel and Judah (2 Kings 10.32–3).

Ben-Hadad II

Ben-Hadad II besieged Samaria in the time of Ahab (874–853 BC). After two unsuccessful attempts to take the city, he was taken prisoner at Aphek and forced to give Israel special trading rights in Damascus. The expansion of Assyria westward was delayed in 853 BC, when Levantine states, including Aram and Israel, joined to confront Shalmaneser III in the battle of Qarqar, but the alliance was short-lived.

Ben-Hadad III

Ben-Hadad III (c. 805–c. 778 BC) suffered from the resurgence of power in Israel. Joash (798–782 BC) recovered the cities that Hazael had taken; Jeroboam II is credited with the conquest of Damascus and Hamath (2 Kings 14.28).

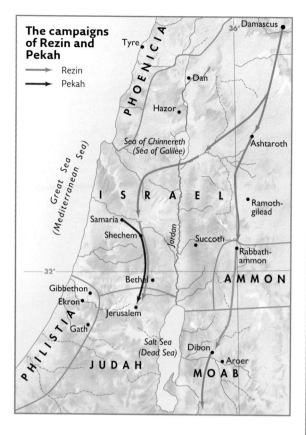

The campaigns of Rezin and Pekah

→ Rezin
→ Pekah

(Map labels: Damascus, Tyre, PHOENICIA, Dan, Hazor, Sea of Chinnereth (Sea of Galilee), Ashtaroth, Great Sea (Mediterranean Sea), ISRAEL, Ramoth-gilead, Samaria, Shechem, Jordan, Succoth, Rabbath-ammon, Bethel, AMMON, Gibbethon, Ekron, PHILISTIA, Jerusalem, Gath, Salt Sea (Dead Sea), Dibon, Aroer, JUDAH, MOAB, 36°, 32°)

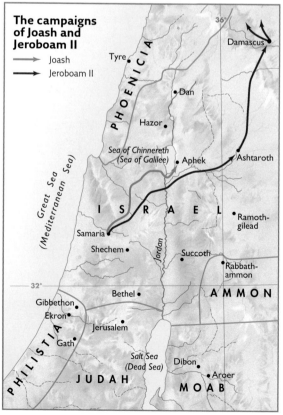

The campaigns of Joash and Jeroboam II

→ Joash
→ Jeroboam II

(Map labels: Damascus, Tyre, PHOENICIA, Dan, Hazor, Sea of Chinnereth (Sea of Galilee), Aphek, Ashtaroth, Great Sea (Mediterranean Sea), ISRAEL, Ramoth-gilead, Samaria, Shechem, Jordan, Succoth, Rabbath-ammon, Bethel, AMMON, Gibbethon, Ekron, PHILISTIA, Jerusalem, Gath, Salt Sea (Dead Sea), Dibon, Aroer, JUDAH, MOAB, 36°, 32°)

Rezin

Rezin (c. 750–c. 732 BC) joined with Pekah of Israel to bring Jotham of Judah into an alliance to oppose Tiglath-pileser III of Assyria. When Jotham refused, Rezin and Pekah captured Jerusalem. Rezin then conquered Ammon, Moab, and Edom. Although Jotham appealed to Tiglath-pileser for help, the latter continued his march, took Damascus, killed Rezin, and undertook a major campaign in Israel. Pekah was assassinated and was succeeded by Hoshea, the last king of Israel.

Aram	Israel		Judah
	909		911
c. 900	Baasha		
	886		Asa
	Elah		
Ben-Hadad I	885		
	Zimri 885		
	Tibni 880		
	Omri 874		
c. 860	Ahab		870
Ben-Hadad II (Adad-Idri)I	853		Jehoshaphat
	Ahaziah 852		848
c. 843	Joram 841		Jehoram 841
Hazael	Jehu		Athaliah 835
	814		Jehoash
c. 805	Jehoahaz 798		
Ben-Hadad III	Joash 798		796
c. 773			Amaziah
	Jeroboam II		767
Hadianu	753		
	Zechariah 752		Uzziah
	Shallum 752		
c. 750	Menahem 742	in Gilead	
Rezin	Pekahiah 742		
	Pekah		740
c. 732	732		Jotham 732
Assyrians	Hoshea		Ahaz 716
	Assyrians		

The reigns of the kings of Aram, Israel, and Judah shown in parallel (*chart above*).

The Assyrians

In order to secure his boundaries against raids by mountaineers to the east and north, King Ashurnasirpal II (883–859 BC), the founder of the Assyrian empire of the 1st millennium BC, began to conquer the foes of the national god Ashur and to impose tribute upon them. In doing this, he opened the way for an Assyrian advance to the Mediterranean, reached in about 875 BC for the first time in two centuries.

Ashurnasirpal was able to move from Carchemish into northern Syria, by a route skirting the powerful state of Hamath. After defeating the state of Patina, he went down the River Orontes as far as the Lebanon range and then to the Mediterranean. There he met no resistance, and the Phoenician states as far south as Tyre sent tribute.

Shalmaneser III

In 853 BC, Ashurnasirpal's son and successor Shalmaneser III (858–824 BC) moved south-westwards via Pethor (*Num 22.5*) and Aleppo into the territory of Hamath. He was met at Qarqar, east of the river Orontes, by a powerful coalition of states (see page 94).

Shalmaneser claimed to have inflicted an enormous slaughter on their coalition, which could be true in view of the difficulties facing over 60,000 men under up to 11 commanders, unused to operating as a coordinated army. However, the resistance was sufficient to check any further southward advance by Assyria for over a decade. Internal problems - particularly the usurpation of Hazael in Damascus and Jehu in Israel (*1 Kings 19.15–18; 2 Kings 8.15, 9.14,* etc.) - caused the coalition to collapse, enabling Shalmaneser to reach Damascus in 841 BC. From there, he marched south to Khaurina and then through Israelite territory, possibly to Mount Carmel; Jehu, Israel's king, is shown paying tribute on a black obelisk found at Nimrud.

Ashurnasirpal II wanted to renew the expansionist policies of Assyria, and he set out to gain tribute from the coastal cities of Phoenicia (*map right*). Our only evidence about Ashurnasirpal II's expedition to Phoenicia is his own account, which is brief and undetailed. The route is virtually certain until he crossed the Orontes, and then it seems he may have gone south down the east side of the river to the Mediterranean. Ashurnasirpal states in the account of the expedition: "At that time I seized the entire extent of the Lebanon mountain and reached the Great Sea of the Amurru country. I cleaned my weapons in the deep sea..." The lists of tribute taken include the usual articles of precious metals and foodstuff, but in addition, there are chairs, beds, and tables made of wood, a commodity readily available in the mountains of Lebanon and highly valued in Assyria.

Ashurnasirpal II's expedition to the Levant

→ Assyrian line of march

▲ tribute sent to Assyria

➤ local military units added to Assyrian army

♣ timber felled for Assyria

Lacking natural boundaries and therefore physical defenses from raiders, the Assyrians constantly needed to extend their kingdom in order to secure surrounding territories (*map below*). The maximum extent of the Assyrian kingdom was brought about by Ashurbanipal, and the boundaries shown combine maximum military penetration with the maximum area credibly claimed as paying tribute. The broken line indicates transitory control. Boundary lines have to be denoted by broad sweeps, which cannot claim accuracy at every point. Where there is a sudden change in the direction of a boundary, there is positive evidence, either from inscriptional data combined with identified sites or from the demands of geography.

http://www.metmuseum.org/Works_of_Art/department.asp?dep=3
Ancient Near Eastern art
http://www.mesopotamia.co.uk/
Mesopotamia: The British Museum
http://oi.uchicago.edu/museum/highlights/assyria.html
Highlights from the Assyrian collection at the Oriental Institute Museum

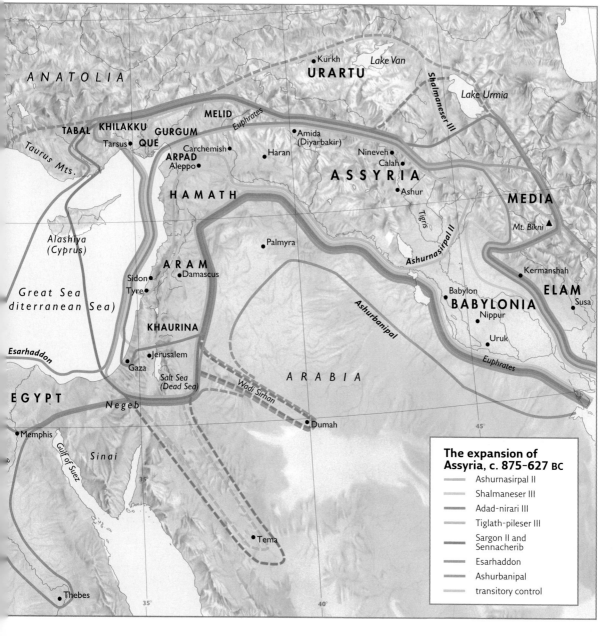

The expansion of Assyria, c. 875–627 BC

- Ashurnasirpal II
- Shalmaneser III
- Adad-nirari III
- Tiglath-pileser III
- Sargon II and Sennacherib
- Esarhaddon
- Ashurbanipal
- transitory control

At the battle of Qarqar, Shalmaneser III defeated a coalition of forces from Phoenicia, Egypt, and Israel and thus gained control over this area (*map right*). The coalition included troops under the command of Ahab the Israelite. According to the Assyrian account, he provided 2000 chariots and 10,000 infantry, but this is almost certainly an Assyrian exagerration designed to make the scale of victory more impressive.

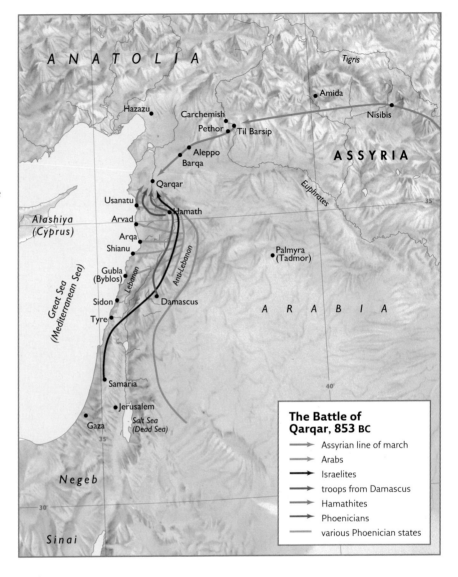

The Battle of Qarqar, 853 BC

→	Assyrian line of march
→	Arabs
→	Israelites
→	troops from Damascus
→	Hamathites
→	Phoenicians
—	various Phoenician states

Forces defeated by Shalmaneser III at Qarqar

Damascus:
infantry 20,000; cavalry 1200; chariots 1200
Hamath:
infantry 10,000; cavalry 700; chariots 700
Israel:
infantry 10,000; chariots 2000

Phoenician states:
Gubla (Gebal, Byblos):
infantry 500
Egyptian garrison in Gubla:
infantry 1000
Irqanata (Arqa):
infantry 10,000; chariots 10

Arvad (of Arvadites of *Gen 10.17*):
infantry 200
Usanatu:
infantry 200
Shianu (cf. Sinites of *Gen 10.17*):
infantry 10,000; chariots 30

others:
Arabs:
camels 1000
"Of Ruhubi of Ammana" (Rehob of *2 Sam 10.8*. Amana was not Ammon in Transjordan but a region in the Anti-Lebanon named in *Song of Sol 4.8*): no details

Shamshi-Adad V and Adad-nirari III

Shamshi-Adad V (823–811 BC) and Adad-nirari III (810–783 BC) reasserted Assyrian dominance between 805 and 796 BC. The latter conquered Damascus, which brought recognition of Assyrian suzerainty by other states including Sidon, Tyre, and cities in Philistia and Israel under Joash. Beginning with attacks in 805 and 804 BC to subdue northern Syria, Adad-nirari III reached the Mediterranean in 803 BC and may have continued down the coast in 802 BC, to ensure the submission of the Phoenician cities. In 796 BC, he moved south to Mansuate (in the Beqa'a Valley) and entered Damascus to receive the submission of its king, Ben-Hadad III.

Tiglath-pileser III

Tiglath-pileser III (744–727 BC, called "Pul" in 2 Kings 15.19, etc.) came to the Assyrian throne following a rebellion. He treated conquered regions west of the Euphrates as tribute-paying vassals and introduced the new strategy of establishing directly ruled provinces in areas that proved troublesome. Vigorous military action established a chain of Assyrian provinces as far as Damascus. Babylonia, unsettled by Chaldean tribesmen, was taken under direct rule.

Tiglath-pileser's policy continued until the end of the empire, with ever-increasing territory. Shalmaneser V (726–722 BC) and Sargon II (721–705 BC) extended Assyrian control in Syria and Palestine, and Sennacherib attacked Judah. From the time of the conquest of Canaan down to the Babylonian exile, Israel had many enemies, varying from small tribal groups of raiders to the major world powers, but none can compare with Assyria for the destruction of property, the amount of tribute taken, or captives carried away to foreign lands.

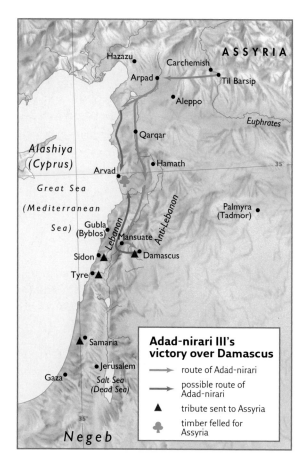

Adad-nirari III was able to take advantage of the Assyrian supremacy achieved by Shalmaneser III over Syria and he received tribute from Damascus. A stone slab found at Calah boasts of his achievements (map above).

Principal Assyrian rulers	
Tiglath-pileser II	966–935 BC
Tukulti-Ninurta II	890–884 BC
Ashurnasirpal II	883–859 BC
Shalmaneser III	858–824 BC
Tiglath-pileser III	744–727 BC
Sargon II	721–705 BC
Sennacherib	704–61 BC
Esarhaddon	680–669 BC
Ashurbanipal	668–627 BC
Ashur-uballit	611–609 BC

"King Pul [Tiglath-pileser III] of Assyria came against the land; Menahem gave Pul a thousand talents of silver, so that he might help him confirm his hold on the royal power. Menahem exacted the money from Israel, that is, from all the wealthy, fifty shekels of silver from each one, to give to the king of Assyria. So the king of Assyria turned back, and did not stay there in the land."

(2 Kings 15.19–20)

Peace and prosperity under Jeroboam II

The kingdom of Israel reached a peak of political importance and prosperity under King Jeroboam II (782–753 BC). Although little is said in 2 Kings about Jeroboam, references in the book of Amos combined with implications drawn from the Samaria ostraca suggest that the time of Jeroboam II was one of economic prosperity as well as geographical expansion.

Judah also saw a revival of political, military, and economic power under Azariah/Uzziah, who launched a campaign against the Philistines (2 *Chron 26.6*) and established strong points in the territory of Ashdod and elsewhere on the coastal plain. His control of the trade routes from Arabia and Sinai was secured by the restoration of Elath after his father died (2 *Kings 14.22*); thus, he received tribute from the Arabs and also the Meunites (2 *Chron 26.7*).

The Samaria ostraca

Among the discoveries of ancient Hebrew texts that contribute as independent sources to biblical geography and history, the finding of a collection of potsherds at Samaria is one of the most important. Most scholars have agreed on the reading and translations of these brief texts, but why they were written is widely debated.

The texts appear to be dated notations of a transaction or shipment of oil or wine from a sender at a particular town and in a certain tribal district to a named recipient in another, presumably Samaria, where the inscriptions were eventually discovered.

The wine and oil were shipped from 18 places, 12 of which are mentioned in the Bible. In Joshua 17.2 the tribes ("children of") Manasseh are listed: Abiezer, Helek, Asriel, Shechem, Hepher, and Shemida. All but one (Hepher) of these names appear as clan names on the Samaria ostraca. This remarkable duplication provides evidence for the geographical reality underlying an otherwise obscure tribal list (*Josh 17.2*). By matching the clan with the town

Towns and clan districts mentioned in the ostraca inscriptions (*map right*). Discovered in 1910, the 63 potsherds record transactions of oil and wine from various regions of Samaria to different officials. They illustrate the concentration of wealth during the eighth century BC, which was criticised by prophets such as Amos and Hosea.

Area of the Samaria ostraca

- ● town
- ■ town mentioned in the ostraca
- *NOAH* clan district
- — tribal boundary

unidentified towns:
Cherem, Yehoeli, Ashereth

associated with it on the ostraca, it has been possible to show the settlement patterns of the various clans of Manasseh.

The ostraca may have been tax receipts issued by officials in charge of administrative districts to those paying taxes in the currency of jars of oil and wine; or they may have been records of commodities received at the royal storehouse in Samaria. The recipients could have been those "eating at the king's table" (cf. 2 Sam 9.10, 13), being sent just enough from their own estates for use while on duty in the capital city.

The recipients of these shipments have typical Hebrew names that end with a form of the divine name Yahweh shorted to "yaw." (This usage seems to be particular to the northern kingdom of Israel, as opposed to the custom of spelling the abbreviated divine name "-yahu" or "-yah" in Judah.)

If this picture reconstructed from archaeological data is correct, it would confirm the existence of a privileged class that was able to own vineyards and olive groves around Samaria in the early 8th century BC. It could have then been this secure class "that lie upon beds of ivory" and that "drink wine in bowls and anoint themselves with the chief oils" whom the prophet Amos so vehemently condemned (Amos 6.1–6).

Israel and Judah at the time of Jeroboam II

- •   city from which prophet originated

- ——   district boundary

The borders of Israel, Judah, and Philistia in the 8th century BC and the cities from which the prophets of this period originated (*map right*).

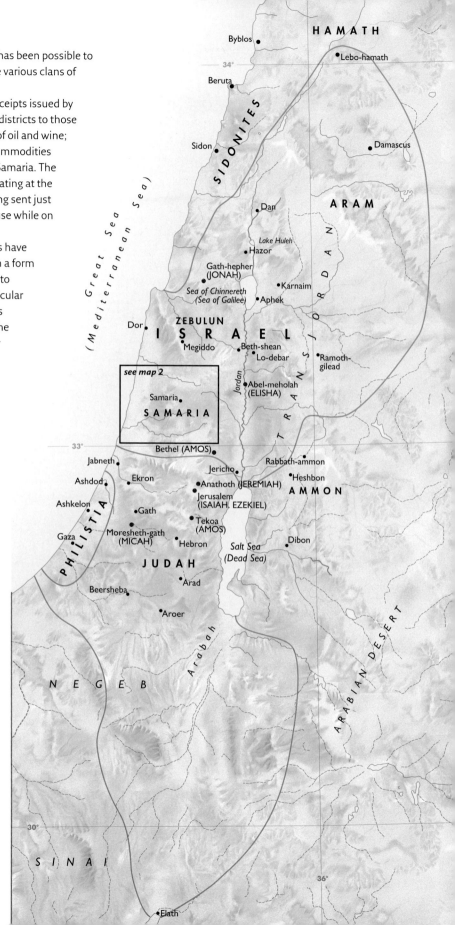

Assyrian sovereignty over Israel

When Tiglath-pileser III came to the throne of Assyria in 774 BC, the kingdoms of Israel and Judah were caught up in world politics to a degree they had not known before. Four of their kings are mentioned by name in cuneiform texts at Nimrud, the distant Assyrian capital. Tiglath-pileser appears three times in the book of Kings. Deportation of Israelite captives to a foreign land was begun, a practice that was followed by the Babylonians with more far-reaching historical consequences.

Until the second half of the 8th century BC, Assyria had treated the river Euphrates as its western boundary. This changed when Tiglath-pileser made provinces out of areas formerly ruled by vassal native kings. A factor in this change of policy was the appearance of a threat to Assyria's major trade route. The kingdom of Urartu (the biblical Ararat) had expanded westward and formed a coalition of northern Syrian states. Tiglath-pileser attacked this Urartian coalition in 743 BC and defeated it. Three years later, Arpad, the main center of resistance, fell and was made the capital of an Assyrian province. It was soon

followed by others: the capital of Unqi, Kullania, was taken in 738 BC and gave its name to a newly created province; Simirra and Khatarikka were made provinces in the same year; and tribute was paid by Rezin of Damascus, Menahem of Samaria, and the kings of Tyre, Byblos, and Hamath. Tiglath-pileser lists a variety of loot: "gold, silver, tin, iron, elephant-hides, ivory, linen garments with multicolored trimmings, blue-dyed wool, purple-dyed wool, ebony-wood, boxwood-wood, whatever was precious [enough for a] royal treasure; also lambs whose stretched hides were dyed purple, [and] wild birds whose

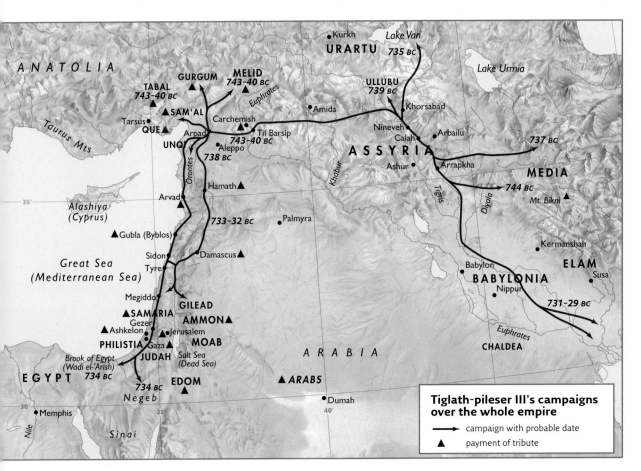

Tiglath-pileser III's campaigns over the whole empire

→ campaign with probable date

▲ payment of tribute

spread-out wings were dyed blue, [furthermore] horses, mules, large and small cattle, [male] camels, female camels with their foals."

After two campaigns in the east and another against Urartu itself, Tiglath-pileser returned west in 734 BC to extend Assyrian control into Philistia. Pekah of Israel had joined with Rezin of Damascus in an anti-Assyrian coalition, which also included Tyre, Ashkelon, and some Arab tribes of northern Arabia and Transjordan. King Ahaz of Judah refused to join the coalition, preferring to accept Assyrian suzerainty and invoke protection against attack (2 *Kings 16.6–7*). Upon the defeat of the coalition, the coastal, northern, and Transjordanian sectors of Israel became the Assyrian provinces of Dor, Megiddo, and Gilead; Pekah was deposed, and what was left of the kingdom of Israel was placed under Hoshea as Tiglath-pileser's nominee and vassal. In 2 Kings 15.29–30, the account of the royal succession mentions only that Hoshea conspiraced against Pekah and slew him. In Tiglath-pileser III's annals, the Assyrian king takes credit for the placing of a new king on the throne: "They overthrew their king Pekah and I placed Hoshea as king over them. I received from them 10 talents of gold, 1000[?] talents of silver as their tribute and brought them to Assyria." The kingdom of Damascus was taken under direct Assyrian rule and divided into the three provinces of Damascus, Karnaim and Khaurina (perhaps Hauran). Following usual Assyrian policy, parts of the populations of both kingdoms were deported and the area repopulated with conquered people from elsewhere.

Between 744 and 727 BC, Tiglath-pileser III carried out a series of campaigns to expand Assyrian influence. His first campaign was against the Urartian coalition in 743 BC. In spite of rebellion by vassal states, he was able to turn his attention to quelling a revolt in Babylonia (*map left*). The Assyrians were not merely destroyers; they evolved a sophisticated system of administration of well-defined provinces. In addition to these were vassal states and peoples who paid tribute. Shown here are the general divisions established by Tiglath-pileser III (*map right*).

Assyrian provinces under Tiglath-pileser III

- province
- vassal state or people

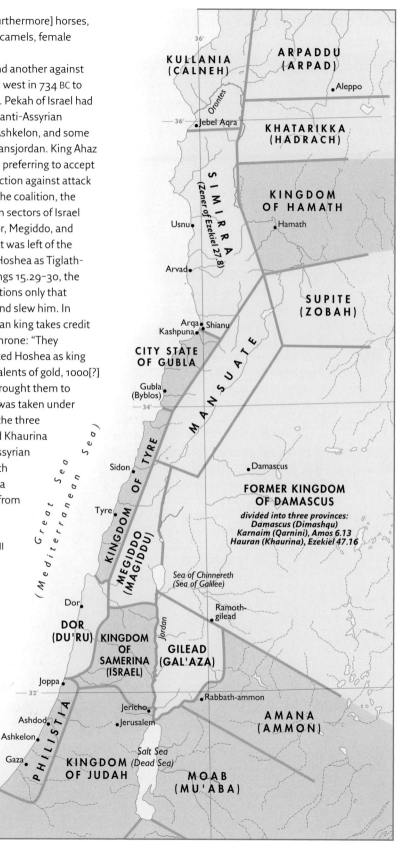

The fall of Israel

The main concern of the rest of Tiglath-pileser III's reign was Babylonia, where a revolt broke out under a Chaldean chieftain. When this had been quelled, Tiglath-pileser himself took the kingship of Babylon from 729 BC.

His briefly reigning successor, Shalmaneser V (726–722 BC), clashed with vested interests in his capital, Ashur. The resulting instability weakened Assyria's hold on the west, and Hoshea, Assyria's appointee as king of Israel, transferred allegiance to Egypt. Assyria replied by sending an army against Samaria, which, after a two-year siege, was taken in late 722 BC. A display inscription on a stone slab of the wall at Khorsabad (Dur Sharrukin) gives the following Assyrian account of the fall of the capital of the northern kingdom of Israel: "I besieged and conquered Samaria, led away as booty 27,290 inhabitants of it. I formed from among them a contingent of 50 chariots and made remaining [inhabitants] assume their [social] positions. I installed over them an officer of mine and imposed upon them the tribute of the former king."

Although this inscription is that of Sargon II (721–705 BC), the successor of Shalmaneser V, this success is not mentioned in his earliest inscription dealing with the events of his campaigns in the west in 720 BC. The Bible implies that the conquest of Samaria took place during the reign of Shalmaneser (2 *Kings* 17.3–6). This can be reconciled with the Assyriological data by assuming that Sargon boasted, in his later inscriptions, of the achievement of his immediate predecessor on the throne of Assyria.

Israel was made into a province called Samerina, possibly incorporating the earlier Dor, although, by the time of Esarhaddon's reign, this was treated as an area of Philistia. Part of the population was subsequently deported to Assyria and then settled in Halah, on the river Khabur (Habor), and in the cities of the Medes (2 *Kings* 17.6). It was the end of the northern kingdom.

Accession of Sargon II

Sargon II's accession was linked to the opposition to Shalmaneser V, but he quickly restored stability. He faced

Military action against Israel

→ Sargon II
→ Shalmaneser V
→ Hamath
↡ anti-Assyrian activities

After the capture of Samaria by Shalmaneser V in 722 BC, his successor, Sargon II, faced with anti-Assyrian activities in major cities of Syria and Palestine, moved to quell the revolts (*map right*). His success in restoring order in Samaria in 720 BC may account for his taking credit, in later records, for the 722 BC victory of his predecessor there.

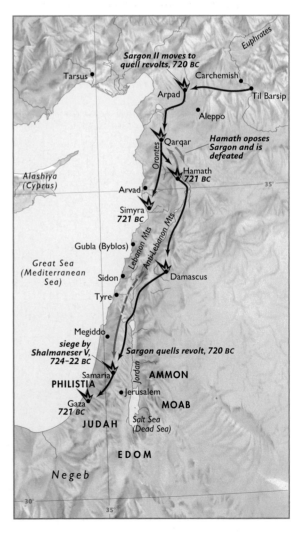

problems in three areas: Babylonia, where Chaldean tribes supported by Elam were attempting to oust Assyrian control; the far north, from south of Lake Urmia to Asia Minor, where Urartu was working to establish a chain of vassal states and allies; and Syria and Palestine, where a resurgent Egypt was seeking to increase its influence.

The most immediate problem was in Babylonia; although a military clash with Elam checked the threat from that quarter, Sargon was powerless against the Chaldean leader Marduk-apil-iddina (Merodach-baladan of the Bible), who usurped the throne of Babylon and held it for a decade. In the west, a widespread revolt broke out, headed by Hamath, with Arpad, Damascus, Samaria, and parts of Phoenicia and Philistia implicated, and Egypt giving support (2 *Kings* 17.4). Sargon quelled the revolt in 720 BC; it was the major siege two years later that allowed him in his records to claim credit for the original capture of the city.

In subsequent years, Assyria had both military and diplomatic successes against Urartian influence in the north. A treaty was made with Urartu's former allies, Midas and Meshech, in Asia Minor - powerful from control of trade routes - and the Assyrians made a decisive invasion of Urartu itself in 714 BC.

> "Then the king of Assyria invaded all the land and came to Samaria; for three years he besieged it. In the ninth year of Hoshea the king of Assyria captured Samaria; he carried the Israelites away to Assyria. He placed them in Halah, on the Habor, the river of Gozan, and in the cities of the Medes. This occurred because the people of Israel had sinned against the LORD their God, who had brought them up out of the land of Egypt from under the hand of Pharaoh king of Egypt. They had worshiped other gods and walked in the customs of the nations whom the LORD drove out before the people of Israel, and in the customs that the kings of Israel had introduced."
>
> *(2 Kings 17.5-8)*

The Assyrians appreciated the benefits of deporting defeated populations and replacing them with captives from elsewhere (*map right*). This policy made it hard for captive people to organize any effective resistance. Halah, the river of Khabur (Habor), and Media are listed in 2 Kings 17.6 as places where Samaritans were deported. In 2 Kings 17.24, Babylon, Cuthah, Hamath, and Sepharvaim are named as cities from which Samaria was repopulated.

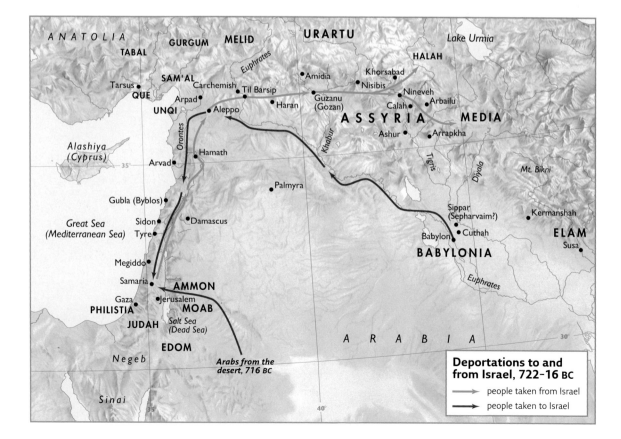

Deportations to and from Israel, 722-16 BC

→ people taken from Israel

→ people taken to Israel

The resurgence of Judah's power

After the split in the kingdoms with the accession of Rehoboam in about 931 BC, Judah emerged as a small and embattled state, greatly reduced both in area and prosperity. In its early years it was continuously at war with Israel, but, with the conclusion of hostilities under Jehoshaphat (870–848 BC), its fortune began to change.

Rehoboam's grandson Asa reigned for some 40 years. The Israelite king, Baasha, took and fortified Ramah (1 *Kings 15.17*), a hill with a good view southward, from which the Israelites could control the route from the coastal plain in the south and also the main road north from Jerusalem, which lay only some five miles away. Asa enlisted the aid of Syria to draw off this threat to Judah's lines of communication and to fortify the towns of Mizpah and Geba against his northern neighbor (1 *Kings 15.22*). Here the northern border of Judah remained, running through the middle of the territory of Benjamin. Jehoshaphat entered an alliance with the dynasty of Omri (sealed by the marriage of his son Jehoram to the Omride princess Athaliah). He also seems to have instituted reform in his realm: he "placed forces in all the fortified cities of Judah, and set garrisons in the land of Judah" (2 *Chron 17.2, 12*). The city list in Joshua (*Josh 15.21–62, 18.21–28*) implies a series of 12 districts, defined by their cities, embracing the known territory of Judah. It is probable that the organizational measures of a number of Judean kings from Jehoshaphat to Josiah are reflected in the city list.

Following the six-year reign of Athaliah (the only non-Davidic to rule in Jerusalem), the line of David was represented once more by Joash. He had to pay the Aramaean king, Hazael, to withdraw from Jerusalem, and in the end he was assassinated. The Judean revival restarted under his successor Amaziah, who defeated the Edomites but was then defeated by Israel in a battle. Eventually he, too, was assassinated and was succeeded by his son Uzziah.

Revival under Uzziah

Uzziah (Azariah) was 16-years-old when he began his 52-year reign; in his later years, he was smitten with leprosy and was forced to live in a separate house (2 *Kings 15.1–7*). According to Chronicles, he achieved a number of military victories over the Philistines. With the capture of the Red Sea port of Elath, he controlled both the land and the sea routes to and from Arabia and the east. He improved the fortifications of Jerusalem with towers at the city's gates, containing equipment for shooting arrows and great stones. Uzziah was also interested in the agricultural development of his kingdom, "for he loved the soil"

This division of Judah into 12 districts is based on a town list that appears in Joshua 15.21–62. This map follows the system suggested by Prof. Y. Aharoni (*map right*).

Districts of Judaean kingdom

▬ national border

── district boundary

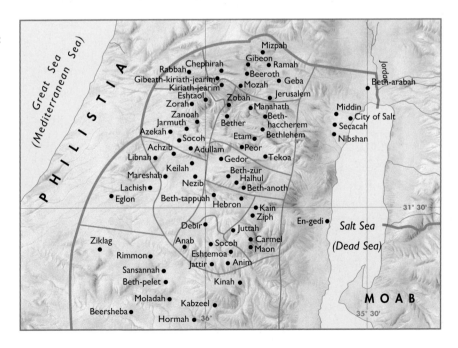

(*2 Chron 26.10*). Uzziah's reign saw an expansion of Judean territory and a resurgence of power such as had not been known since the division of the kingdom.

The role of the prophet

A radical change in the nature of prophecy appeared in the 8th century BC with the appearance of oracles of carefully prepared poetic form, spoken on special occasions and afterwards written down. Amos, Hosea, and Isaiah were such "writing" prophets, distinguished principally for their words rather than for any miraculous deeds. Prefaced by "thus saith the Lord," the prophet made use of analogies, simile, and even irony and sarcasm.

In substance as well as in form, prophecy took a new turn. Amos, for example, proclaimed the deity's concern for the underprivileged in society. Ethical and moral dimensions were added to the more traditional religious practices. Isaiah was deeply involved in advising the kings of Judah in the crises of the Assyrian invasions of Tiglath-pileser III, Sargon II, and Sennacherib. Examples of his poetic genius can be seen in the account of his call (*Isa 6.1–12*), the figure of the worthless vineyard (*Isa 5.1–12*), and the lament over the ruin of Judah (*Isa 1.4–9*). These and other passages indicate that the resurgence of power in Judah was matched by a flowering of its literature.

> "The LORD, the God of their ancestors, sent persistently to them by his messengers, because he had compassion on his people and on his dwelling place; but they kept mocking the messengers of God, despising his words, and scoffing at his prophets, until the wrath of the LORD against his people became so great that there was no remedy."
>
> (*2 Chron 36.15–16*)

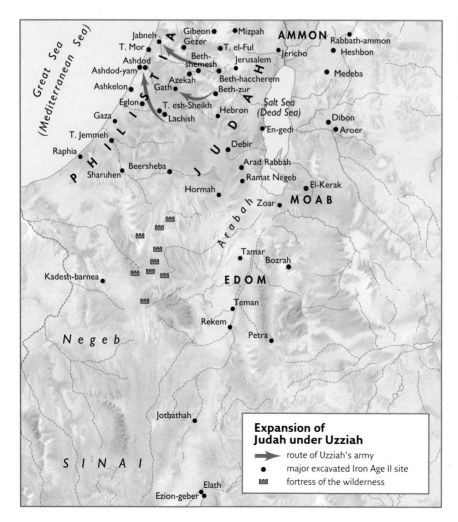

Uzziah's expansion of the Judean kingdom west and his attempts to gain control of the far south (*map left*).

Assyrian attacks on Philistia and Judah

The attempts of Sargon II and Sennacherib to control Philistia and Judah were a continuation of the policy of Tiglath-pileser III. The policy was not just about taking booty and levying a regular tribute, it was also an attempt to control the trade routes along the eastern rim of the Mediterranean.

Assyrian treatment of subject peoples varied. If tribute payment was forthcoming, the Assyrians could be accommodating, but determined resistance was met with force and even brutality. One method for quelling revolt against Assyria was the deportation of a local population to another land, with foreigners brought in to replace it (2 Kings 17.6, 24).

Sargon II

Upon the death of Shalmaneser V in 722 BC, Sargon II seized the throne of Assyria, taking the name of the famous Sargon who had ruled Akkad almost 2000 years earlier. In 720 BC, he captured Qarqar and Hamath and put down a rebellion of Hanno of Gaza, which had been aided by the Egyptians. By 716 BC, Sargon had extended his boundary to the Brook of Egypt, where he established a colony and encouraged trade with Egypt. In 712 BC, Sargon was faced with a rebellion on the part of Ashdod, which had attempted to involve other Philistine city-states, as well as Judah, Edom, and Moab, in revolt against Assyrian rule. Sargon removed Azuri, king of Ashdod, because he had refused to send tribute, and placed his pro-Assyrian brother Ahimiti on the throne. After conquests in Syria, Palestine, and Armenia, Sargon defeated Mardukapaliddin (biblical Merodach-baladan) and proclaimed himself governor of Babylon. He extended the borders of Assyria from the Caucasus to Egypt and from Elam to Cyprus - the largest area of Assyrian domination until this time.

Campaigns of Sargon II

→ anti-Assyrian activity
→ Assyrian campaigns, 720 and 716 BC
→ Assyrian campaigns, 713-12 BC

Sargon II conquered Gaza in 720 BC after the revolt of 721. In 716, he extended his control to the Brook of Egypt (Wadi el-'Arish). In 712, he acted against Ashdod, which had tried to form an anti-Assyrian coalition with other Philistine states plus Judah, Moab, and Edom (*map right*).

Sennacherib

Sargon II's death in 705 BC precipitated widespread revolt, involving both Hezekiah of Judah and Merodach-baladan of Babylonia (2 Kings 20, 12, etc.). Sennacherib (704-681 BC), Sargon's son, defeated Merodach-baladan, who had regained the throne and installed Bel-ibni as vassal king. He then crushed rebellions in Syria and Palestine (701 BC) before moving southward, capturing Ashkelon, and surrounding cities and setting up a pro-Assyrian king and

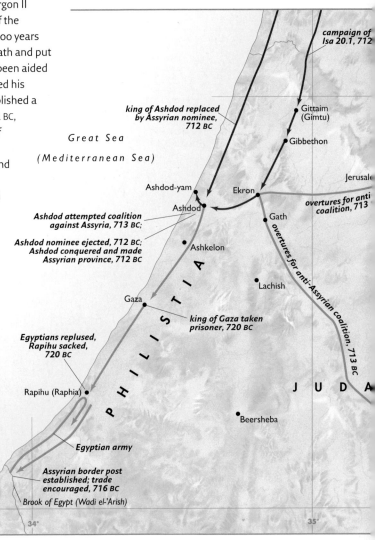

campaign of Isa 20.1, 712

king of Ashdod replaced by Assyrian nominee, 712 BC

Gittaim (Gimtu)

Gibbethon

Great Sea
(Mediterranean Sea)

Ashdod-yam

Ekron

Jerusale

Ashdod

overtures for anti coalition, 713

Ashdod attempted coalition against Assyria, 713 BC;

Gath

overtures for anti-Assyrian coalition, 713 BC

Ashdod nominee ejected, 712 BC; Ashdod conquered and made Assyrian province, 712 BC

Ashkelon

Lachish

Gaza

P H I L I S T I A

king of Gaza taken prisoner, 720 BC

Egyptians replused, Rapihu sacked, 720 BC

J U D A

Rapihu (Raphia)

Beersheba

Egyptian army

Assyrian border post established; trade encouraged, 716 BC

Brook of Egypt (Wadi el-'Arish)

34°

35°

imposing tribute. At Eltekeh, he defeated the Egyptians and Ethiopians who had been summoned by the insurgents at Ekron. Padi, king of Ekron, had been put into fetters and given over to Hezekiah, king of Judah. Sennacherib attacked Hezekiah in Jerusalem, released Padi, and restored him to his throne. Assyrian officers (the Tartan, the Rabsaris, and the Rabshakeh) went to Hezekiah in Jerusalem to demand surrender of the city, but Hezekiah refused (2 Kings 18.17). A second embassy from Sennacherib likewise failed. From the Assyrian account, it is clear that Jerusalem was not captured, an event that the biblical account credits to miraculous intervention (2 Kings 19.35–37).

In 681 BC, Sennacherib was murdered by two of this sons, one of whom has been identified in a cuneiform source as Arad-mulishshi, whose name has been identified in the Bible as Adrammelech (2 Kings 19.37).

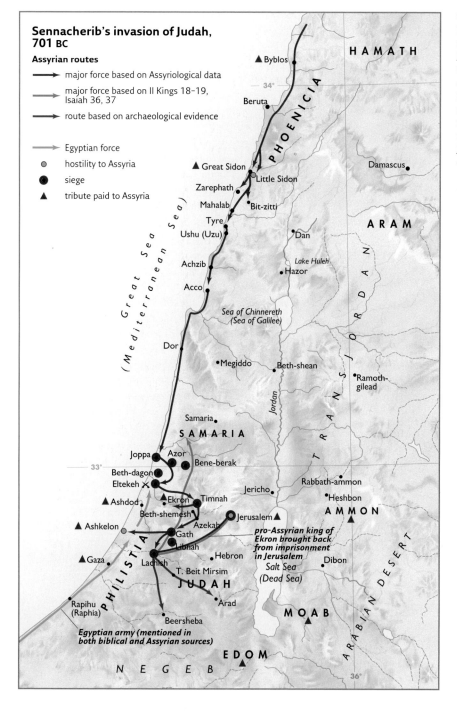

Sennacherib's campaign of 701 BC was occasioned by rebellions in Syria, Philistia and Judah (map left). He subdued the whole coast from Byblos to Ashdod, placed pro-Assyrian kings on the thrones of rebellious cities, and imposed tribute. Hezekiah of Judah was forced to submit, but Jerusalem itself was not captured.

Judah under Hezekiah and Manasseh

King Hezekiah (716–687 BC) and his son Manasseh (687–643 BC), the two kings of Judah who reigned longer than any other two consecutive kings, lived under the shadow of Assyria's power.

When King Hezekiah came to the throne in 716 BC, he tried to unite "all of Israel and Judah" in the worship at the Jerusalem temple (2 *Chron* 30.1–5). When Sargon II died in 605 BC, Hezekiah followed the lead of many subject nations and raised the flag of revolt. The Assyrian army under Sennacherib appeared and extracted revenge, capturing 46 Judean cities, the foremost of which was Lachish. Though Jerusalem was not taken (2 *Kings* 18.13–19, 30), the kingdom was devastated and its Shephelah and Negeb districts largely transferred to Philistine control. Hezekiah found himself without direct access to the major trade routes.

On the eve of the Assyrian siege of Jerusalem, Hezekiah "made a pool and a tunnel, and brought water into the city" (2 *Kings* 20.20). According to 2 Chronicles 32.5, he "built up the entire wall that was broken down, and raised towers on it, and outside it he built another wall; he also strengthened the Millo in the city of David." The "wall without" probably refers to a new wall around two residential and commercial quarters of the city: the second (*mishneh*) quarter (2 *Kings* 22.14) on the Western Hill and the Makhtesh quarter (*Zeph* 1.10–11) in the Central Valley. Houses belonging to the *mishneh* quarter have been unearthed as well as the fortification wall, 23 feet wide, and part of a tower that may have belonged to a gateway, perhaps the "Middle Gate" (*Jer* 39.3).

Manasseh

Manasseh was appointed coregent by his father in 696 BC (2 *Kings* 21.1). By the time of Hezekiah's death in 686 BC, all trade routes were in the hands of his neighbors, and Sennacherib had reduced Judah to the area of the hill country and the wilderness. Manasseh sought to overcome the isolation in which Judah found itself after the crushing defeat at the hands of Sennacherib. He entered into diplomatic relations with countries that were enjoying the benefits of Assyrian control. He invited embassies from Tyre and other adjacent countries and restored shrines to their respective deities in Jerusalem for their use (2 *Kings* 21.3, 23.13). The population of the city at that time probably numbered about 20,000.

Large storage jars dating to Hezekiah's reign have been found in many Judean excavations. They bear on their handles a royal-seal impression with "for the king" (*lamelech*) followed by one of four place names: Ziph, Socoh, Hebron, or *mmst*. Elsewhere, jars appear with impressions of both the royal seal and a personal-name seal. The purpose of these impressions is debated by scholars, but the simplest explanation is that the geographical names were the four centers where royal wineries were located and that the personal names may have been those of officials who inspected and certified the contents. On the map of Judah's districts, based on Joshua 15 (*page 110*), Socoh appears in a southern district, Ziph in a southeastern, and Hebron in a central; mmst was possibly located in the Bethlehem or Jerusalem district.

For half a century, Judah was subservient; Manasseh not only assisted in delivering timber to Assyria for Esarhaddon's palace but also had to send troops to accompany the Assyrian army under Ashurbanipal in his campaigns against Egypt (667/6 and 664/3 BC). However, under pressure from Ashurbanipal (2 *Chron* 33.11–17), Manasseh renounced all his treaties with Tyre and other neighbors (indicated by turning away from their gods) and became on good terms with the Assyrians. Permission was granted to rebuild the fortresses of Judah, which indicates that Judah was trusted with the supervision of trade routes. Manasseh's new lease of life opened the way for a renaissance of Judean power as the decline of the Assyrian empire allowed a degree of freedom to neighboring states.

Manasseh, the longest-reigning king of Judah, is described as the king who "misled" Judah into doing "more evil than the nations had done that the Lord destroyed" (2 *Kings* 21.9). It was the introduction of foreign religious practices into the Jerusalem temple by Manasseh that occasioned the reform of King Josiah for which he was famous.

Judah and surrounding provinces and states in the time of Hezekiah and Manasseh and sites where royal seals have been found (*map right*).

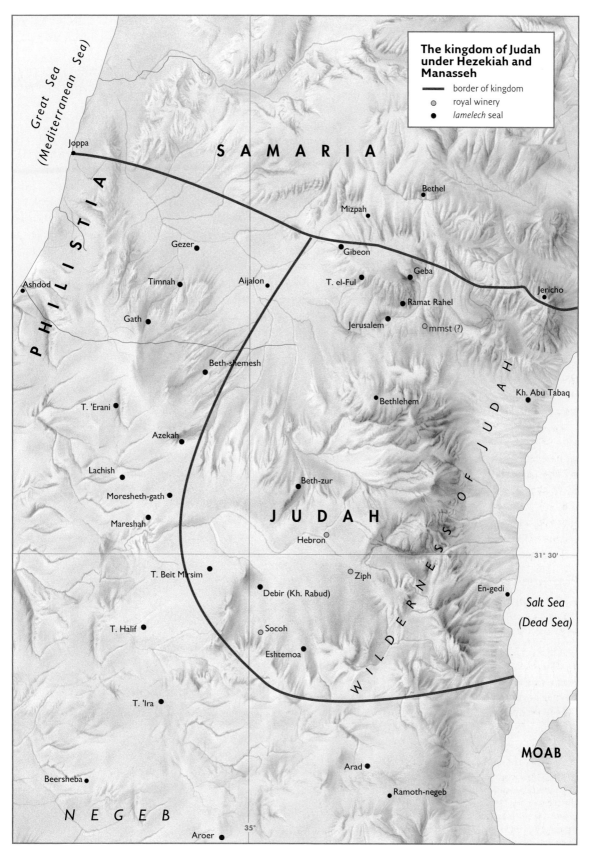

Great Sea
(Mediterranean Sea)

The kingdom of Judah under Hezekiah and Manasseh

— border of kingdom
○ royal winery
● *lamelech* seal

S A M A R I A

P H I L I S T I A

Joppa

Bethel

Mizpah

Gezer

Gibeon

Timnah

Aijalon

T. el-Ful

Geba

Ashdod

Jericho

Gath

Ramat Rahel

Jerusalem

mmst (?)

Beth-shemesh

Kh. Abu Tabaq

T. 'Erani

Bethlehem

Azekah

W I L D E R N E S S   O F   J U D A H

Lachish

Beth-zur

Moresheth-gath

J U D A H

Mareshah

Hebron

31° 30'

T. Beit Mirsim

Ziph

En-gedi

Debir (Kh. Rabud)

*Salt Sea
(Dead Sea)*

T. Halif

Socoh

Eshtemoa

T. 'Ira

MOAB

Arad

Beersheba

Ramoth-negeb

N E G E B

35°

Aroer

The end of the Assyrian empire

For more than a century (beginning with Tiglath-pileser III in 734 BC), Assyria had collected tribute from the small states of Israel and Judah, destroyed cities, and taken captives away into exile.

Esarhaddon

Esarhaddon (680–669 BC), Sennacherib's son and successor, made major innovations in Assyrian imperial strategy. He reversed his father's harsh policy, by rebuilding devastated Babylon with the help of vassals from the west and appointing his son Shamash-shum-ukin to rule. He made treaties with his more powerful vassals, notably the Medes, the kingdom of Tyre, the Scythian tribes in the north, and the desert Arabs.

Esarhaddon's attitude toward Egypt also represented a radical change of policy. Egypt had frequently supported anti-Assyrian movements in Palestine and Phoenicia; in 669 BC, Esarhaddon sought to curb this policy by invasion through Sinai, an undertaking made possible only through friendship with the Arabs. His plan was to hold the Nile Delta area through native kings supervised by Assyrian officials.

Ashurbanipal

At Esarhaddon's death, his heir, Ashurbanipal (668–627 BC), continued his father's policy in Egypt. He undertook two major campaigns: the first, in 667 BC, was to quell a rebellion in support of the former Egyptian king, Tirhakah, returning from his southern capital of Thebes to retake Memphis; the second, in 664 BC, followed an attack on Assyrian garrisons by Tirhakah's Ethiopian successor,

Tanuatamun. This time, Ashurbanipal conquered Egypt as far south as Thebes and confirmed one of the vassal kings, Necho of Sais, as paramount ruler. Ashurbanipal's control of Egypt, however, depended on the loyalty of the vassal king, and when Necho's successor Psammetichus proclaimed independence, Assyrian withdrawal became inevitable.

Problems were also developing elsewhere. Instability in Elam threatened Babylonia and required repeated Assyrian intervention from 667 BC onwards, producing tensions that led to civil war (652–648 BC) between Ashurbanipal and his brother Shamash-shum-ukin of Babylonia, ending

Esarhaddon, son of Sennacherib, made use of Assyrian vassals in the west to rebuild the devastated city of Babylon during 670 BC (*map right*). He extended Assyrian influence as far as Egypt, as his troops were escorted through Sinai by friendly Arabs. His son and heir Ashurbanipal undertook two campaigns through Phoenicia and Judah in order to strengthen Assyrian control along the Nile. The first, in 667 BC, was against Pharoah Tirhakah, who had attempted to take Memphis. In the second campaign three years later, he responded to an attack of Pharoah Tanuatamun upon an Assyrian garrison. In

664 BC, he conquered Egypt as far south as Thebes and confirmed the vassal king Necho. When Necho's successor, Psammetichus, proclaimed independence, Assyria was forced to withdraw.

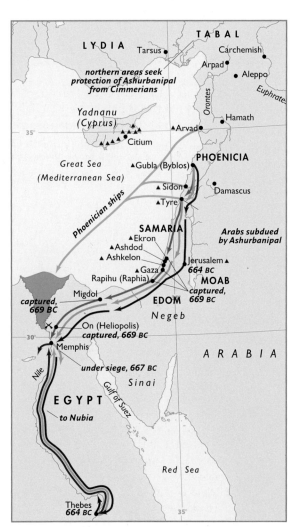

Assyrian conquests, mid 7th century BC

→ Esarhaddon, 669 BC
→ Ashurbanipal, 667 BC
→ Ashurbanipal, 664 BC
→ Tirhakah
→ Tanuatamun

taken under Assyrian control with vassal kings

▲ king required by Esarhaddon to assist in the rebuilding of Babylon in the 670s BC

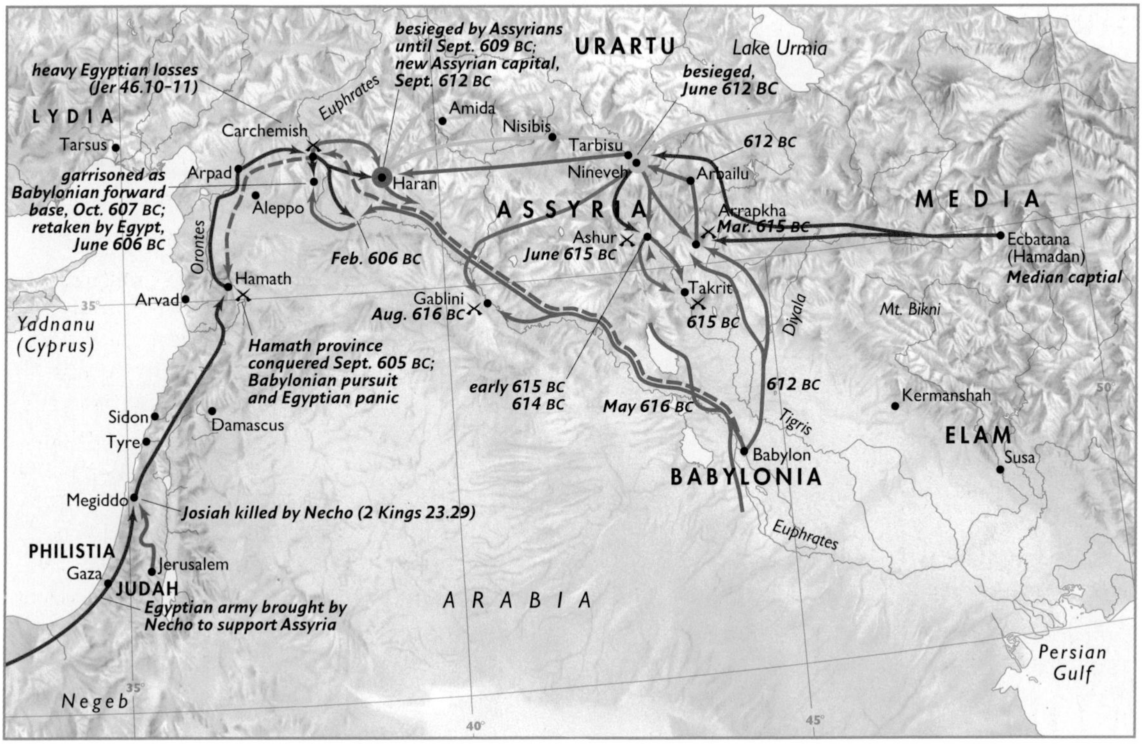

besieged by Assyrians until Sept. 609 BC; new Assyrian capital, Sept. 612 BC
URARTU
Lake Urmia
heavy Egyptian losses (Jer 46.10-11)
besieged, June 612 BC
Euphrates
LYDIA
Amida
Nisibis
Carchemish
Tarsus
Tarbisu
612 BC
garrisoned as Babylonian forward base, Oct. 607 BC; retaken by Egypt, June 606 BC
Arpad
Nineveh
Arbailu
Haran
Aleppo
ASSYRIA
MEDIA
Arrapkha
Mar. 615 BC
Ashur
Ecbatana (Hamadan)
Orontes
Feb. 606 BC
June 615 BC
Median captial
Hamath
Takrit
Gablini
Arvad
Aug. 616 BC
615 BC
Mt. Bikni
Diyala
Yadnanu (Cyprus)
Hamath province conquered Sept. 605 BC; Babylonian pursuit and Egyptian panic
early 615 BC
612 BC
614 BC
May 616 BC
Kermanshah
Sidon
Damascus
Tigris
ELAM
Tyre
Babylon
Susa
BABYLONIA
Megiddo
Josiah killed by Necho (2 Kings 23.29)
Euphrates
PHILISTIA
Jerusalem
Gaza
JUDAH
Egyptian army brought by Necho to support Assyria
ARABIA
Persian Gulf
Negeb
35°
40°
45°
50°

in Shamash-shum-ukin's defeat and death. The death of Ashurbanipal in 627 BC unleashed many tensions inherent within the empire, but the most significant development was the seizing of the kingship of Babylon by a Chaldean chieftain, Nabopolassar, in 626 BC. It was to lead to the fall of the Assyrian empire.

The downfall of Assyria

Four specific factors contributed to the downfall of the Assyrian empire: a struggle for succession between two sons of Esarhaddon; Nabopolassar's assumption of the kingship of Babylonia in 626 BC; the Medes, who, under Cyaxares, attacked Assyria; and, lastly, the Ummanmanda - tribal hordes from the north, who overran Assyrian territory.

After several years of fighting to break the Assyrian hold on Babylonia, Nabopolassar moved against Assyria itself by 616 BC. In 612 BC, Nineveh fell, surprisingly quickly, to a combined siege by Babylonians, Medes, and Ummanmanda. The Assyrian army withdrew, first to Haran, and then to Carchemish, where they called on Egypt for assistance. The Egyptians sent a large army northward under Necho. Josiah of Judah, an ally of the Babylonians, attempted to intercept the Egyptians at Megiddo and was killed (*2 Kings 23.29*). The Egyptians joined the Assyrian remnant at Carchemish. In 605 BC Crown Prince Nebuchadnezzar, placed in charge of the Babylonian army, attacked the Egyptian army at Carchemish, with massive slaughter (*Jer 46.2-12*).

After twelve years of attacks, Assyria finally succumbed to Babylon (*map above*). In 616 BC, the Babylonian king, Nabopolassar, moved into Assyrian territory. The Medes invaded Ashur in 615 BC, taking the old capital a year later. In 612 BC, Nineveh, besieged by Babylonians, Medes, and Ummanmanda hordes, fell quickly. The Assyrian army fled to Haran, then to Carchemish. Pharoah Nechnoh, while marching north to aid the Assyrians, was opposed by Josiah of Judah at Megiddo; Josiah was fatally wounded. Finally, the Babylonian Crown Prince Nebuchadnezzar defeated the Egyptians at Carchemish in 605 BC.

Destruction of Assyria, late 7th century BC

- Babylonians, 616–606 BC
- Babylonians under Nebuchadnezzar, 605 BC
- Medes, 615–612 BC
- Ummanmanda, 612–609 BC
- Assyrians, 616–609 BC
- Egyptians, 609–605 BC
- Josiah, king of Judah, 609 BC
- captured city (color coded)

The rise of Babylon

With the fall of Nineveh in 612 BC, Assyrian might came to an end, weakened by an internal struggle for the throne, invasion by foreign hordes from the north and east, and a revolt by Babylon. It was the start of the Babylonian empire, the next great power in the Near East. Although Assyria had so often threatened the peoples of Israel and Judah, it was left to Babylon to deal the final and heaviest blow in the destruction of Jerusalem, taking its people into exile.

The Chaldean chieftan Nabopolassar had tried for many years to shake off the shackles of Assyrian lordship. In 616 BC he moved against Assyria. He was joined in this action by the Medes, under Cyaxares, who attacked a year later and took the old capital, Ashur, in 614 BC. Following this success, Nabopolassar and Cyaxares made a formal pact, an alliance that was to bear fruit in 612 BC when a combined force of Babylonians, Medes, and Ummanmanda – tribal hordes from the north - captured Nineveh.

It was the start of the orderly dismemberment of the Assyrian empire. The principal heir was Babylonia, with the Medes taking control of the most northerly area in Asia Minor and the regions east of the Zagros Mountains.

Nabopolassar's son Nebuchadnezzar, the crown prince, proceeded to lead his own army against the hostile north-eastern hill tribes. The Egyptians established a garrison at the important city of Carchemish, forcing the Babylonians at Quramati to retreat. Nebuchadnezzar, with the help of Greek mercenaries, then embarked on a reprisal raid. Moving up the east bank of the Euphrates, he crossed to the west below Carchemish, surprised the enemy, and captured the city in August 605 BC. The Egyptians who fled were cut off and the whole force destroyed so that, according to the *Babylonian Chronicle*, a reliable source, "not a single Egyptian escaped home." The whole region of Hamath was taken over, including Riblah, a former

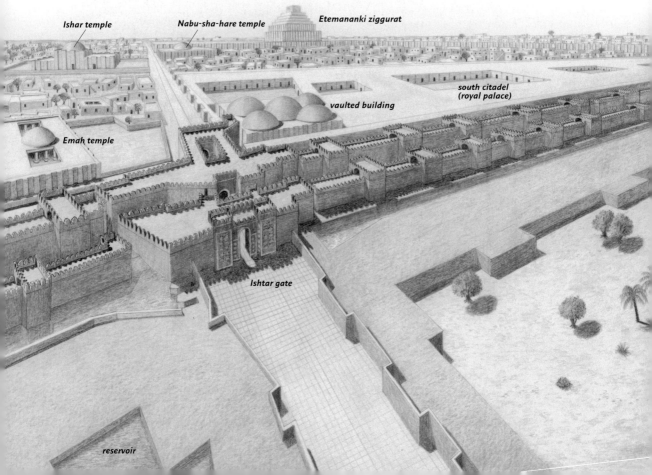

Ishar temple

Nabu-sha-hare temple

Etemananki ziggurat

Emah temple

vaulted building

south citadel
(royal palace)

Ishtar gate

reservoir

Egyptian stronghold dominating the road south and the routes to the Mediterranean coast. From here, the Babylonians claimed sway over Palestine as far south as the Egyptian border at Wadi el-'Arish.

Nebuchadnezzar also took action in Khilakku (Cilicia) and neighboring areas in the northwest, a region in which Neriglissar (559–556 BC), the successor after Nebuchadnezzar's briefly reigning son Evil-merodach (2 Kings 25.27), had to undertake a further campaign to consolidate the Babylonian hold.

For the most part, the major powers of the 7th century BC, - Assyria, Egypt, and Babylonia - did not concern themselves with the relatively isolated kingdom of Judah. It survived, for more than a century, the conquest of the northern kingdom of Israel, and even saw the fall of the Assyrian empire. It was Nebuchadnezzar's campaign against Judah in 587 BC that proved to be a turning point in the history of ancient Israel. He brought an end to the dynasty of David, which had lasted for more than three and a half centuries, and took Judeans to Babylon, where they developed the practices of Judaism to replace the worship once performed in the Jerusalem temple.

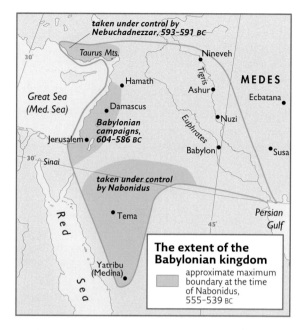

The extent of the Babylonian kingdom

approximate maximum boundary at the time of Nabonidus, 555–539 BC

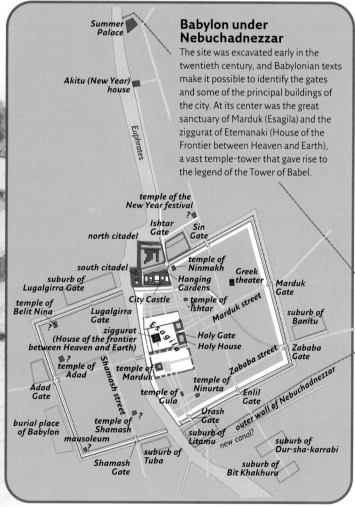

Babylon under Nebuchadnezzar

The site was excavated early in the twentieth century, and Babylonian texts make it possible to identify the gates and some of the principal buildings of the city. At its center was the great sanctuary of Marduk (Esagila) and the ziggurat of Etemanaki (House of the Frontier between Heaven and Earth), a vast temple-tower that gave rise to the legend of the Tower of Babel.

Hanging Gardens

Illustration of Babylon based on archaeological evidence.

The reign of Josiah

Josiah came to the throne of Judah as a boy of eight years, placed there by an assembly of common people at a time of national crisis. Josiah's aim was to restore the area once held by the house of David and thus reunite the divided kingdom.

The death of Ashurbanipal of Assyria (c. 627 BC) allowed Judah to gain independence and expand territory (2 *Kings* 23.25). He seems quickly to have regained the land of Ephraim and could claim to rule from Beersheba to Geba. He controlled Bethel (2 *Kings* 17.28) and, in the south, took territory back from Philistia. Archaeological evidence indicates that he fortified Arad and En-gedi in readiness against possible Egyptian reprisals. In the north, he held sway as far as Naphtali.

Religious reform

The extension of political authority was accompanied by the most radical religious reforms in the history of Judah. The account in 2 Kings 22–23 indicates that reform was underway by Josiah's eighteenth year. The repair of the Jerusalem temple revealed the "book of the law" of Moses (2 *Kings* 22.9), and it is generally agreed that the book of Deuteronomy, or a part of it, provided the legal basis for the religious reforms of King Josiah.

All evidence of foreign religious practices was quickly removed. Worship was concentrated in Jerusalem at the Temple of Yahweh. False priests were slain and their altars desecrated. The male and female prostitutes employed in pagan ritual were removed. Special attention was paid to blotting out the old Canaanite worship of Molech (Moloch), which had been reintroduced by Ahaz and seems to have involved child sacrifice.

In 609 BC, the Egyptian ruler Necho II sent word to Josiah that he required passage to a garrison post - "the house with which I am at war" (2 *Chron* 35.21) - presumably Megiddo or Carchemish. Josiah, fearing, perhaps, either a resurgent Egypt or a revival of Assyrian power, moved swiftly to where the pass across Mount Carmel enters the Plain of Esdraelon. He clashed with the Egyptians in open warfare. In the ensuing battle, Josiah was badly wounded, taken to Jerusalem, and died. Despite the tragedy of his death, Josiah was characterized in the Deuteronomic appraisal of the kings of Israel and Judah as having done what was "right in the eyes of the Lord."

Necho's attack at Carchemish ended in disaster in 606 BC, with the complete annihilation of the Egyptian army (*Jer* 46.2–12). He withdrew to Egypt, where he fought one final battle against the Babylonians, in 601 BC. Although the Babylonians were repulsed, the Egyptians were never again to enter Palestine in force. "The king of Egypt did not come again out of his land, for the king of Babylon had taken over all that belonged to the king of Egypt from the Wadi of Egypt to the river Euphrates" (2 *Kings* 24.7).

The role of Jeremiah

The prophet Jeremiah came from a priestly family from Anathoth in the territory of Benjamin and was active during the reigns of Josiah, Jehoiakim, and Zedekiah (*Jer* 1.2–3). He had serious confrontations with the latter two kings, was imprisoned by Zedekiah, and rescued from death by an Ethiopian commander (*Jer* 37–38).

In Jeremiah's view, the rise and fall of empires were controlled by a divine hand; the impending invasion by the Babylonians, which he consistently predicted (*Jer* 25, 28), was therefore a punishment for the moral corruption of the people and their failure to perform the ritualistic demands of their law (*Jer* 29.5–7). He was convinced that the exiles would eventually return and the monarchy be restored in Judah (*Jer* 30–33).

Despite his protestations that he and the remnants left in the land after most of population had been taken into captivity by the Babylonians should remain there, Jeremiah was taken to Egypt by the refugees from Jerusalem (*Jer* 42–43). It is possible that he died there in exile.

> "Go, inquire of the LORD for me, for the people, and for all Judah, concerning the words of this book that has been found; for great is the wrath of the LORD that is kindled against us, because our ancestors did not obey the words of this book, to do according to all that is written concerning us."
>
> *(2 Kings 22.13)*

Extent of Josiah's kingdom
with the routes of Josiah's and
Necho's armies in 509 BC and
sanctuaries abolished by Josiah
in his reform (*map right*).

Haran

Carchemish
Til Barsip

Arpad

Balikh

Alalakh

Aleppo

Euphrates

36°

Rezeph

Ugarit

Orontes

Hamath

Arvad

Riblah

Byblos

34°

Beruta
(Beirut)

Sidon

Damascus

DAMASCUS

SIDON

A R A M

Tyre

Dan

NAPHTALI

Acco

Karnaim

Mt. Carmel

*Sea of Chinnereth
(Sea of Galilee)*

GALILEE

Plain of Esdraelon

Dora

MEGIDDO   Beth-arbel

Megiddo

Ramoth-gilead

Valley of Jezreel

Beth-shean

GILEAD

Samaria

Jordan

Wadi 'Ara

SAMARIA

Shiloh

Ramath-mizpeh

AMMON

Joppa

Ono

32°

Mesad Hashavyahu

Lod

Bethel

Rabbath-ammon

Anathoth

Gilgal

Ashdod

Gezer

Geba

Jericho

Nebo

Libnah

Jerusalem

Ashkelon

PHILISTIA

Lachish

Hebron

Dibon

M O A B

Gaza

En-gedi

Aroer

JUDAH

*Salt Sea
(Dead Sea)*

Arad

36°

Beersheba

*Great Sea
(Mediterranean Sea)*

38°

The kingdom of Josiah and
the campaign of Necho

— former provincial boundary
— border of Josiah's kingdom
● abolished sanctuary
✕ major battle
→ route of Necho's army
→ route of Josiah's army

Nebuchadnezzar and the fall of Jerusalem

The Babylonian king Nebuchadnezzar II (605–562 BC) was the most powerful of the six kings that constituted the Chaldean dynasty, whose rule extended over a period of 86 years (625–539 BC). In biblical history, his name is most widely known for the capture of Jerusalem and the exile of its inhabitants at Babylon.

In 605 BC, Nebuchadnezzar, then the crown prince, fought the Egyptians at the city of Carchemish, capturing the city in August 605 BC. The result was that the Babylonians now controlled the road south and the routes to the Mediterranean coast. From here, the Babylonians claimed sway over Palestine as far south as the Egyptian border at Wadi el-'Arish.

Following the death of his father, Nabopolassar, in 605 BC, Nebuchadnezzar claimed the throne as Nabu-kudurri-usur (Nebuchadnezzar). In 604 BC, Jehoiakim of Judah was among a number of rulers who paid a heavy tribute (2 Kings 24.1). Nebuchadnezzar attempted to invade Egypt in 601 BC, but was forced to return to Babylon to refit his army. King Jehoiakim of Judah, thinking that the tide had turned against the Babylonians, changed his allegiance to Egypt. It was a catastrophic misjudgment, and the Babylonians sought an opportunity for revenge.

Capture of Jerusalem in 597 BC

In December 598, the Babylonians marched on Judah. Jehoiakim - who received no support from his new Egyptian allies - died during the siege and was succeeded by his son Jehoiachin. The *Babylonian Chronicle* records Nebuchadnezzar's victory: "On the second day of the month Addar in his seventh year [16 March 597] he captured the city of Judah [Jerusalem] which he had besieged. He seized its kings and appointed there a king of his own choice. Taking heavy spoil he sent it to Babylon." As they had done some 10 years earlier, the Babylonians marked the fall of Jerusalem by exporting yet more soldiers, administrators, and skilled Judeans. According to Jeremiah, in 597 BC they took 3023 people; in 587 BC, 832; and in 582 BC, 745 (Jer 52.28–30).

The destruction of Jerusalem

Nebuchadnezzar placed Jehoiachin's uncle on the throne and renamed him Zedekiah. When, contrary to the advice of Jeremiah (Jer 27.1–11), Zedekiah planned an anti-Babylonian coalition with Edom, Moab, Ammon, Tyre, and Sidon, Nebuchadnezzar besieged Jerusalem again. After two years, the Babylonians steadily closed in. Hill forts and watch posts in the surrounding hills were taken and walls breached. The temple fell in August 586 BC and the city fell a month later.

At the capture of Jerusalem, the Babylonians took a major group of 10,000 army and skilled Judeans off into exile, followed, at the fall of the city, by further bands totalling 3023, 832 and 745 prisoners (Jer 52.28–30).

The reign of Nabonidus

After the death of Nebuchadnezzar in 562 BC, there were three kings of Babylon in seven years, only one of whom died a natural death. Eventually, Nabonidus (555–539 BC) assumed the throne. In 552, he moved to northwestern Arabia to win military control of an area around the oasis of Tema. He stayed there, in virtual voluntary exile, for 10 years because of opposition from the Babylonians. This unpopularity had two causes: he had become increasingly eccentric, possibly due to some health problem, and he was suspected of harboring unorthodox religious views. In 542 BC, Nabonidus finally returned to Babylon where his son and coregent Bel-sharra-usur (the biblical Belshazzar) had been left in charge.

By now, the Babylonians were under pressure from the Medes and the Persians, and elaborate defenses against any attack on the capital were prepared. The flood defenses and the Median Wall across the narrow land

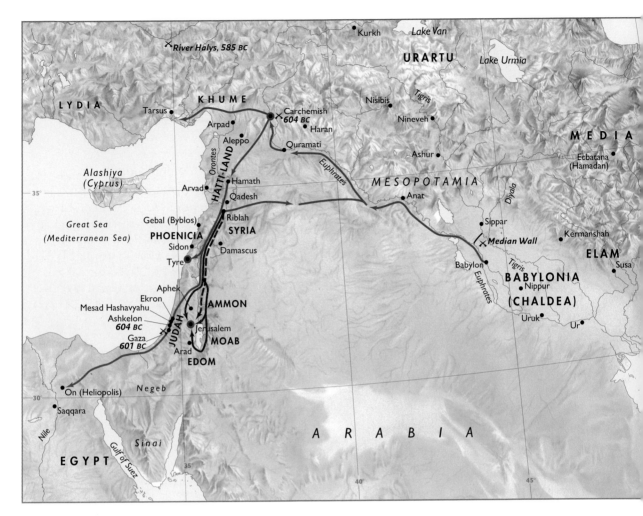

bridge between the Euphrates and Tigris south of Sippar and Opis became the scene of a pitched battle in which the Babylonians were defeated. The sudden fall of the city may have been due in part to a diversion of the river, which subverted the defenses. Belshazzar was killed and Nabonidus was captured. Cyrus entered Babylon on October 30, 539 BC, and brought Babylonian domination of the Near East to an end.

Under Nebuchadnezzar, the Babylonians dominated the ancient Near East (*map above*). Using the traditional invasion routes, they invaded Judah, destroyed Jerusalem, and subjugated the Jews.

The campaigns of Nebuchadnezzar

⟶ Nebuchadnezzar's early campaigns

⟶ attack on Jerusalem, 597 BC

---➤ attack on Jerusalem, 587 BC

● siege

http://www.greatbuildings.com/buildings/Ishtar_Gate.html
Ishtar Gate, Babylon
http://www.thebritishmuseum.ac.uk/explore/galleries/middle_east/room_55_mesopotamia.aspx
Babylonian tablets at the British Museum

The Persian empire

When in 546 BC the Persian king, Cyrus the Great, captured the Lydian capital Sardis from Croesus and his troops looted the city, Croesus asked Cyrus, "What are those men doing?" "Plundering your city," replied Cyrus. "Not my city, but yours," said Croesus.

In 498 BC, Sardis was burnt again when the Ionians, supported by the Athenians, rebelled. Persia invaded Greece, to be defeated on land at Marathon (490 BC) and on sea at Salamis (480 BC). For the next two centuries, Greeks and Persians eyed each other warily across the Aegean.

Up to that point, the Persian empire had expanded rapidly. Cyrus took Babylon in 539 BC, his son Cambyses annexed Egypt in 525 BC, and Darius I took Sind about 516 BC. The resulting empire was the greatest the world had yet known.

Palestine in the Persian period

Palestine under the Persians was part of the satrapy called "Beyond the River" (Ezra 4.10, 8.36; Neh 2.7–9). The province of Judah was subdivided into districts and half-districts (Neh 3). It is generally agreed that the Persians inherited the divisions created under Assyrian and Babylonian rule. The Assyrians divided the land into the northern provinces of Megiddo, Dor, and Samaria, and the Transjordanian provinces of Hauran, Karnaim (biblical

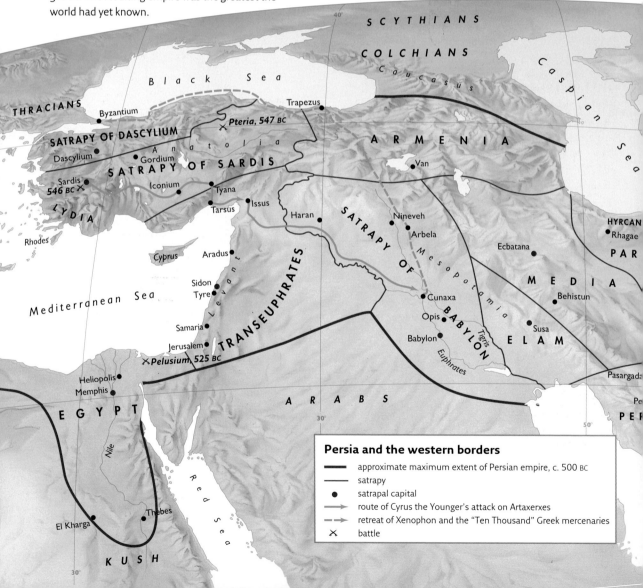

Persia and the western borders

▬▬▬	approximate maximum extent of Persian empire, c. 500 BC
▬▬▬	satrapy
●	satrapal capital
➡	route of Cyrus the Younger's attack on Artaxerxes
⇢	retreat of Xenophon and the "Ten Thousand" Greek mercenaries
✕	battle

Bashan), and Gilead. The Babylonians annexed new provinces: Judah, Ashdod, and Idumaea (the southern Judean hills) in the west, and the Ammonite and Moabite regions in Transjordan. Some of these provinces may have been created only at the beginning of the Persian period.

In the time of Ezra and Nehemiah, mention is made of the provinces of Samaria in the north, Ashdod in the west, and the Ammonites in the east; the southern region was occupied by Geshem the Arab. The existence of a province of Moab may be indicated by the reference to "the sons of Pahath-Moab" (Ezra 2.6; Neh 7.11). Contemporary evidence of the existence of the provinces of Samaria and Judah is found in the Elephantine papyri and in the documents from Wadi ed-Daliyeh.

Very little is known of the history of Judah under the Persians. The biblical writers remember it basically for three major events: the rebuilding of the temple in Jerusalem under the high priest Joshua and the governor Zerubbabel in 520–515 BC, (Hagg; Zech 1–8; Ezra 1–6); the rebuilding of the walls of Jerusalem and the development of some limited autonomy for Judah under Nehemiah (444–432 BC) (Neh 1–13); and the establishment in Judah of the Jewish law under Ezra (458 or perhaps 398 BC) (Ezra 7–10; Neh 8–9). Persian culture and history thus left no lasting impression in Judah; Persia's destruction by Alexander the Great is vividly depicted in Daniel 8.5–8.

Archaeological excavation has begun to throw light on this obscure period. The county was culturally divided into two regions: the mountain region of Judah, Transjordan, Samaria to a lesser extent, and Galilee; and the coastal plain. The culture of the mountains was basically Eastern: a continuing Israelite culture with influence from Assyria, Babylonia, and Egypt. The culture of the coast, in contrast, contained the essentially Western East Greek, Cypriot, and Attic elements. The material culture of Greece thus appeared in Palestine much earlier than the Macedonian conquest, carried there by the Phoenicians, and, to a lesser extent, Greek soldiers and colonists.

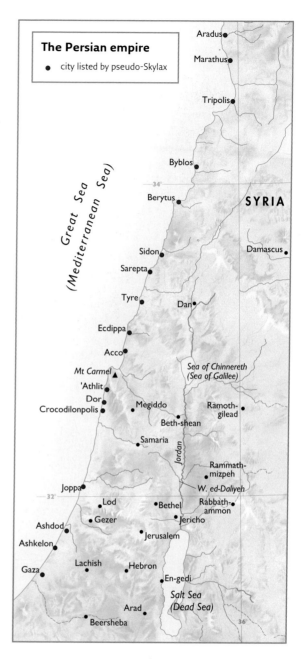

The Persian empire

● city listed by pseudo-Skylax

Aradus
Marathus
Tripolis
Byblos
Berytus
SYRIA
Damascus
Sidon
Sarepta
Tyre
Dan
Ecdippa
Acco
Sea of Chinnereth (Sea of Galilee)
Mt Carmel
'Athlit
Dor
Crocodilonpolis
Megiddo
Ramoth-gilead
Beth-shean
Samaria
Jordan
Rammath-mizpeh
Joppa
W. ed-Daliyeh
Lod
Bethel
Rabbath-ammon
Gezer
Jericho
Ashdod
Jerusalem
Ashkelon
Lachish
Hebron
Gaza
En-gedi
Salt Sea (Dead Sea)
Arad
Beersheba
Great Sea (Mediterranean Sea)

The western satrapies of the Persian empire, and the route of Cyrus's attack on Artaxerxes II (map left). Evidence for the history of the Persian empire comes mainly from the Bible and from Greek writers.

Wrongly attributed to Skylax of Cayanda (6th–5th century BC) is a late 4th-century description of the Mediterranean Sea giving useful details of the Palestinian coast (map above right).

SEVEN

BETWEEN THE TESTAMENTS

**Courtyard of the synagogue of Sardis, Turkey
(third century AD).**
The inter-testamental period saw Jewish populations grow in cities
throughout the Mediterranean. Crucial to their identity was the
synagogue, which first developed in the Hellenistic period.

Judah in the Hellenistic world

Though they pretended to despise it, the Greeks were always fascinated by Persia and its wealth. Many Greeks before Alexander the Great went east, and throughout the Persian territory of coastal Asia Minor, cities were built or rebuilt in the Hellenistic grid pattern.

Alexander and the east

It was Alexander who dramatically quickened the pace of Hellenization. In 334 BC he crossed the Hellespont with approximately 35,000 men, to fight the Persians. Having defeated the Persians at the river Granicus in 334 BC and at Gaugamela in 331 BC, Alexander then continued north to the Caspian Gates and the Hindu Kush in his unsuccessful search for the mythical river that was thought to encircle the world. He was forced to return to Babylon from India when his troops refused to advance any further into the unknown.

Alexander labored to unite Greeks and non-Greeks, encouraging intermarriage, founding Hellenistic cities, and settling Greek colonists.

After his death in Babylon in 323 BC, his generals continued his policy in their new kingdoms: Cassander held Greece and Macedonia; Lysimachus, Thrace; Antigonus and his son Demetrius Poliorcetes ("the Besieger"), Asia Minor; Seleucus, Babylon and Syria; and Ptolemy, Egypt.

The Seleucid kings founded new colonies to secure their communications with the east, sometimes merely renaming old towns with Greek dynastic names or granting Greek city status to such places for a fee. The Ptolemies similarly renamed cities:

Having crossed the Hellespont in 334 BC with around 35,000 men, Alexander defeated the Persians at the river Granicus. He then advanced into Syria and Egypt and moved into Armenia, where he had a second decisive victory against the Persians at Gaugamela in 331 BC. He then advanced through Media and Persia and north to the Caspian Gates and the Hindu Kush. In India, however, he had to turn back, as his troops refused to advance any further into the unknown. Some troops returned by sea under Nearchus, while the rest returned by land through Gedrosia to Babylon, where Alexander died in 323 BC.

Alexander's campaigns

- empire of Alexander, 323 BC
- route of Alexander the Great
- route of Nearchus's naval expedition, 325 BC
- return route of Alexander's veterans and elephants under Craterus, 325 BC
- battle

for example, Acco became Ptolemais, and Rabbath-ammon became Philadelphia. Both dynasties had large empires to control, and a strong, bureaucratic administration, conducted in Greek and conversant with the local Egyptian or Aramaic, served their need. The spread of Greek language and culture went hand in hand with the purposes of government.

The Maccabees were well aware of the Hellenistic Mediterranean world. Judas Maccabeus himself sent an embassy to Rome (*1 Macc 8.17*), and Jonathan entertained diplomatic relationships with Sparta (*1 Macc 12.2*). Hellenistic lifestyle is illustrated by the town of Marisa, where tombs contain Greek inscriptions and wall paintings of animals captioned with Greek names. Hellenistic administration is evident at Scythopolis (Beth-shean), where a Greek inscription records orders issued by Antiochus III and his son.

Jewish writings

This was an age of Jewish expansion abroad. Many Mediterranean Hellenistic cities had a growing Jewish population, which began to adopt Greek as its own language. At Alexandria, the Jewish Law was translated into Greek in the 3rd century BC. There were many other notable writings from Alexandrine Jewish communities in the period from the 2nd century BC to the 1st century AD, including the translation into Greek of Ecclesiasticus, 2 Maccabees, the Wisdom of Solomon, and the writings of Philo. Jewish literature in Greek was also found in Jerusalem. The coins of Alexander Jannaeus (103–76 BC) had a Hebrew inscription on one side and a Greek inscription on the other. By the 1st century AD, Greek was written even at Qumran, the home of an Essene community, and Greek was spoken among the early Christian Hellenizers (*Acts 6.1*). According to John 19.20, Pontius Pilate used Greek, with Latin and Hebrew, for the title on the cross of Jesus.

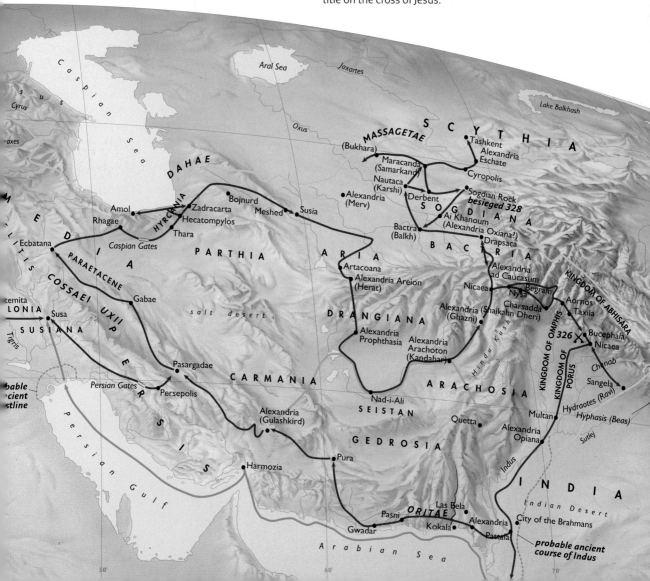

Judah and the Ptolemies

In the intertestamental era, Egypt once more played a crucial role in the history of the Jewish people. Alexandria became the home of a very lively Jewish community, anxious to be included in the citizenship of the capital of Hellenistic Egypt.

It was here that the Hebrew scriptures were first translated into Greek - a translation that became known as the Septuagint (Greek *septuaginta*) after the legend that 72 elders of Israel translated the Hebrew Bible in 72 days.

Ptolemaic interest in the Levant

Ptolemy I Soter was a Macedonian general of Alexander the Great. On the death of Alexander, Ptolemy seized Egypt. At the height of their power, the Ptolemies held most of the Levant, the south and southwestern coasts of Anatolia, Cyprus, and some coastal areas of Thrace.

Ptolemy annexed Cyrenaica and then Syria and Phoenicia to improve his access to the Mediterranean and his defense against his rivals, Antigonus and Seleucus.

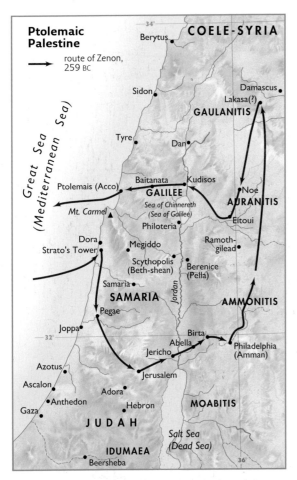

Ptolemaic Palestine

→ route of Zenon, 259 BC

Great Sea (Mediterranean Sea)

COELE-SYRIA
Berytus
Sidon
Tyre
Damascus
Lakasa(?)
GAULANITIS
Dan
Baitanata
Kudisos
Ptolemais (Acco)
GALILEE
Noe
AURANITIS
Mt. Carmel
Sea of Chinnereth
(Sea of Galilee)
Eitoui
Philoteria
Dora
Megiddo
Ramoth-gilead
Strato's Tower
Scythopolis
(Beth-shean)
Berenice
(Pella)
Samaria
SAMARIA
Pegae
AMMONITIS
Joppa
Birta
Abella
Philadelphia
Jericho
(Amman)
Azotus
Jerusalem
Ascalon
Adora
Anthedon
Hebron
MOABITIS
Gaza
JUDAH
Salt Sea
(Dead Sea)
IDUMAEA
Beersheba
Jordan

He transferred the capital from Memphis to Alexandria, occupied Coele-Syria and Judah (301 BC), and established control over Cyprus and the Aegean. In 288/7 BC, he took Tyre and Sidon, securing a defensive ring of territory, and also created close contacts with the Hellenistic world. The Ptolemies held Judah until 200 BC, when Ptolemy V fought the Seleucid Antiochus III at Panion. The resulting defeat meant that control of Coele-Syria, Sidon, Gaza, and Judah passed to the Seleucids.

Jews in Egypt

Under the Ptolemies, the Jewish population in Egypt increased. Jews had settled in Egypt after the fall of Jerusalem in 587 BC (*Jer 43.5–7, 44.1*), and the Elephantine papyri reveal a Jewish colony near Aswan. In 312 BC, Ptolemy added Jewish captives from Jerusalem; some, according to the Letter of Aristeas, were later repatriated in exchange for a copy of the Torah, which was taken from Jerusalem to Alexandria and translated into Greek for Ptolemy II's library (or, more likely, for the benefit of the growing Jewish population in Alexandria). Ptolemy III was well disposed towards the Jews, and many appear settled as farmers, artisans, soldiers, policemen, tax collectors, and administrators during his reign. Jewish synagogues are known at Alexandria, Crocodilopolis in the Fayum, Athribis, and elsewhere.

Some Jews favored Hellenistic culture, others rejected it; but all of them were anxious to persuade fellow Jews and gentiles alike that the Jewish traditions compared well with those of the gentiles. Jews may boast of their contribution to the world of learning and of their loyalty to society, to demonstrate that persecution was unjustified. The story of Ptolemy IV's trying to massacre Jews packed into a hippodrome by setting intoxicated elephants on them is legendary, but it does reflect the fear felt by the Jews living in alien surroundings.

Route described by Zenon, mid-third century BC. From 261 BC, Zenon accompanied his master Apollonius as he visited the cities and regions under Ptolemy II's control (*map left*).

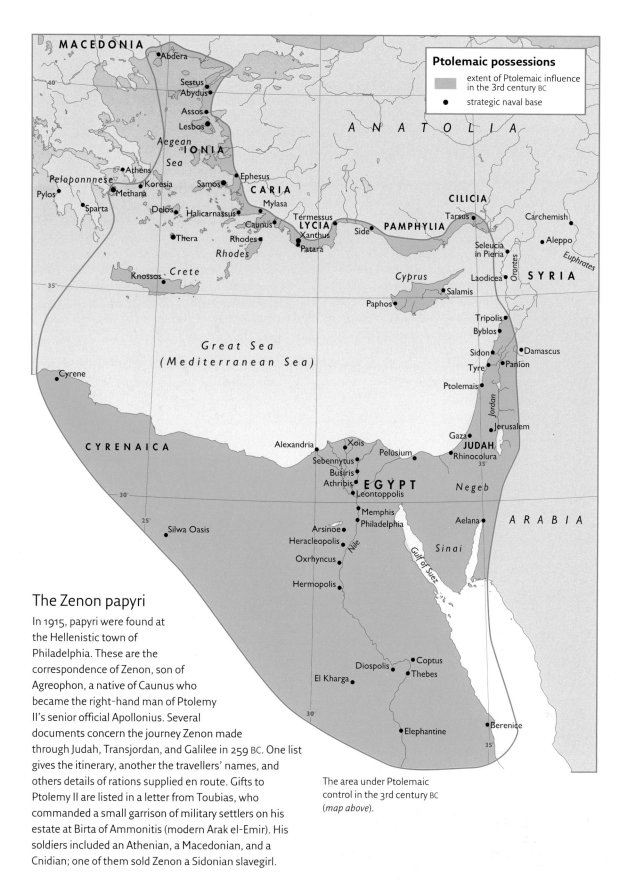

Ptolemaic possessions

extent of Ptolemaic influence in the 3rd century BC

● strategic naval base

MACEDONIA

Abdera

Sestus
Abydus
Assos
Lesbos

Aegean Sea

ANATOLIA

IONIA

Athens
Koresia
Methana
Pylos
Sparta
Delos
Halicarnassus
Samos
Ephesus
CARIA
Mylasa
Caunus
Termessus
LYCIA
Xanthus
Patara
Side
PAMPHYLIA
Thera
Rhodes
Rhodes

CILICIA
Tarsus
Carchemish
Aleppo
Seleucia in Pieria
Laodicea
Orontes
SYRIA
Euphrates

Knossos
Crete

Cyprus
Salamis
Paphos

Great Sea
(Mediterranean Sea)

Tripolis
Byblos
Sidon
Damascus
Tyre
Panion
Ptolemais
Jordan
Jerusalem

Cyrene

CYRENAICA

Alexandria
Xois
Pelusium
Sebennytus
Busiris
Athribis
Leontoppolis
EGYPT
Gaza
JUDAH
Rhinocolura
Negeb

ARABIA

Silwa Oasis

Memphis
Philadelphia
Arsinoe
Heracleopolis
Oxrhyncus
Nile
Hermopolis

Aelana

Sinai

Gulf of Suez

Diospolis
El Kharga
Coptus
Thebes

Elephantine
Berenice

The Zenon papyri

In 1915, papyri were found at the Hellenistic town of Philadelphia. These are the correspondence of Zenon, son of Agreophon, a native of Caunus who became the right-hand man of Ptolemy II's senior official Apollonius. Several documents concern the journey Zenon made through Judah, Transjordan, and Galilee in 259 BC. One list gives the itinerary, another the travellers' names, and others details of rations supplied en route. Gifts to Ptolemy II are listed in a letter from Toubias, who commanded a small garrison of military settlers on his estate at Birta of Ammonitis (modern Arak el-Emir). His soldiers included an Athenian, a Macedonian, and a Cnidian; one of them sold Zenon a Sidonian slavegirl.

The area under Ptolemaic control in the 3rd century BC (*map above*).

The Seleucid empire

Seleucas had taken Babylon and Syria on Alexander's death. He founded a new capital, Seleucia, on the Tigris, but his political interests were in the west, where his main rival, Antigonus the One-eyed, aimed to reunite and rule Alexander's empire.

In 301 BC, Seleucus and his son Antiochus, together with Lysimachus of Thrace and Cassander of Macedon, allied against Antigonus and his son Demetrius Poliorcetes. Antigonus was killed and Demetrius fled to Ephesus. The center of the Seleucid empire now shifted west, and Seleucus moved his capital, first to the port of Seleucia Pieria and then to Antioch on the Orontes in Syria.

The eastern empire

The eastern empire became something of a burden. In 308–3 BC, Seleucus yielded the eastern provinces of Arachosia and Gedrosia to Chandragupta of India in exchange for 300 elephants. Bactria, however, well settled with Macedonian colonists and Hellenistic cities, and linked to the west by a

good road, remained Seleucid until 250 BC, when it gained independence under Diodotus. In 247 BC, the less Hellenized Parthia seized independence, but by 205 BC it was under the control of Antiochus III. However, after Antiochus' humiliation by the Romans in the Treaty of Apamea (188 BC), the Seleucids were unable to hold the east. Antiochus IV (166–5 BC) (*1 Macc 3.30–37, 6.1–16*), Demetrius II (141 BC) (*1 Macc 14.1–2*), and Antiochus VII (129 BC) all tried and failed to regain Parthia, whose king, Mithridates II (124–87 BC) welcomed ambassadors from China.

The Seleucid empire was founded in 312 BC by Seleucus I (*map right*). The capital was moved from Babylon to Antioch on the Orontes in 300 BC. Seleucus intergrated the full extent of Alexander's eastern conquests, but Arachosia, Gedrosia, Bactria, and Parthia were successfully lost to the Seleucids. Antiochus III "the Great" temporarily restored Seleucid control of Parthia. The Seleucids, however, were more interested in the west, but were checked by the rising power of Rome, which prevented Antiochus III from seizing Greece (189 BC) and Antiochus IV from seizing Egypt (169–168 BC).

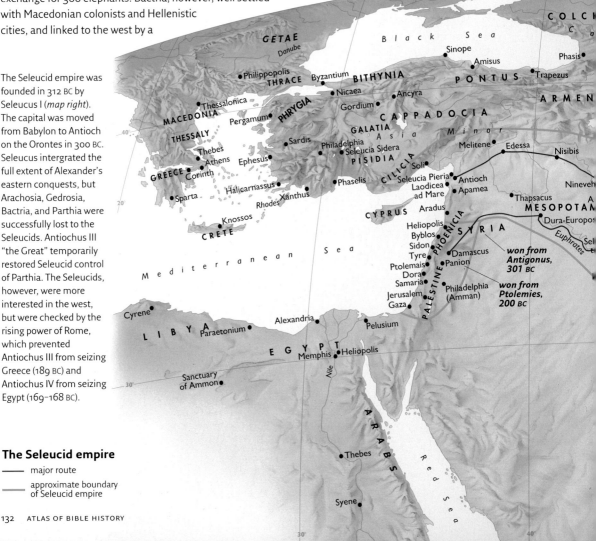

The Seleucid empire

—— major route

—— approximate boundary of Seleucid empire

The western empire

The Seleucids were equally unsuccessful in the west. They never controlled Armenia, Cappadocia, Pontus, or Bithynia. They met opposition from the Galatians, from the growing states of Pergamum and Rhodes, from the Romans in Greece, and from the Ptolemies along the Mediterranean coasts, leaving them effectively limited to Cilicia and Syria. The acquisition of Coele-Syria, Palestine, and Transjordan after the battle of Panion (200 BC) was a major Seleucid success. Antiochus IV's anxiety to secure Judah as a buffer towards Egypt was probably a major factor in his reaction to the Maccabaean rebellion.

Seleucid administration

The Seleucid rulers were of Macedonian origin; their subjects included both city dwellers and nomads between the Aegean and India. A major feature was the settlement of Macedonian soldiers into colonies, which developed into cities. New towns, usually with names taken from Macedonia (Larissa, Beroea) or from the Seleucid royal family (Antiochia, Laodicea), gave the king more direct control. Temple cities also had a certain independence and the right of asylum; Jerusalem seems to have been one of these (1 Macc 10.43). The Seleucid aim was to make cities loyal to the crown, and so hold the empire together by peaceful rather than military means.

The army and navy

The Seleucid army was composed of heavy infantry (originally drawn from Macedonian colonists) and local groups of light infantry and cavalry. The navy operated in the Mediterranean from Seleucia and Ephesus, and in the Persian Gulf. The Seleucid empire, however, never looked solid. Its eastern borders were too far from Antioch, its Greek colonists too insecure. From the mid-2nd century BC, the Seleucids were under pressure from the Parthians and Armenians, east and north, and from Rome in the west. The empire fell to Rome with Pompey's arrival in 64 BC.

The Maccabees

When the Seleucids took Judah from the Ptolemies in 200 BC, most Jews probably welcomed the tax concessions and the freedom to live in accordance with the traditional Jewish Law granted by Antiochus III.

The trouble began when Seleucus IV attempted to raise money by robbing the Jerusalem temple (2 *Macc 3*). The high priest Onias resisted but was deposed by his brother Jason, who offered Antiochus IV increased tribute in exchange for the high priesthood for himself and Greek city status for Jerusalem. Jason, in turn, was replaced as high priest by Menelaus. When Jason tried to regain the high priesthood by force, Antiochus saw it as rebellion, attacked Jerusalem, and pillaged the temple.

In autumn 167 BC, Antiochus enforced increased control over his unruly subjects; he banned Jewish sacrifices, Sabbath observance, circumcision, and the Jewish Law, and enforced gentile forms of religion (*1 Macc 1.41–61; 2 Macc 6.2*). He sought to prohibit the very things that consituted Jewish independence: a measure of self-rule through their own ancestral laws and the exclusivity of their temple in Jerusalem. The result was rebellion.

The Maccabean rebellion

The Maccabees came from Modin, a village north-west of Jerusalem. The rebellion began when they killed a Jewish official as he tried to force them to participate in pagan worship (*1 Macc 2.15–28*). They then killed the governor of Samaria as he led a small force against them, and ambushed a larger force in the pass of Beth-horon. In 165 BC, their leader Judas, called Maccabeus ("hammerlike"), defeated a larger Seleucid army at Emmaus, and in December 164 BC, (just as Antiochus died) Judas seized the temple area. The area was purged of its gentile cult and rededicated. In 162 BC, Lysias, Antiochus V's vice-regent, invaded Judah, took Beth-zur, defeated Judas at Beth-zechariah, and besieged Judas' troops in the temple. A threatened coup in Syria forced Lysias to offer terms to Judas; he repealed the decree of 167 BC, executed Menelaus, and left the Syrian garrison in control of Jerusalem.

The Seleucids and the Maccabees

— boundary of Seleucid eparchy

--- original extent of eparchy of Judaea

◉ attacked by Jonathan

Maccabean campaign

● given to Jonathan by Alexander Balas, 147 BC

● given to Jonathan by Demetrius II, 145 BC

● taken and fortified by Simon, 144–43 BC

In 161 BC, the new Seleucid king, Demetrius, appointed a new high priest, Alcimus, and a new general, Nicanor. After initial attempts at peace, Nicanor was killed at Adasa (161–160 BC); Judas himself was killed at the battle of Elasa (160 BC). The new general, Bacchides, garrisoned the land (*1 Macc 9.50–53*) but failed to defeat or capture Judas' successor Jonathan.

Towards independence

Jonathan bargained with successive contenders for the Seleucid throne. Through a series of alliances he acquired honors and territory and, with his brother Simon, proceeded by various conquests to consolidate the Jewish position. This Jewish resurgence alarmed Trypho, guardian of Antiochus VI, who captured Jonathan treacherously at Ptolemais. Simon, however, took over the leadership, and continued to develop Judah's political and military strength, culminating in the expulsion of the Seleucid garrison from Jerusalem (141 BC). He renewed diplomatic relationships established earlier with Rome (*1 Macc 8.17–32, 12.1–4*) and Sparta (*1 Macc 12.5–23*), and negotiated the formal abolition of tribute with Demetrius II. This meant, in effect, that the Seleucid dynasty had lost, and Israel had gained independence.

1 and 2 Maccabees

The principal sources for the history of the Maccabean rebellion are 1 Maccabees and 2 Maccabees. The book of 1 Maccabees emphasizes the political and military history and the importance of the Hasmonaean family; it was originally written in Hebrew, perhaps in the reign of John Hyrcanus. The book of 2 Maccabees underlines religious motivation and was written in Greek, probably a little later.

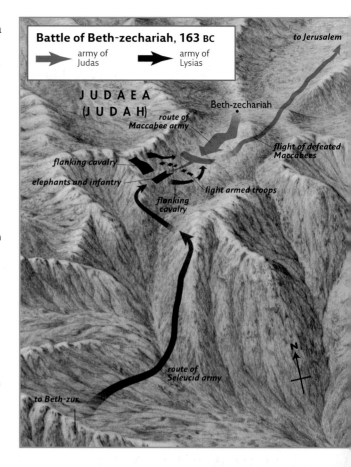

Battle of Beth-zechariah, 163 BC
→ army of Judas   → army of Lysias

JUDAEA (JUDAH)
to Jerusalem
Beth-zechariah
route of Maccabee army
flight of defeated Maccabees
flanking cavalry
elephants and infantry
light armed troops
flanking cavalry
route of Seleucid army
to Beth-zur
N

After the Maccabees' early campaigns against the Seleucids, their strategy changed under the leadership of Jonathan (*map left*). Political maneuver worked where military action had failed, and Jonathan and his brother, Simon, were able to consolidate the Jewish position, culminating in 141 BC with the expulsion of the Seleucid garrison from Jerusalem. In 163 BC, the Seleucid general Lysias, with Antiochus V, campaigned against Judas Maccabeus in Judaea. Lysias' elephants and infantry marched through the center of the valley protected by flanking cavalry on the hillsides and light-armed troops in front.

Judas' troops attacked the heavy infantry phalanx head on but were defeated by the cavalry on the high ground and forced to flee to Jerusalem and beyond (*map above right*). In 160 BC Judas camped at Elasa, and Bacchides faced him at Berea, half a mile away (*map right*). Bacchides had 20,000 infantry and 2000 cavalry. Judas' army is said to have suffered loss of morale, his original 3000 men being reduced by desertion to 800; if so, his defeat of Bacchides' right wing is astonishing. Judas' men were pursuing Bacchides' army when the Syrian left wing swung round in their rear. Judas was among those killed.

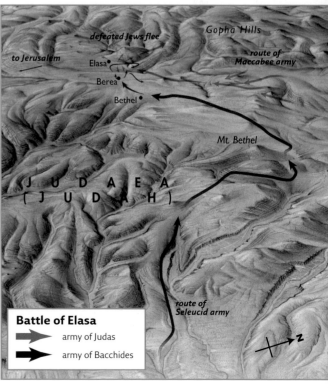

defeated Jews flee
Gopha Hills
to Jerusalem
Elasa
route of Maccabee army
Berea
Bethel
Mt. Bethel
JUDAEA (JUDAH)
route of Seleucid army

Battle of Elasa
→ army of Judas   → army of Bacchides

Jewish independence - the Hasmonaean monarchy

Under Simon, in the 170th year of the Seleucid era (142 BC), "the yoke of the gentiles was removed from Israel" (*1 Macc 13.41*), and the first year of a new era began. From now until the arrival of the Romans in 63 BC, the Jews were free to develop their own independent state.

The main features of the period are the final emancipation from Seleucid rule, the expansion of Judaea's territory, the development of a monarchy, and opposition to this development. Demetrius II (145–40 BC) exempted Judaea from tribute (*1 Macc 11.30–37*), thus granting Judaea virtual independence, and Antiochus VII (138–29 BC) even granted Simon the right to mint coins (*1 Macc 15.1–9*). Antiochus soon demanded the return of disputed territory and attacked Simon. After Simon's death (134 BC), he successfully besieged Simon's son John Hyrcanus in Jerusalem, forcing from him hostages and tribute. But in 129 BC, Antiochus died fighting the Parthians (129 BC), and thereafter the Seleucids were no threat to Judah.

Expansion of Judaea

The Seleucid collapse gave Judah the opportunity to expand. Jonathan had already won some territory in the coastal region (Paralia) and Samaria (*1 Macc 10.30, 89; 11.28, 34*), and Simon had annexed Gazara and Joppa (*1 Macc 10.76, 13.11, 14.5*).

Over the next 50 years, Judaea continued to grow. Along the coast, Hyrcanus took Apollonia, Jamnia, and Azotus, to which Jannaeus added Strato's Tower (the later Caesarea) and Dora to the north and Anthedon, Gaza, Raphia, and Rhinocolura towards Egypt. Inland, Hyrcanus took Samaria in two stages, first defeating the people and destroying their temple on Mount Gerizim near Shechem, and later (108 BC) capturing the cities of Samaria and Scythopolis. A few years later, Aristobulus (103 BC) took Galilee. To the south, Hyrcanus invaded Idumaea, forcibly Judaizing the people (with the unexpected result that, a century later, an Idumaean, Herod, reigned in Jerusalem). The location of forts at Alexandrium, Hyrcania, Masada, and Machaerus reveals Jannaeus' concern for his southern and eastern borders.

Hasmonaean rule

The Hasmonaeans ruled with difficulty. Simon was assassinated and Hyrcanus I was opposed by the Pharisees, who objected to his high priesthood. The right of the dynasty to assume the role of high priest was a constant source of unrest. Jonathan's assumption of the office in 152 BC probably caused the Qumran sect to call him "the Wicked Priest." When Jannaeus later presided as high priest at the feast of Tabernacles, he was pelted with citrons; his response was a massacre, which led to civil war. The Pharisees enlisted the Seleucid Demetrius III against Jannaeus, who revenged himself by crucifying 800 opponents and killing their families. On his deathbed Jannaeus advised his wife Alexandra to make her peace with the Pharisees, and she did.

After her death, her ambitious younger son Aristobulus forced his older brother Hyrcanus to resign the throne and the high priesthood. However, the even more ambitious Idumaean Antipater tried to reestablish Hyrcanus as his puppet with the help of Nabataean Aretas III, and they besieged Aristobulus in the temple. Meanwhile, the Romans under Pompey had eventually taken over Syria, and both parties appealed to Hyrcanus. Pompey supported Hyrcanus, leading Aristobulus and his supporters to stage a last-ditch defense in the temple. After a protracted siege, the Romans captured the temple. Pompey himself entered the Holy of Holies to see what it contained; later, when he was assassinated, Jews saw it as divine retribution for this act of desecration. Hyrcanus was declared high priest; Aristobulus was taken to Rome as a captive; the Romans were now in charge.

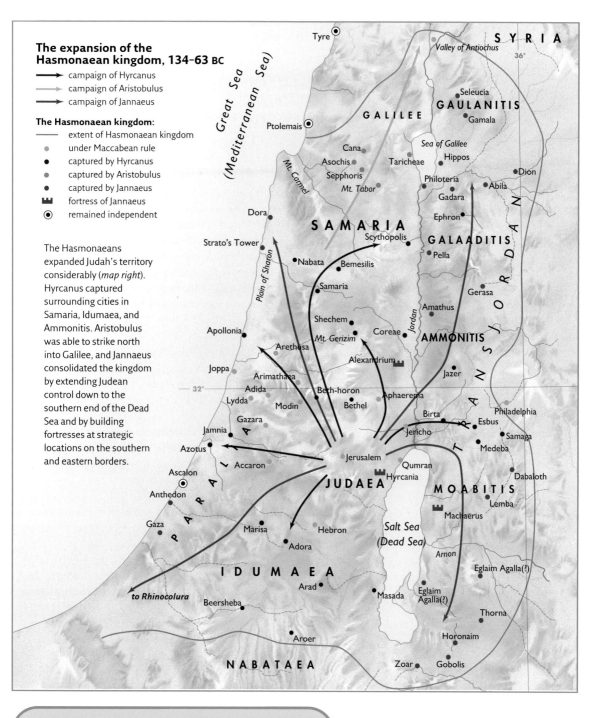

The expansion of the Hasmonaean kingdom, 134–63 BC

➤ campaign of Hyrcanus
➤ campaign of Aristobulus
➤ campaign of Jannaeus

The Hasmonaean kingdom:

— extent of Hasmonaean kingdom
• under Maccabean rule
• captured by Hyrcanus
• captured by Aristobulus
• captured by Jannaeus
ᗒ fortress of Jannaeus
◉ remained independent

The Hasmonaeans expanded Judah's territory considerably (*map right*). Hyrcanus captured surrounding cities in Samaria, Idumaea, and Ammonitis. Aristobulus was able to strike north into Galilee, and Jannaeus consolidated the kingdom by extending Judean control down to the southern end of the Dead Sea and by building fortresses at strategic locations on the southern and eastern borders.

Map labels:
SYRIA • Valley of Antiochus • 36° • Tyre • Seleucia • GAULANITIS • GALILEE • Gamala • Ptolemais • Great Sea (Mediterranean Sea) • Cana • Sea of Galilee • Hippos • Asochis • Taricheae • Sepphoris • Dion • Mt. Tabor • Philoteria • Abila • Gadara • Mt. Carmel • Ephron • Dora • SAMARIA • GALAADITIS • Strato's Tower • Scythopolis • Nabata • Pella • Bemesilis • Samaria • Gerasa • Plain of Sharon • Amathus • Shechem • Coreae • AMMONITIS • Apollonia • Mt. Gerizim • Arethusa • Alexandrium • Joppa • Jazer • Arimathaea • TRANSJORDAN • Adida • Beth-horon • Aphaerema • 32° • Lydda • Modin • Bethel • Birta • Philadelphia • Gazara • Jericho • Esbus • Jamnia • Samaga • Azotus • Medeba • Accaron • Jerusalem • Qumran • Ascalon • Hycania • MOABITIS • Anthedon • Dabaloth • Gaza • Lemba • PARALIA • Marisa • Hebron • Salt Sea (Dead Sea) • Machaerus • Adora • Arnon • IDUMAEA • Arad • Eglaim Agalla(?) • to Rhinocolura • Masada • Eglaim Agalla(?) • Beersheba • Thorna • Aroer • Horonaim • NABATAEA • Zoar • Gobolis

"In the one hundred seventieth year the yoke of the gentiles was removed from Israel, and the people began to write in their documents and contracts, 'In the first year of Simon the great high priest and commander and leader of the Jews.'"

(Exod 13.17–18)

The development of the synagogue

Just when the institution of the synagogue first began is uncertain. Some have suggested that it arose among the Babylonian exiles; others, that it came from the Second Temple period as part of Ezra's reform in Judaea. In general, the evidence points to the Hellenistic period.

The Temple of Jerusalem was the central place for Jewish worship through the priesthood and the sacrificial cult. After AD 70, when Herod's temple was destroyed, new modes of worship were needed, and the synagogue (from the Greek word *synagoge*, meaning "assembly") emerged as the central institution of Jewish prayer and study of Torah.

Archaeological evidence

Although synagogues were a common feature of Jesus' day, there is no archaeological evidence of synagogue buildings in 1st century AD Palestine. Most archaeological evidence for synagogue buildings (including building remains, inscriptions, and papyri) during the 2nd century AD comes from the Diaspora. Synagogue remains from Palestine come from the 3rd century AD and later.

There were probably two distinct lines of development: one from the Diaspora, the other from the homeland. In the Diaspora, the needs of minority Jewish communities seeking to maintain their worship and identity in an alien environment gave rise to communal centers as places of prayer. In the homeland, local places of civic assembly (*beth ha-knesset*) and small associations for the study of Torah (*beth ha-midrash*) were brought together under the new religious leadership of the Pharisees. After AD 70, these distinct lines of development began to merge.

Architecture

Jewish places of prayer (*proseuchai*) were common from Egypt to Greece during the Hellenistic period. Most of the excavated synagogues from the Diaspora have been renovated from houses. In urban centers such as Alexandria, where the Jewish population was substantial, there were several synagogues. These congregations were loosely organized under a governing "council of elders" (*gerousia*). At Rome, more than 11 synagogues are known after the 1st century AD, but there is no indication of a central governing body.

In the 2nd and 3rd centuries AD, houses where congregations had held casual assemblies were taken over and converted. At Dura-Europos, a Roman garrison on the Euphrates, a house-synagogue was converted into a large, opulent synagogue hall with a forecourt (*see page 162*). The hall had a Torah shrine, and the walls were lavishly painted with biblical scenes.

Synagogue buildings in Palestine come from the 3rd–6th centuries AD, when rabbinical Judaism was being consolidated with the compilation of the Mishnah and the Talmud. Strict architectural forms were not enforced, although some regional patterns evolved. Some buildings show elaborate artistic decorations, such as mosaic floors with depictions of the zodiac, the Torah shrine, menorah, and other Jewish symbols.

Worship

Initially, great variety existed in worship and order. Women were not excluded from the assembly until later times and often served in leadership roles, especially in the Diaspora. With the demise of the temple, weekly prayers and annual feasts were centered in the synagogue; however, the synagogue liturgy did not have a fixed form in the 1st century AD.

Reading of scripture became a central act of worship. Depending on location, the scriptures were read in Greek translation (the Septuagint) or were paraphrased in Aramaic vernacular (Targum). Two of the major synagogue prayers (the Shema and Eighteen Benedictions) were already in use by the end of the 1st century AD, though not in their later fixed forms.

Synagogue sites in Roman Palestine

✴ synagogue remains

Distribution of synagogue remains in Roman Palestine (*map right*). There are no remains of identifiable synagogue buildings from the 1st century AD or before. Most of the sites shown date from the 4th to 6th centuries AD, though there are some indications that architectural development had begun by the end of the 2nd century AD, and a few date to the 3rd century AD.

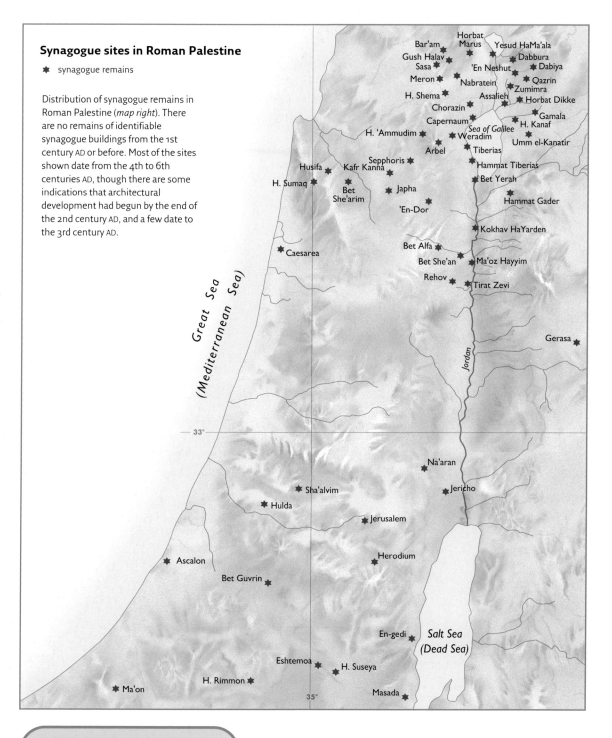

Bar'am
Horbat Marus
Yesud HaMa'ala
Gush Halav
Sasa
Dabbura
Dabiya
'En Neshut
Meron
Nabratein
Qazrin
Zumimra
H. Shema
Assalieh
Horbat Dikke
Chorazin
Gamala
Capernaum
H. Kanaf
Sea of Galilee
Weradim
Umm el-Kanatir
H. 'Ammudim
Arbel
Tiberias
Husifa
Sepphoris
Hammat Tiberias
Kafr Kanna
H. Sumaq
Bet Yerah
Bet She'arim
Japha
'En-Dor
Hammat Gader
Caesarea
Kokhav HaYarden
Bet Alfa
Bet She'an
Ma'oz Hayyim
Rehov
Tirat Zevi

Great Sea
(Mediterranean Sea)

Gerasa

Jordan

33°

Na'aran

Sha'alvim
Jericho

Hulda

Jerusalem

Herodium

Ascalon

Bet Guvrin

En-gedi
Salt Sea (Dead Sea)

Eshtemoa
H. Suseya

H. Rimmon
Ma'on
Masada

35°

EIGHT

PALESTINE UNDER THE ROMANS

The Herodion, Israel.
One of a string of hill-top fortresses constructed by Herod the
Great, the Herodion (or Herodium) was constructed c. 24 BC.
Once topped by a palace complex with bathhouse, synagogue,
and banqueting hall, it was also the site of Herod's burial.

Rome's expansion

Whereas the Greek monarchies had partitioned the eastern Mediterranean, the west had remained under the sway of several powerful city-states. By the end of the 3rd century BC, one of these - Rome - gradually expanded its power throughout all of Italy and surrounding regions. After the Third Punic War (146 BC), Rome was master of the west and began to establish a provincial system to control its far-flung holdings.

Rome's conquests and trading interests brought increasing diplomatic interests in the east. Rome gained a foothold in Asia Minor by serving as protector of the client kingdom of Pergamum, and when the last Attalid ruler of Pergamum died in 133 BC, its territories were bequeathed to Rome and reconstituted as the Province of Asia.

Gradually, much of the east came under Roman provincial organization through similar diplomatic measures. Rome's policy was to weaken the strong powers and enlist the favor of local rulers who might be allied to Rome. In 168 BC, Rome forced the Seleucid Antiochus IV to retire from his campaign on Ptolemaic Egypt, an intervention that probably had an impact in Judaea (Judah) at the beginning of the Maccabean revolt.

Pompey's eastern settlement

In 67 BC, a crisis faced Rome when pirates from Cilicia threatened to disrupt the corn fleets from Egypt. The Senate granted "extraordinary" powers to the general Pompey, who consolidated power in Asia Minor and forced Armenia to sue for peace. He then marched on Syria, reaching Damascus in 64 BC. Pompey formed a line of provinces along the coastline of Asia Minor and around to Syria. Beyond this, allied kingdoms with the status of clientele served as buffer states. Local rulers became "client-kings" and were diplomatically termed "friends" (*amici*) or "allies" (*socii*) of Rome.

Judaea, too, came under Pompey's control. Just as Pompey was moving from Asia Minor into Syria, the

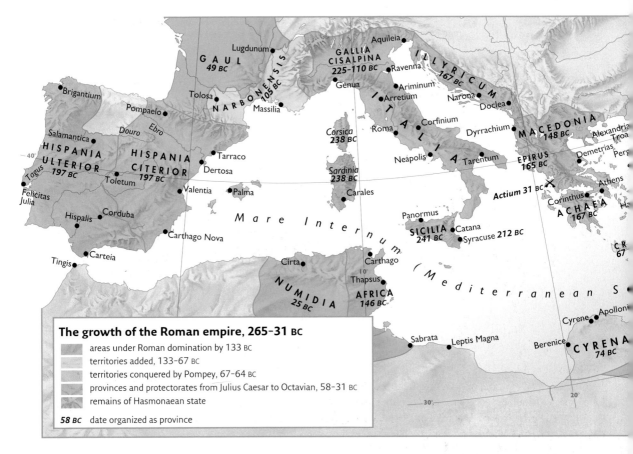

The growth of the Roman empire, 265–31 BC

- areas under Roman domination by 133 BC
- territories added, 133–67 BC
- territories conquered by Pompey, 67–64 BC
- provinces and protectorates from Julius Caesar to Octavian, 58–31 BC
- remains of Hasmonaean state

58 BC date organized as province

Hasmonaean state fell into a civil war. To ensure peace, Pompey reorganized Palestine and deposed Aristobulus II in favor of Hyrcanus II, who ruled as high priest and ethnarch from 64–40 BC. The Hasmonaean state was reduced to three areas: Judaea (including Idumaea), Galilee, and Peraea. Samaria was partitioned as a separate client state.

Judaea during the Roman civil war

Pompey was involved in a contest for power with Julius Caesar. When Pompey was killed in Egypt by Ptolemy XIII, Julius Caesar avenged Pompey's death and began his fateful encounter with Ptolemy's sister, Cleopatra VII. Julius Caesar was assassinated (44 BC) by Republican sympathizers, who were defeated by Marc Antony and Caesar's nephew, Octavian. Finally, Antony and Octavian fell out, and in 31 BC Octavian defeated the forces of Antony and Cleopatra. By 27 BC, Octavian claimed for himself the title of Augustus (Sebastos in Greek), Emperor of Rome.

During this time of unrest and factionalism, the client-king of Judaea, Hyrcanus, employed as his chief adviser a prince called Antipater. When they switched allegiance from Pompey to Caesar, they were duly rewarded. Antipater's son, Herod, was declared King of Judaea by the Senate in 37 BC. When the political wind shifted yet again, Herod sided with Octavian against Antony and Cleopatra. As a reward, Octavian confirmed and rewarded Herod as client-king, thus producing the new Jewish state that existed under the early Roman empire.

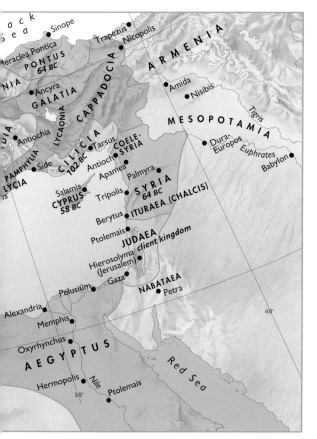

Pompey's settlement of the Hasmonaean Jewish state

— Hasmonaean state before Pompey's settlement

⬜ Jewish state after Pompey's settlement

⬛ Jewish territories ceded to Ituraea and Ptolemais

⬛ Samarian state

◉ cities of the Decapolis

● large towns within the borders of non-Jewish states

• other independent cities

◉ Gabinius' synedria

🏰 fortress of Jannaeus

— other political boundary

In the 2nd century BC, Rome was at war on every front (map left). To the west ,as a result of the wars with Carthage, Rome gained the provinces of Spain (Hispania) in 197 BC and Africa in 146 BC. In the east, Roman legions defeated the Seleucids in 190 BC and Macedonia and Asia were annexed in 148 BC and 133 BC. Under Sulla Lucullus and Pompey, the Romans gradually defeated the princedoms of Asia Minor and extended their control of Bithynia, Pontus Cilicia, Syria, Crete, and Cyprus.

The decline of Seleucid rule had allowed the Hasmonaean Jewish state under Jannaeus (103–76 BC) to expand (map above). In 64 BC, the Roman general Pompey and his successor Gabinius reduced the kingdom to Judaea, Galilee, and Peraea, and allowed the 20 or so Greek cities that Jannaeus had captured to become independent. Under Gabinius (57–55 BC), a short-lived attempt was made to divide up the Jewish state yet further into five synedria (districts).

The Herodian kingdom

Herod the Great and his brother Phasael were the sons of Antipater, the Idumaean who had risen to prominence under Hyrcanus II (64–40 BC). His success in brokering alliances throughout the region gained great favors for his family from the Roman rulers.

Antipater had interceded with Pompey to install Hyrcanus II as king and high priest of Judaea instead of his rival Aristobulus II and subsequently orchestrated the political maneuvering of Judaea over to Julius Caesar. As a result, Hyrcanus II retained the title of high priest, but Antipater was named procurator (governor), and he named his sons *strategoi* ("commanders").

However, Antipater was assassinated by supporters of Aristobulus II and Marc Antony designated Phasael and Herod as tetrarchs (rulers) over Judaea and Galilee, respectively. Antigonus, the son of Aristobulus II, enlisted the help of Parthian armies to attack. Phasael was captured and executed, and Antigonus captured Jerusalem, where he disfigured Hyrcanus II and claimed the titles of king and high priest (40–37 BC).

Herod escaped to Rome, where, supported by Antony and Octavian, he was made king of Judaea. Herod returned to Judaea with a mandate and military support from Rome to pacify the region. By 37 BC, Herod had captured all of Judaea (with Idumaea), Samaria, Peraea, and Galilee. Antigonus was captured and executed along with 45 Sadducean priests who had supported him. In the meantime, Herod had married the Hasmonaean princess Mariamne, granddaughter of both Hyrcanus II and Aristobulus II.

Organization of Herod's kingdom

When Marc Antony assumed control over the east, Herod was forced to cede several territories to Cleopatra. These territories were eventually returned to Herod in 30 BC by Octavian, after Herod denounced Cleopatra in the wake of the battle of Actium (31 BC). Shortly thereafter, Herod quietly eliminated the aged Hyrcanus II, along with the remaining members of the Hasmonaean line, including Herod's wife Mariamne and her mother. In 23 BC, Octavian, now the emperor Augustus, conferred on Herod the territories of Batanaea, Trachonitis, and Auranitis, and in 20 BC Gaulanitis was added to his realm of Ituraea. With this, Herod's kingdom reached its greatest extent, greater in fact than under the Hasmonaean kings.

Herod's kingdom was divided into city-territories and toparchies, regions without any settlement of free-city status. Some cities remained independent of Herod's direct control, while others were autonomous. The rest were organized into five regions: Idumaea, Judaea, Samaria, Galilee, and Peraea.

While a Jew in religion, Herod was socially and ethnically of mixed background. He was an Idumaean, a remnant of the Edomites, who in the Persian and Hellenistic periods had been pushed from the Negeb by the expanding Nabataean kingdom. In the Hasmonaean expansion of John Hyrcanus (134–104 BC), Idumaea was annexed to Judaea and its population was forcibly Judaized.

This background surely influenced Herod's governance of his realm's diverse population, which included non-Jews (goyim, or gentiles) as well as other subethnic groups, such as the Samaritans, Ituraeans, or Galileans. Following the lead of Augustus, Herod inaugurated a program of royal bequests to these groups, chief among which was an elaborate building program in major cities, such as Jerusalem, Jericho, and Masada.

In his later years, Herod was ruthless in eliminating rivals for his throne, even among his own children, several of whom died suspiciously or were executed for treason. Rumors of such atrocities probably contributed to the story of Herod's ordering a slaughter of children around the time of the birth of Jesus (*Matt 2.16*).

Judea after Pompey: Herod's kingdom

- Jewish state, 40 BC
- added, 40 BC
- added, 30 BC
- added, 23 BC
- added, 20 BC
- taken by force from the Nabataeans
- maximum extent of Herod's kingdom

PHOENICIA

Paneas

Caesarea Philippi (Paneas)

GAULANITIS

— 33°

— 35°

Ptolemais

BATANAEA

'Arav

Migdal

Sea of Galilee

TRACHONTIS

Arbela

Hippos

Gabae

Sepphoris

Dion

AURANITIS

GALILEE

Gabae

Dora

Gadara

Agrippina

Strato's Tower

Scythopolis (Beth-shean)

Pella

SAMARIA

DECAPOLIS

Qayum

Amathus

Samaria

Gerasa

Shechem

Mt Gerizim▲

Acrabbein

CUTHEANS

Apollonia

Alexandrium (Sartaba)

Arethusa

Jordan

Gedor

Joppa (Japha)

Ramatayim

Timnah

PERAEA

— 32°

Philadelphia

Patros

Lydda

Ephraim

JUDAEA

Gezer

Jericho

Jamnia

Emmaus

Beth-ramatha (Julias)

Esbus

...us Parialus

Accaron

Jerusalem

Azotus

Bethletepha

Hyrcania

Qumran

Ascalon

Bet Guvrin

Herodium

Marisa

Qe'ilah

Betogabris

Machaerus

Adoraim

En-gedi

Lacus Asphaltites (Dead Sea)

Adora

IDUMAEA

Masada

Beersheba

Arad

Malatha

NABATAEA

(...unean Sea)

Jerusalem under Herod the Great

Herod transformed Jerusalem, building a new palace, fortifying the city walls, and adding the buildings and amenities of a sophisticated Greco-Roman city. However, his most famous building was emphatically Jewish: the enormous, magnificent temple complex, which dominated the city.

In Jerusalem, Herod renovated the Hasmonaean palace and built a new one on the western wall of the city. He fortified the city walls, added defensive towers, and built the Antonia fortress to the north of the temple complex. He refurbished the Hellenistic theater, added a stadion or hippodrome, and employed Roman engineers to build an aqueduct.

The most famous of Herod's projects was the new temple, built on a platform of massive quarried blocks (still visible at the so-called Wailing or Western Wall) surmounted on all sides by porticoes with Corinthian colonnades. The east colonnade was called Solomon's Portico. On the southern rampart, overlooking the massive steps that led up from the old City of David, stood the

Royal Basilica (or Royal Portico) with audience halls. The temple complex towered over the rest of the city and was reached from all sides by steps, stairs, bridges, or ramps. In the open center of the complex (called the Court of Gentiles) stood the temple proper, enlarged and refurbished to include an outer court (the Court of Israel). The scale of this project was so vast that construction went on for over 80 years (from c. 19 BC to AD 64).

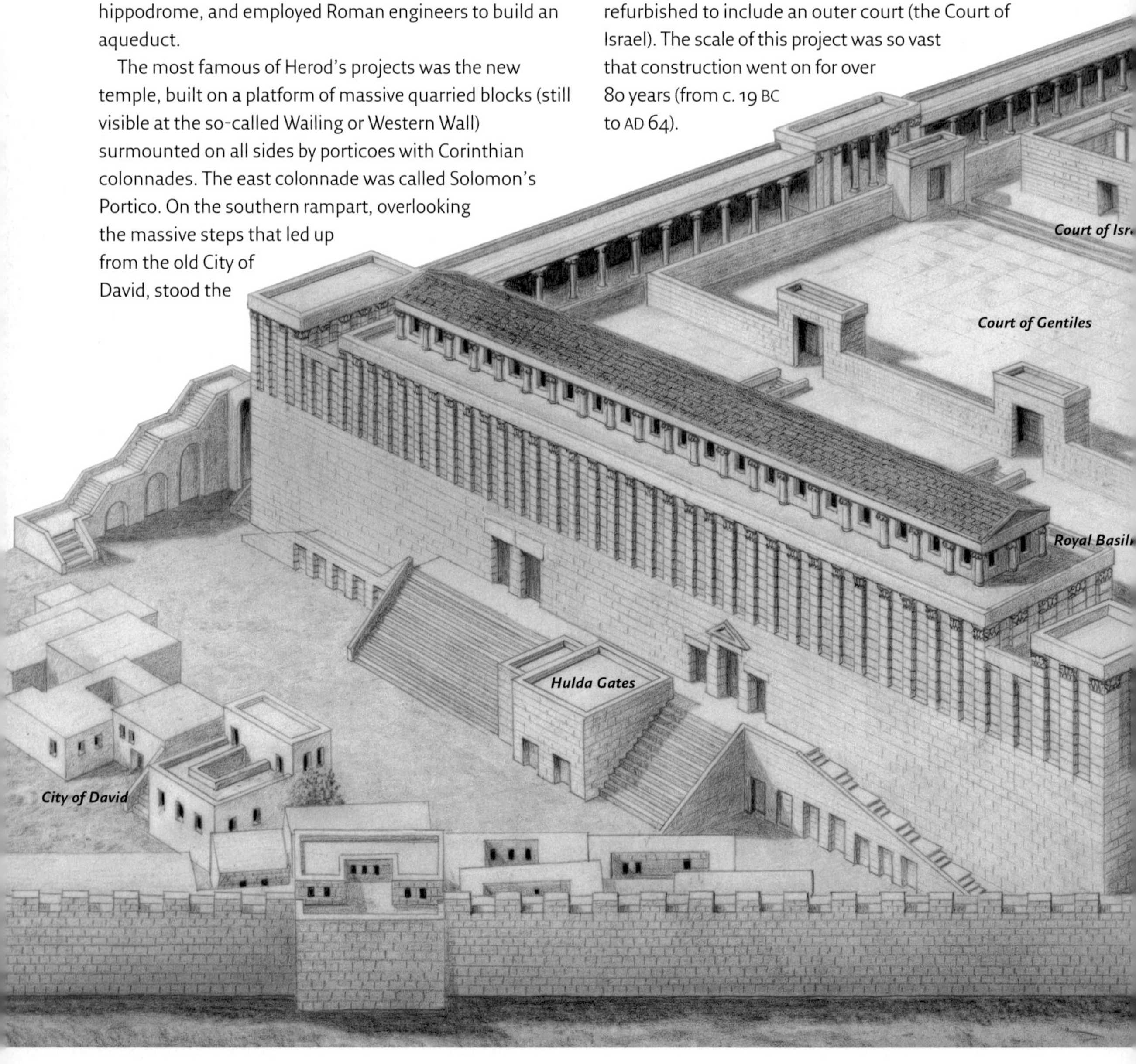

Court of Isr.

Court of Gentiles

Royal Basil.

Hulda Gates

City of David

Although his benefactions to Jerusalem showed Herod's support for Judaism, Herod also built pagan temples and public buildings in many cities, both inside and outside his realm. At Paneas (later called Caesarea Philippi), Herod built a temple dedicated to Pan, the city's patron deity, while at Samaria, the city was enhanced with a huge temple dedicated to Augustus.

Palaces and fortresses

Lavish Herodian palaces were built at Sepphoris, Livias, Ascalon, and Jericho (the so-called Winter Palace). He also constructed mountain-top fortresses, such as Herodium, Machaerus, and Masada. The fortress named after him, the Herodium, incorporated a summer palace with gardens and pools. It was also his burial place, and a recent archaeological dig has finally identified his tomb.

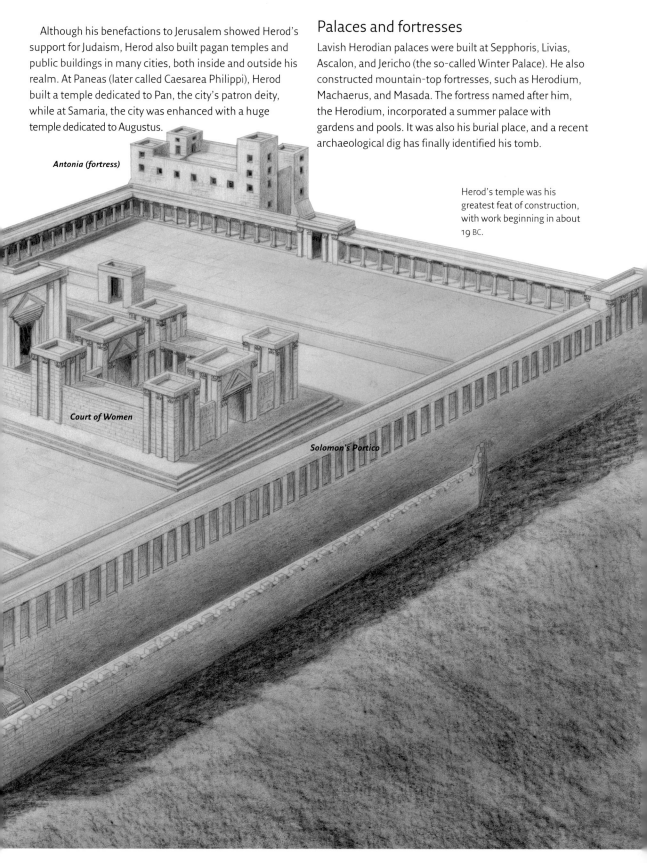

Herod's temple was his greatest feat of construction, with work beginning in about 19 BC.

Antonia (fortress)

Court of Women

Solomon's Portico

Caesarea by the sea

One of Herod's most ambitious projects was Caesarea Maritima, where his engineers built a huge artificial harbor. A temple dedicated to Roma and Augustus rose above the harbor at the entrance to the city, where he also built a theater, amphitheater, hippodrome, two aqueducts, Roman-style baths, warehouses, administrative buildings, and a seaside palace. Caesarea was the center of trade with the rest of the Roman world. In subsequent years, it would also become the center of the Roman provincial administration, the military command, and capital for the procurators of Judaea.

The kingdom after Herod

On the death of Herod in 4 BC, the kingdom was divided between his three surviving sons: Philip, Antipas, and Archelaus. Philip received Ituraea and Trachonitis; Antipas received Galilee and Peraea; while Archelaus received Judaea, Idumaea, and Samaria. Some city territories were placed under direct Roman control by ceding them to the province of Syria. While Antipas and Philip had long and prosperous reigns in their respective tetrarchies, the reign of Archelaus was unsatisfactory in Judaea. In AD 6, Archelaus was removed from office and his territories placed under the direct Roman administration of a military procurator who answered to the Legate of Syria.

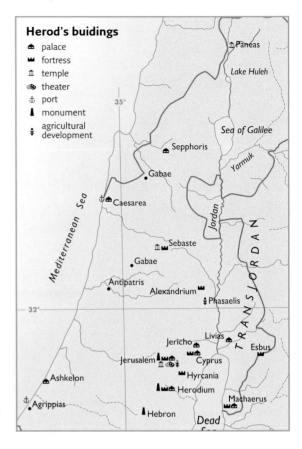

Herod's buidings

♣ palace
⚏ fortress
🏛 temple
🐚 theater
⚓ port
▮ monument
⚐ agricultural development

The fortress of Herodium was a triumph of engineering skill (*right*). The illustration shown is based on the remains found by archaeologists. The mound that encased the lower portion of the fortress was wholly artificial and helped to make the structure secure against attack. However, Herodium was not only a fortress - Herod furnished it magnificently to also serve as a palace. The great variety and quantity of Herod's building projects is demonstrated by this map showing the distribution of Herodian buildings in Palestine (*map above*).

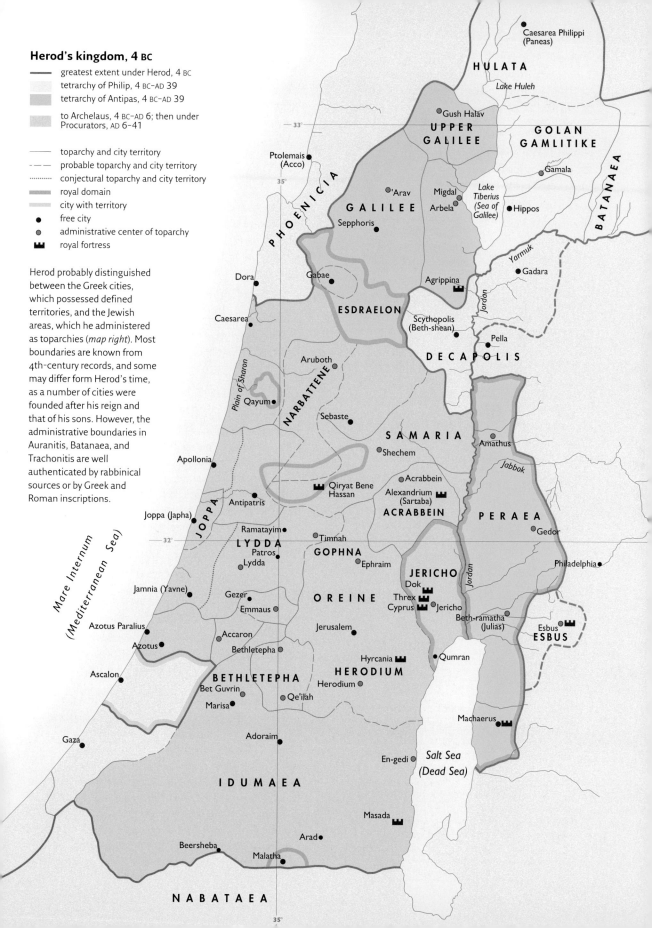

Herod's kingdom, 4 BC

- greatest extent under Herod, 4 BC
- tetrarchy of Philip, 4 BC–AD 39
- tetrarchy of Antipas, 4 BC–AD 39
- to Archelaus, 4 BC–AD 6; then under Procurators, AD 6–41

- toparchy and city territory
- probable toparchy and city territory
- conjectural toparchy and city territory
- royal domain
- city with territory
- ● free city
- ● administrative center of toparchy
- royal fortress

Herod probably distinguished between the Greek cities, which possessed defined territories, and the Jewish areas, which he administered as toparchies (*map right*). Most boundaries are known from 4th-century records, and some may differ form Herod's time, as a number of cities were founded after his reign and that of his sons. However, the administrative boundaries in Auranitis, Batanaea, and Trachonitis are well authenticated by rabbinical sources or by Greek and Roman inscriptions.

Caesarea Philippi (Paneas)

HULATA

Lake Huleh

33°

Gush Halav

UPPER GALILEE

GOLAN GAMLITIKE

35°

Ptolemais (Acco)

PHOENICIA

'Arav

Migdal
Arbela

Lake Tiberius (Sea of Galilee)

Gamala

BATANAEA

GALILEE

Sepphoris

Hippos

Dora

Gabae

Agrippina

Yarmuk

Gadara

Caesarea

ESDRAELON

Scythopolis (Beth-shean)

Jordan

Pella

DECAPOLIS

Plain of Sharon

Aruboth

NARBATTENE

Qayum

Sebaste

SAMARIA

Shechem

Amathus

Jabbok

Apollonia

Acrabbein

Alexandrium (Sartaba)

PERAEA

Antipatris

Qiryat Bene Hassan

ACRABBEIN

Gedor

Joppa (Japha)

JOPPA

Ramatayim

32°

LYDDA

Timnah

GOPHNA

Philadelphia

Patros

Ephraim

Lydda

JERICHO

Jamnia (Yavne)

Gezer

OREINE

Dok

Threx
Cyprus

Jericho

Jordan

Beth-ramatha (Julias)

Emmaus

Esbus

ESBUS

Azotus Paralius

Accaron

Jerusalem

Azotus

Bethletepha

Qumran

Ascalon

BETHLETEPHA

Hyrcania

HERODIUM

Mare Internum (Mediterranean Sea)

Herodium

Bet Guvrin

Qe'ilah

Gaza

Marisa

Machaerus

Adoraim

En-gedi

Salt Sea (Dead Sea)

IDUMAEA

Masada

Beersheba

Arad

Malatha

NABATAEA

35°

The Dead Sea Scrolls and their writers

In winter 1947, a cache of seven scrolls was discovered in caves overlooking the Dead Sea and near the ruins of Khirbet Qumran. Soon after, scholars discovered many more scrolls and fragments in the caves surrounding Qumran. They proved to be perhaps the greatest archaeological discovery of the 20th century.

In all, 11 caves were found to contain manuscripts. Nearly 800 manuscripts were brought to light, although many of these were duplicates. Allowing for duplication, some 400 different works have been discovered.

The most famous cave - Cave 4 - contained more than 500 different manuscripts, all in fragments. Publication of the entire collection was a matter of controversy; the manuscripts from Cave 1 were published relatively quickly and the contents of Caves 2-3 and 5-10 appeared in 1962. But the material from Cave 4 took many years to emerge, held back by a mixture of official reluctance to publish, and the sheer weight of material available. Today, however, the vast majority of scrolls and fragments have been made public.

Scholars have dated the scrolls to between 250 BC and 68 AD, when the Romans overran the area during the first Jewish revolt. The scrolls fall into two main categories: scriptural manuscripts, including the entire Hebrew Bible (except for the book of Esther), and pseudepigraphia and apocryphal writings; and other, previously unknown Jewish writings, including the rules of the community. Their importance lies in the fact that the Dead Sea Scrolls represent specimens of biblical books that were being read by Jews in the time of Herod the Great. Before the discovery of the scrolls, the oldest extant Hebrew text was a copy of Isaiah dated to 895 AD. The Isaiah scroll from Cave 1 is around a thousand years older.

The Essenes

Although it is a matter of considerable debate, many scholars identify the Essenes as the sect that occupied Qumran and owned the scrolls. Their origins are obscure, but it appears that the Essenes split off from a conservative faction, known as the *Hasidim* (pious ones) in the Maccabean revolt (*1 Macc* 2.42). They came from a priestly order who abandoned the temple after the Hasmonaean kings became high priests, sometime between 150 and 134 BC. The founder, probably a deposed Zadokite priest known as the Teacher of Righteousness, fled to the wilderness of Judaea to fulfil the words of Isaiah: "In the wilderness, prepare the way of the Lord" (*Isa 40.3*). They established the New Covenant to study the law night and day until the advent of two Messiahs: one a royal figure, called the Messiah of Israel; the other a priestly figure, called the Messiah of Aaron, who would restore the pure temple.

The sect went through several phases. Declining in the later Hasmonaean period, the settlement was abandoned after an earthquake (c. 31 BC). Sometime after Herod there was a new phase of occupation and growth, which lasted until the community was destroyed in AD 68. Other members of the sect probably lived in nearby farming settlements, and there may have been enclaves living in distant towns that would gather periodically for a covenant renewal. The sect provided their own livelihood by herding or farming on the plain above the cliffs and at the nearby oasis of Ein Fashka.

The scrolls and the community

One of the major concerns of the religious life of the Dead Sea sect was "studying the law night and day" (*Rule of the Community 6.6-8*). Along with the Hebrew scritpures, there was also an extensive set of commentaries (called *pesharim*) on key prophetic texts, the best preserved of which are the commentaries on Habakkuk and Nahum. The community also produced hymns for their communal worship. Further information about the sect comes from scrolls dealing with community discipline (the Rule of the Community), the plan for the ideal temple (the Temple Scroll), and a scroll that imagines an eschatological war between the people of Israel and the nations that rule the world (the War Scroll). The latter was taken seriously, as the community was destroyed by the Romans during the First Revolt. The settlement was burned and eventually became a military camp (c. AD 70-74). It is probable, therefore, that

http://www.virtualqumran.com/
UCLA Qumran visualization project
http://www.imj.org.il/eng/shrine/index.html
Shrine of the Book, Israel Museum
http://oi.uchicago.edu/research/projects/scr/
Dead Sea Scrolls project at the Oriental Institute,
University of California
http://www.biblicalarchaeology.org/
deadseascrolls/bswbDSSHomePage.asp
The Dead Sea Scrolls and why they matter - Biblical
Archaeology Review

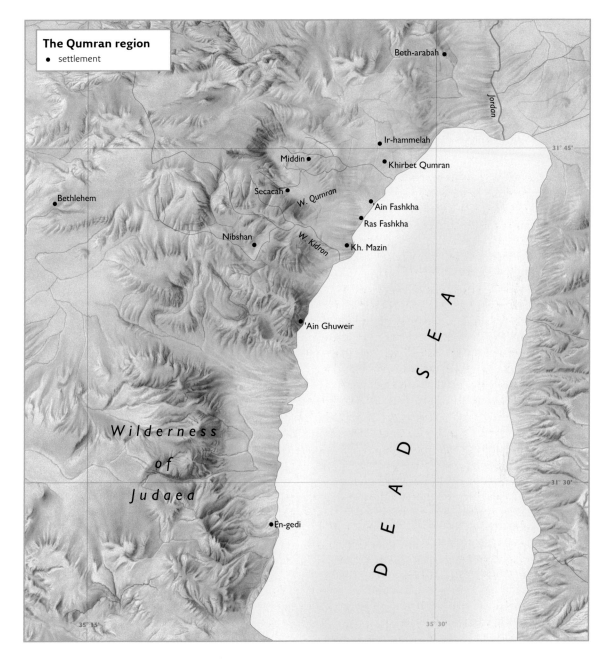

The Qumran region
- settlement

Beth-arabah

Jordan

Ir-hammelah

Middin

Khirbet Qumran

Secacah

W. Qumran

'Ain Fashkha

Ras Fashkha

Bethlehem

Nibshan

W. Kidron

Kh. Mazin

31° 45'

'Ain Ghuweir

D E A D   S E A

Wilderness

of

Judaea

31° 30'

En-gedi

35° 15'

35° 30'

the scrolls, if not already stored in the caves, were hidden there in anticipation of this final confrontation.

The Copper Scroll

One of the most curious finds was a scroll made of two rolls of copper, engraved with Hebrew writing, and listing the location of a huge amount of hidden treasure. Whether these treasures were real or imaginary is a matter of dispute. Some scholars argue that the scroll is a list of the treasures of the Second Temple, hidden before the Bar Kochba revolt. Whatever the case, all attempts to locate treasure have ended in failure.

The settlement at Khirbet Qumran was most probably founded by a religious sect known as the Essenes, who withdrew from Jerusalem sometime during the Hasmonaean period (c. 150–134 BC). Excavations revealed an extensive community at Qumran, with several farming settlements nearby at Ein Fashkha and Ein Ghuweir, that may have supplied the community (*map above*).

Roman rule after Herod

In Jesus' time, the Kingdom of Herod was administered as three separate districts. Herod Antipas ruled as tetrarch of Galilee and Peraea (from 4 BC to AD 37); Herod Philip ruled the region of Gaulanitis, Ituraea, and Trachonitis (from 4 BC to AD 34); while Judaea was governed by a Roman military procurator.

Judaea (including Samaria and Idumaea), was originally under the rule of Herod's son Archelaus. However, he was deposed in AD 6, and in his place a Roman procurator administered Judaea from Caesarea, under the direct authority of the Province of Syria. Pontius Pilate was procurator of Judaea from AD 26–36.

Palestine under Gaius and Claudius

With the demise of Herod's sons, the entire region might have come under procuratorial control; however, Tiberius' successor, Gaius (AD 37–41), favored personal friends to serve as client-kings in the east. Among these was Herod Agrippa I, grandson of Herod the Great and an heir of the Hasmonaean line, brought to Rome by his mother Berenice. Agrippa I was well connected both at Rome and in the east. His sister was Herodias, who had married Herod Antipas in AD 28, and her daughter (his niece) was married to Herod Philip. In AD 37, Gaius bequeathed to Agrippa the tetrarchies of Philip and Lysanias, and in AD 40 Galilee and Peraea.

When Gaius was assassinated in AD 41, Agrippa supported the accession of Claudius (AD 41–54), another of his companions from days in Rome. Claudius granted him the procuratorial territory of Judaea; Agrippa's kingdom now equalled that of Herod the Great. His pro-Jewish policies favored the old aristocrats as well as the Pharisees, and his rule seems to have been popular. However, his role in ordering the death of James and the arrest of Peter (*Acts 12.1–23*) suggests a less favorable picture.

When Agrippa I died suddenly at Caesarea in AD 44, his son and heir Agrippa II was only 17. Consequently, Claudius transferred the entire kingdom to procuratorial control as the Province of Judaea. In AD 50, Agrippa II was made client-king of Chalcis. Then, in AD 53 Claudius gave him the territories of Abila and Arca along with all the Tetrarchy of Philip in exchange for Chalcis.

Agrippa II

Agrippa's sister Drusilla was married to the Roman procurator Antonius Felix (AD 52–c. 60), and both are reported to have dealt with Paul after his arrest (*Acts 24.24, 25.13*). Under Nero (AD 54–68), eastern Galilee, including the cities of Tiberias and Taricheae, and the

---

Roman emperors

Augustus (January 16, 27 BC–August 19, AD 14)
Tiberius (September 17, 14–March 16, 39)
Gaius (March 16, 37–January 24, 41)
Claudius (January 24, 41–October 13, 54)
Nero (October 13, 54–June 9, 68)
Galba (June 10, 68–January 15, 69)
Otho (January 15, 69–April 14, 69)
Vitellius (January 2, 69–December 20, 69)
Vespasian (July 1, 69–June 24, 79)
Titus (June 24, 79–September 13, 81)
Domitan (September 14, 81–September 16, 96)
Nerva (September 16, 96–January 25, 98)
Trajan (January 25, 97–August 8, 117)
Hadrian (August 11, 117–July 10, 138)

Roman governors of Judaea (AD 6–132)

Prefects/procurators subject to supervision by the Imperial Legate in Syria (AD 6–66):

Copnius (AD 6–66)
Marcus Ambibulus (6–9)
Annius Rufus (c. 12–15)
Valerius Gratus (15–26)
Pontius Pilate (26–36)
Marcellus/Marullus (36–41)
King Herod Agrippa I (41–44)
Cuspius Fadus (44–?46)
Tiberius Iulius Alexander (?46–48)
Ventidius Cumanus (48–c. 52)
Antonius Felix (c. 52–?60)
Porcius Festus (?60–62)
Lucceius Albinus (62–64)
Gessius Florus (64–66)
[Jewish Revolt 66–70]
Commanders of the Legio X Fretensis with praetorian rank (AD 70–?120). Only isolated names are known:
Sex. Vettulenus Cerialis (70–?71)
Lucilius Bassus (?71–73)
L. Flavius Silva (73–?)
Cn. Pompeius Longinus (86)
Sex. Hermetidius Campanus (93)
Atticus (?99/100–?102/3)
C. Iulius Quadratus Bassus (c. 102/3–104/5)
Q. Roscius Coelius Pompeius Falco (c. 105–107)
?Tiberianus (c. 114)
Lusius Quietus (c. 117)

territory of Julias in Peraea, were ceded to Agrippa II. He would have been granted the remaining Herodian lands but for the outbreak of hostilities in Judaea leading up to the First Jewish Revolt in AD 66.

In the revolt, Agrippa II lost much of his territory to the rebels, but it was restored afterward, with the exception of eastern Galilee. He was further rewarded with other territories, which he ruled until about AD 93. While he never ruled Judaea proper, he was accorded the hereditary right to appoint the high priest in Jerusalem throughout much of his reign, until the destruction of the temple in AD 70. During the First Revolt, there was considerable resistance to Agrippa's pro-Roman policies, and his appointed high priest was replaced by a supporter of the revolutionary party.

Political boundaries after Herod

- Judaea, 4 BC–AD 41 (Tetrarchy of Archelaus, 4 BC–AD 6)
- Tetrarchy of Herod Antipas, 4 BC–AD 34
- Tetrarchy of Philip, 4 BC–AD 34
- —— Agrippa I's kingdom, AD 37–44
- —— Agrippa II's kingdom, AD 52–93

Claudius placed Judaea under Herod Agrippa I in AD 41 as a gesture of reconciliation after the cruelty of Gaius Caesar (Caligula) (*map right*). Agrippa II was granted much of his father's northern territory under Claudius and Nero.

High priests

Appointed by King Herod the Great (37–4 BC)
Ananel (37–36, and again from 34 BC)
Aristobulus II (35 BC)
Jesus son of Phiabi (to c. 23 BC)
Simon son of Boethus (c. 23 –5 BC)
Matthias son of Theophilus (5–4 BC)
Joseph son of Ellem (one day)
Joazar son of Boethus (4 BC)
Appointed by the Tetrarch Archelaus (4 BC–AD 6)
Eleazar son of Boethus (from 4 BC)
Jesus son of See (to AD 6)
Appointed by Quirinius, Legate of Syria (AD 6)
Ananus/Annas son of Sethi (6–15)
Appointed by Gratus, Procurator of Judaea (15–26)
Ismael son of Phiabi (c. 15–16)
Eleazar son of Ananus (c. 16–17)
Simon son of Camithus (c. 17–18)
Josephus Caiaphas (c. 18–37)

Appointed by Vitellius, Legate of Syria (35–39)
Jonathan son of Ananus/Annas (two months in 37)
Appointed by King Agrippa I (41–44)
Simon Cantheras son of Boethus (from 41)
Matthias son of Ananus/Annas (dates unknown)
Elionaeus son of Cantheras (c. 44)
Appointed by Herod of Chalcis (44–48)
Joseph son of Kami (dates unknown)
Ananias son of Nedebaeus (47–c. 59)
Appointed by King Agrippa II (50–?92)
Ismael son of Phiabi (c. 59–61)
Joseph Cabi son of Simon (61–62)
Ananus son of Ananus/Annas (three months in 62)
Jesus son of Damnaeus (c. 62–63)
Jesus son of Gamaliel (c. 63–64)
Matthias son of Theophilus (65–?)
Appointed by people during the revolt (66–70)
Phannias/Phanni/Phanasos (dates unknown)

Galilee and the ministry of Jesus

Jesus was a Galilean from the village of Nazareth, born during the last years of Herod the Great (died 4 BC). The Gospel of Matthew suggests that Jesus' family was from Judaea, near Bethlehem, and fled to Egypt to escape Herod. Afterwards, they resettled in Galilee to avoid returning to Judaea under Archelaus (4 BC–AD 6). Luke associates the birth in Bethlehem with a census under P. Sulpicius Quirinius, the legate of Syria (AD 6–7?) after Archelaus was deposed. The family then returned by way of Jerusalem to Nazareth.

Until the Hasmonaean period, the northern hill country was not considered part of the Jewish homeland; instead, "Galilee of the Gentiles" (*Isa 8.23, 9.1; cf. Matt 4.15*) was hostile to Judaea (*1 Macc 5.15*). Its capital was Sepphoris, a few miles southeast of which was the village of Nazareth. Because of its remoteness, the region remained more rural, a haven for refugees from the time of Herod until after the First Revolt. The valleys of Lower Galilee provided the major trade route around the Sea of Galilee and across the Mediterranean coast or south to the Valley of Jezreel.

Economy and society

The social organization of Galilee was built around village economies and trade networks. The terrain, especially in Lower Galilee, was productive for farming or herding. Some villages specialized in other goods, such as coarseware pottery produced from local clay beds. The Sea of Galilee (also called Lake Chinnereth, Gennesaret, or Tiberias) supported a thriving fishing industry, centered at Magdala.

The amount to which the region was influenced by Greco-Roman culture is a matter of debate. Certainly Aramaic was the vernacular, though documents have been found in duplicate, one copy in Aramaic and another in Greek. Tomb inscriptions from catacombs at Bet She'arim assume that Greek was the first tongue for many Galilean Jews. Excavations of Sepphoris have revealed an elaborate Roman city with a palace, theater, and fortress from the 1st century AD. While there was clearly a prominent Jewish population, Sepphoris was a center for Roman administration and Hellenistic culture as well. Between 17 and 20 AD; Herod Antipas founded Tiberias (in honor of the Emperor) as the new capital of his tetrarchy.

Jesus the Galilean

To some, Galilean meant "extremist" (*Luke 13.1*). To others, being from Galilee might mean that Jesus was among the "people of the land" (*amme ha-aretz*) who did not observe Torah scrupulously. Either way, it seemed doubtful that messianic claims should come from the region.

Jesus' public ministry began around AD 27–29, when Galilee and Peraea were ruled by Herod Antipas (4 BC–AD 39) and Judaea was under the procurator Pontius Pilate (AD 26–36). In the synoptic Gospels, most of Jesus' public career occurred in the villages of Lower Galilee. Capernaum became the center of his early activity (*Mark 2.1*), but after being rejected at Nazareth (*Mark 6.1–6*), Jesus and his followers began to move more broadly in the region surrounding Lower Galilee. He also ventured to Tyre and Sidon (*Mark 7.24*). After returning by way of the Decapolis or Ituraea (*Mark 7.31*), Jesus moved from Capernaum to Bethsaida and Caesarea Philippi (*Mark 8.27*). He journeyed to Judaea only at the end of his career.

"Jesus went throughout Galilee, teaching in their synagogues and proclaiming the good news of the kingdom and curing every disease and every sickness among the people. So his fame spread throughout all Syria, and they brought to him all the sick, those who were afflicted with various diseases and pains, demoniacs, epileptics, and paralytics, and he cured them. And great crowds followed him from Galilee, the Decapolis, Jerusalem, Judaea, and from beyond the Jordan."

(Matt 4.23–25)

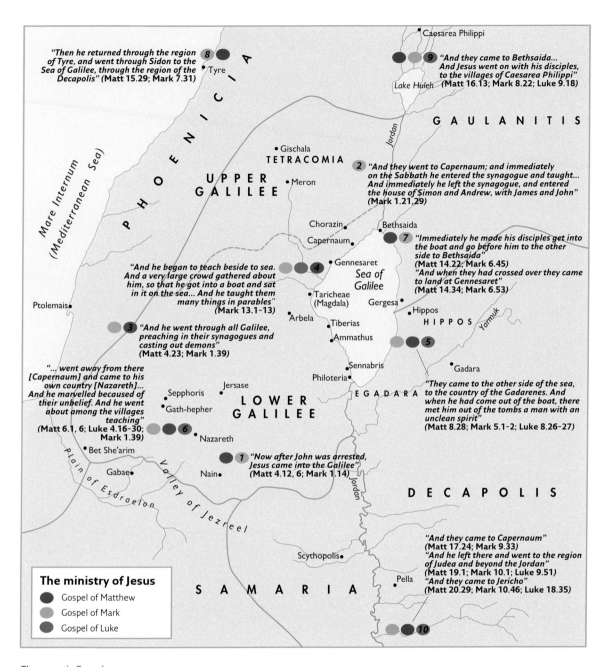

"Then he returned through the region of Tyre, and went through Sidon to the Sea of Galilee, through the region of the Decapolis" (Matt 15.29; Mark 7.31) **8**

"And they came to Bethsaida... And Jesus went on with his disciples, to the villages of Caesarea Philippi" (Matt 16.13; Mark 8.22; Luke 9.18) **9**

"And they went to Capernaum; and immediately on the Sabbath he entered the synagogue and taught... And immediately he left the synagogue, and entered the house of Simon and Andrew, with James and John" (Mark 1.21,29) **2**

"Immediately he made his disciples get into the boat and go before him to the other side to Bethsaida" (Matt 14.22; Mark 6.45) "And when they had crossed over they came to land at Gennesaret" (Matt 14.34; Mark 6.53) **7**

"And he began to teach beside to sea. And a very large crowd gathered about him, so that he got into a boat and sat in it on the sea... And he taught them many things in parables" (Mark 13.1-13) **4**

"And he went through all Galilee, preaching in their synagogues and casting out demons" (Matt 4.23; Mark 1.39) **3**

"They came to the other side of the sea, to the country of the Gadarenes. And when he had come out of the boat, there met him out of the tombs a man with an unclean spirit" (Matt 8.28; Mark 5.1-2; Luke 8.26-27) **5**

"... went away from there [Capernaum] and came to his own country [Nazareth]... And he marvelled becaused of their unbelief. And he went about among the villages teaching" (Matt 6.1, 6; Luke 4.16-30; Mark 1.39) **6**

"Now after John was arrested, Jesus came into the Galilee" (Matt 4.12, 6; Mark 1.14) **1**

"And they came to Capernaum" (Matt 17.24; Mark 9.33) "And he left there and went to the region of Judea and beyond the Jordan" (Matt 19.1; Mark 10.1; Luke 9.51) "And they came to Jericho" (Matt 20.29; Mark 10.46; Luke 18.35) **10**

The ministry of Jesus

- Gospel of Matthew
- Gospel of Mark
- Gospel of Luke

The synoptic Gospels – Matthew, Mark, and Luke – represent the ministry of Jesus as being based around the Sea of Galilee (*map above*).

Jesus' last days

A week before his death, Jesus' entered Jerusalem in triumph (*Mark 11.1-10; Matt 21.1-9; Luke 19.28-38*). According to the synoptic Gospels – Matthew, Mark, and Luke – this was his first appearance in Jerusalem, the city where he was to be arrested, tried, and executed.

The synoptic Gospels place the ministry of Jesus in the region around the Sea of Galilee until Jesus turns toward Jerusalem. There, after the triumphal entry, he attacks the merchants in the temple, angering the leaders (*Mark 11.15-19*). Later in the week, after eating the Passover meal with his followers, he is arrested and tried during the night and crucified the following day, just outside the city. Jesus' resurrection appearances in the synoptic Gospels show much greater diversity. In both Matthew and Mark, the disciples are told to go to Galilee to see Jesus (*Matt 28.7; Mark 16.7*). In Luke, the post-Resurrection appearances occur in and around Jerusalem (*Luke 24.13-53; Acts 1.4-12*).

The Gospel of John

The fourth Gospel presents a different chronology. In John, Jesus visits Jerusalem from the beginning of his career, and three different Passover feasts are mentioned. In the third feast, Jesus eats the last supper and is crucified on the day

of preparation just before the Passover is to begin (*John 13.1, 18, 28, 19.14*). In John, Jesus hangs on the cross while the Passover lambs are being slaughtered in preparation for the feat, harking back to the words of John the Baptist (*John 1.29*).

Thus Jerusalem plays a greater role in John's Gospel, while the Galilean links are somewhat blurred. In reporting events after the resurrection, John's Gospel mentions appearances both in Jerusalem and, sometime later, beside the Sea of Galilee.

The Gospels record the appearances of Jesus after the Resurrection. In Luke, all the appearances, including the ascension, occur in and around Jerusalem, but the final appearance and departure occur beside the Sea of Galilee (*map below*).

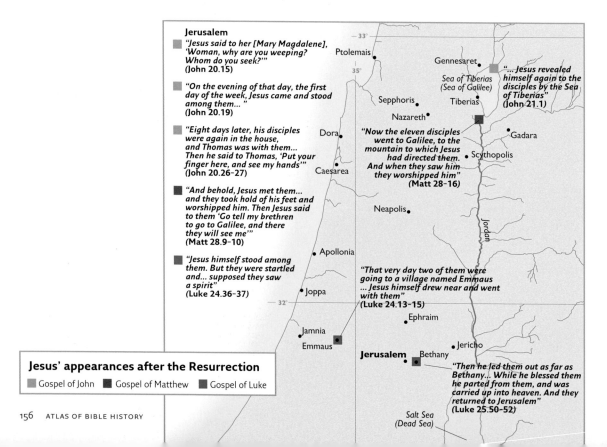

Jerusalem
"Jesus said to her [Mary Magdalene], 'Woman, why are you weeping? Whom do you seek?'"
(John 20.15)

"On the evening of that day, the first day of the week, Jesus came and stood among them... "
(John 20.19)

"Eight days later, his disciples were again in the house, and Thomas was with them... Then he said to Thomas, 'Put your finger here, and see my hands'"
(John 20.26-27)

"And behold, Jesus met them... and they took hold of his feet and worshipped him. Then Jesus said to them 'Go tell my brethren to go to Galilee, and there they will see me'"
(Matt 28.9-10)

"Jesus himself stood among them. But they were startled and... supposed they saw a spirit"
(Luke 24.36-37)

"... Jesus revealed himself again to the disciples by the Sea of Tiberias"
(John 21.1)

"Now the eleven disciples went to Galilee, to the mountain to which Jesus had directed them. And when they saw him they worshipped him"
(Matt 28-16)

"That very day two of them were going to a village named Emmaus ... Jesus himself drew near and went with them"
(Luke 24.13-15)

"Then he led them out as far as Bethany... While he blessed them he parted from them, and was carried up into heaven. And they returned to Jerusalem"
(Luke 25.50-52)

Ptolemais
Gennesaret
Sea of Tiberias (Sea of Galilee)
Sepphoris
Tiberias
Nazareth
Dora
Gadara
Scythopolis
Caesarea
Neapolis
Jordan
Apollonia
Joppa
Ephraim
Jamnia
Emmaus
Jerusalem
Bethany
Jericho
Salt Sea (Dead Sea)

Jesus' appearances after the Resurrection
Gospel of John   Gospel of Matthew   Gospel of Luke

The trial of Jesus

The charges on which Jesus was condemned reflect Jewish concerns, but ultimately they were politically motivated. Crucifixion was a punishment meted out by the Romans to rebels and slaves. Jesus was perceived as a seditious threat (*Luke 23.5*), claiming to be the king of the Jews, as the plaque on the cross proclaims the charge (*Mark 15.26*). The location of Jesus' trial is disputed. It is most likely that Pilate would have occupied the former palace of Herod the Great - the best quarters in the city. A 1968 excavation of Jewish burials unearthed an ossuary containing the bones of a young man who was apparently crucified. Although one of the heel bones still has the nail in it, it is uncertain whether nails or ropes were used to secure the arms to the cross.

The place of crucifixion

The execution took place in an old quarry, which in Jesus' day was just outside the city walls. In the angle of the first and second walls, marked by the Gennath Gate, was a quarry dating to the 7th century BC. It was not brought within the bounds of the city until Herod Agrippa I (AD 41–44) extended the city to the north. The present-day Church of the Holy Sepulchre, which was built in the 4th century AD, stands over the northern section of this quarry. In excavations it was found that a protrusion on the southern side was never quarried, and this may have been the place known as Golgotha, resembling a "skull" (*Mark 15.22; Luke 23.33*). Facing it were several tombs cut out of the cliff, dating from the 1st century AD.

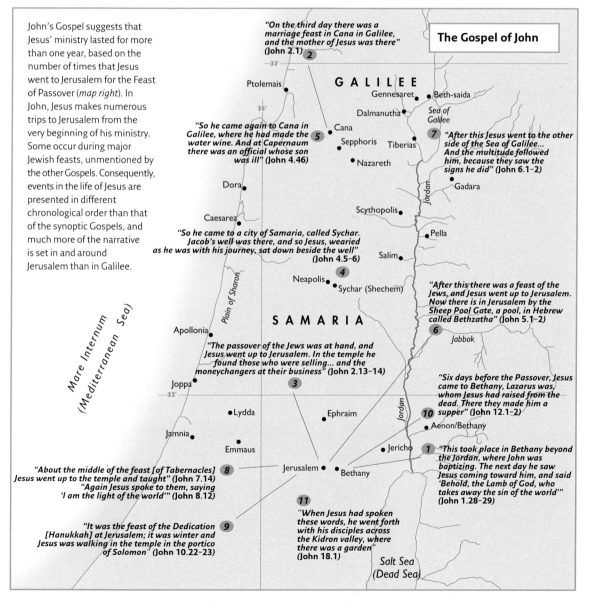

John's Gospel suggests that Jesus' ministry lasted for more than one year, based on the number of times that Jesus went to Jerusalem for the Feast of Passover (*map right*). In John, Jesus makes numerous trips to Jerusalem from the very beginning of his ministry. Some occur during major Jewish feasts, unmentioned by the other Gospels. Consequently, events in the life of Jesus are presented in different chronological order than that of the synoptic Gospels, and much more of the narrative is set in and around Jerusalem than in Galilee.

The Gospel of John

"On the third day there was a marriage feast in Cana in Galilee, and the mother of Jesus was there" (John 2.1) ②

"So he came again to Cana in Galilee, where he had made the water wine. And at Capernaum there was an official whose son was ill" (John 4.46) ⑤

"After this Jesus went to the other side of the Sea of Galilee... And the multitude followed him, because they saw the signs he did" (John 6.1-2) ⑦

"So he came to a city of Samaria, called Sychar. Jacob's well was there, and so Jesus, wearied as he was with his journey, sat down beside the well" (John 4.5-6) ④

"After this there was a feast of the Jews, and Jesus went up to Jerusalem. Now there is in Jerusalem by the Sheep Pool Gate, a pool, in Hebrew called Bethzatha" (John 5.1-2) ⑥

"The passover of the Jews was at hand, and Jesus went up to Jerusalem. In the temple he found those who were selling... and the moneychangers at their business" (John 2.13-14) ③

"Six days before the Passover, Jesus came to Bethany, Lazarus was, whom Jesus had raised from the dead. There they made him a supper" (John 12.1-2) ⑩

"This took place in Bethany beyond the Jordan, where John was baptizing. The next day he saw Jesus coming toward him, and said 'Behold, the Lamb of God, who takes away the sin of the world'" (John 1.28-29) ①

"About the middle of the feast [of Tabernacles] Jesus went up to the temple and taught" (John 7.14) "Again Jesus spoke to them, saying 'I am the light of the world'" (John 8.12) ⑧

"When Jesus had spoken these words, he went forth with his disciples across the Kidron valley, where there was a garden" (John 18.1) ⑪

"It was the feast of the Dedication [Hanukkah] at Jerusalem; it was winter and Jesus was walking in the temple in the portico of Solomon" (John 10.22-23) ⑨

Ptolemais · GALILEE · Gennesaret · Beth-saida · Dalmanutha · Sea of Galilee · Cana · Sepphoris · Tiberias · Nazareth · Gadara · Dora · Scythopolis · Caesarea · Pella · Salim · Neapolis · Sychar (Shechem) · SAMARIA · Apollonia · Jabbok · Joppa · Lydda · Ephraim · Jamnia · Aenon/Bethany · Emmaus · Jericho · Jerusalem · Bethany · Plain of Sharon · Mare Internum (Mediterranean Sea) · Jordan · Salt Sea (Dead Sea)

NINE

THE EARLY CHURCH

The Library of Celsus Library, Ephesus.
Built between AD 110 and 135, the library was home to
some 12,000 scrolls. Ephesus was one of the main centers
of early Christianity; Paul spent some 18 months here
between AD 51 and 53.

The Jewish Diaspora

While contact with other lands had been common since Solomon's day, the sense of national identity of the people of Israel remained intact. But with the Assyrian conquest of northern Israel (722 BC), and even more so with the Babylonian conquest of Judah (586 BC), many Israelites were deported, exiled, or "dispersed" to other lands.

These communities, striving to maintain their heritage and identity in alien contexts, came to be known in later times as the Jews of the Diaspora (from the Greek word for dispersion). While some of the Babylonian exiles returned to rebuild Jerusalem, others remained in the Mesopotamian regions through the Persian period and after, making it a center of Jewish culture and tradition. Nor were all Diaspora Jews forcibly removed from their homeland. During the Babylonian period, many Judahites fled to Egypt. Later, Jewish mercenaries of the Persian state commanded a garrison (5th–4th centuries BC) at Elephantine, in Upper Egypt, and from it an archive of correspondence (in Aramaic) has been preserved.

The Diaspora after Alexander

The great expansion of the Diaspora occurred after the conquests of Alexander the Great (332–323 BC), especially from Jews who had once again become associated with the homeland and the new temple. Some Jews were again carried off as war captives under Ptolemy I Soter (323–285 BC) and yet again after the siege of Pompey (64 BC). Others emigrated voluntarily as the political unification of Mediterranean lands provided them with ample opportunities abroad, either as merchants or mercenaries.

According to Josephus, the biggest Jewish population outside Israel was in Syria, especially Antioch and Damascus (*map right*). Philo claimed that there were one million Jewish inhabitants in Egypt, while Rome had at least 7000 at the beginning of the reign of Augustus. Leaving aside the accuracy of these figures, they at least imply a large population of Jews throughout the Mediterranean world. Not all of these would have been born Jewish: many would have converted to the Jewish faith.

The Diaspora during the Roman period

areas of Jewish settlement
- 1st century AD
- late Roman period
- possible settlement in late Roman period

Jewish population in 1st century AD
- very large
- large
- population attested
- population attested during late Roman period

In the 3rd–2nd centuries BC, Jewish mercenaries under a rival priest, Onias IV, were commissioned by the Ptolemaic court and founded a colony at Leontopolis, where they built their own temple.

The Diaspora during the Roman period

By the end of the 1st century BC, when Rome had taken over the eastern Mediterranean, Jewish communities could be found in many cities of the east. The nearer regions of Syria and Egypt had sizable Jewish populations, making proximity to the homeland, travel, and commerce profitable. Two of the most prominent Diaspora communities were located in the capital cities, Antioch and Alexandria. From the Hellenistic period, enclaves followed Ptolemaic and Seleucid trade to other centers of the Greek world. In the later Hasmonaean period and during the time of Julius Caesar, Jewish communities were thriving in Asia Minor and Greece. The growth of communities outside the homeland

would continue to expand through the 1st and 2nd centuries AD as a result of the two Jewish Revolts. By the 3rd–4th centuries, well-established Jewish communities could be found in most major cities of the eastern Roman empire and through the western provinces as well.

It is impossible to guess the population of the homeland or the Diaspora by the 1st century AD; however, Philo, the Jewish philosopher of Alexandria, claims that there were a million Jews in Egypt alone. Estimates place the Jewish population of Alexandria at over 100,000, or approximately 12% of the total inhabitants. The percentage of Jewish residents at Antioch was probably higher, though the total population was smaller. By the 2nd–4th centuries AD, it is estimated that the Jewish population of the city of Rome might have been approaching 100,000 as well, and after the two Jewish Revolts, it is likely that more Jews lived in the Diaspora than in the homeland.

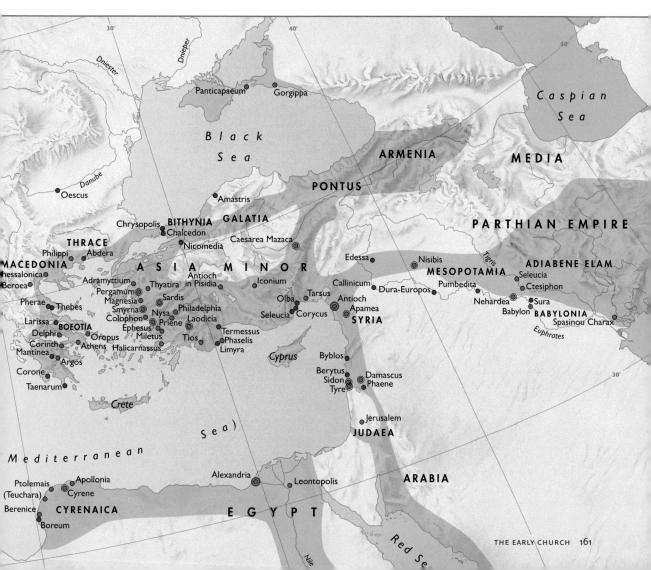

Jewish life in the Diaspora

The evidence of Jewish life in the Diaspora is scattered, and any picture of this period must take account of Jewish literature as well as inscriptions and archaeological remains. One of the prime sources is the New Testament itself, especially Paul, a Jew from Tarsus in Cilicia, who traveled through Asia Minor and Greece.

Josephus also gives scattered information about Diaspora communities; he lived out his life as a retainer of the emperors at Rome, while maintaining contacts with Jews in Cyrene and Egypt. Other occasional pieces of Jewish literature come from the Diaspora, including *The Epistle of Jeremiah*, *Joseph and Asenath*, *The Wisdom of Jesus Son of Sirach*, the Greek additions to the book of Daniel, and others.

Philo of Alexandria

One of the best-known Jewish writers of the Diaspora is Philo of Alexandria (c. 25 BC–AD 50). He was born into a wealthy Jewish family that was already well-established in Alexandrian society. His elder brother served as *alabarch* (official government tax agent) for Alexandria, and the family made a huge donation of gold for the decoration of Herod's temple. Philo's nephew Mark was married to a daughter of Herod Agrippa I. Another nephew, Tiberius Julius Alexander, abandoned his Jewish faith to enter Roman civil service; he served as procurator of Judaea (c. AD 46–48) before becoming prefect of Egypt. Philo himself seems to have resisted public life for his scholarly and philosophical pursuits, although, following pogroms against the Jews of Alexandria in AD 37–38, he led a delegation to Rome and secured from Emperor Claudius official protection for the rights of Alexandrian Jews.

Identity and community

The social standing of Diaspora Jews varied from place to place. Some communities faced prejudice and sporadic persecution, and many pagan authors perpetuated hostility towards or misinformed rumors about the Jews. Other Jewish communities enjoyed a favorable social position. Jews participated regularly in theater and gymnasia and could aspire to the ranks of local aristocracy, city councillors, or magistrates. Extensive Jewish papyri and inscriptions show that Jewish activities stretched across all walks of life and social levels. In many cases, Jewish residents were given equal citizenship (*isopoliteia*) status with the Greek residents; in other cases, they were given a measure of autonomy in dealing with internal Jewish affairs.

Plan of the municipal complex of Sardis (Asia Minor), showing the position of the basilical hall that was taken over and renovated as a synagogue (3rd-6th centuries AD) (*box right*). Plan of the synagogue at Dura-Europos (Roman Syria), in two phases of development (*box right*). In the earlier phase (*top*), it was a typical house, with one room serving as a hall of assembly. In the later phase (*bottom*), the entire structure was renovated into a formal hall with forecourt (mid-3rd century AD).

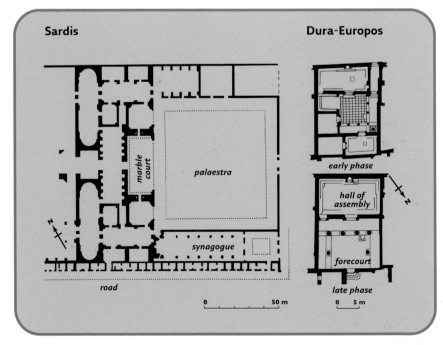

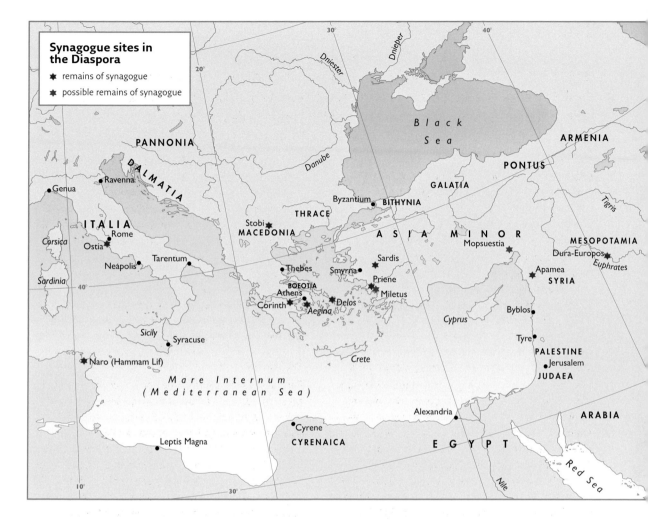

Synagogue sites in the Diaspora

★ remains of synagogue

★ possible remains of synagogue

Both the literary remains of the Diaspora and archaeological evidence of synagogues show a high degree of Hellenistic influence. Like Philo, most Jews of the Diaspora spoke Greek and participated to some extent in the surrounding culture. Diaspora Jews (and Christians) would have read the Septuagint, the Greek translation of the Hebrew scriptures. Yet devotion to temple and Torah remained the central marks of Jewish faith. Many Diaspora Jews attempted to make the pilgrimage to Jerusalem for one of the major feasts as long as the temple stood, and in later generations it became common among more wealthy Jews to be reburied in the homeland. However, among Diaspora Jews, there was still the tension of trying to balance their tradition with the surrounding culture. The result is that there were many diverse forms of Jewish theological reflection in the Diaspora, with greater or lesser degrees of pagan influence. The community itself, eventually becoming identified with its place of assembly (in Greek, *synagoge*), became the focus of Jewish identity for the Diaspora.

The great majority of synagogue remains throughout the Diaspora date from the late Roman and Byzantine periods (*map above*).

http://www.torreys.org/bible/philopag.html
Philo of Alexandria resource page
http://www.geocities.com/apollonius_theocritos/home.html
The Library of Alexandria
http://www.pbs.org/wgbh/pages/frontline/shows/religion/portrait/diaspora.html
A portrait of Jesus' world: The Jewish Diaspora

The cities of Paul

Jesus focused on the villages of Galilee, Paul on the cities of the Roman empire. Paul himself was a Diaspora Jew from Tarsus, a cosmopolitan city in Cilicia. Following his conversion, his travels took him to many of the major cities of the time.

Philippi

Philippi lies on the Egnatian Way, the major road across Greece connecting the Levant with the Adriatic coast. It was a Roman colony with the air of an imperial outpost. The bulk of the official inscriptions were in Latin. Greek and Roman gods blended with local Thracian deities; there was also a sanctuary to the Egyptian gods Isis and Sarapis. Paul may have faced opposition in Philippi (*1 Thess 2.2; cf. Acts 16.24-34*). Over the years he made several visits, and the church in Philippi continued to support his work (*Phil 4.10-20; cf. 2 Cor 8.1*).

Corinth

Paul stopped in Athens for a short time (*1 Thess 3.1-6; Acts 17.16-34*) before moving on to Corinth. Athens was the intellectual and tourist center, but Corinth was the administrative and economic hub of the region. It owed this position to its two ports, one on each side of the isthmus, so that it served as the major shipping center between the Adriatic (and Italy) and the Aegean (and Asia Minor).

Priscilla and Aquila had come to Corinth from Italy (*Acts 18.2*) and their home - like several in the city - became a Christian meeting place (*1 Cor 16.19; Rom 16.3*). Paul indicates that worship took place around the table, in the dining room (*triclinium*) of each house (*1 Cor 11.17-34*). Social convention would have ranked the guests in importance by where they sat and what they were served. Paul argued that such social stratification was inappropriate to Christian communion and worship. It was from Corinth on this last visit that Paul wrote his letter to the church at Rome (*Rom 15.22-27, 16.1-24*).

The two letters to Corinth in the New Testament preserve only a part of Paul's extensive dealings with them. Paul visited Corinth at least three times; Timothy and Titus were sent on other occasions, and Paul wrote them at least four letters.

Ephesus

Ephesus was the capital of the Roman province of Asia and a leading port city. Famed for its magnificent Temple of Ephesian Artemis, the city faced the harbor along a colonnaded thoroughfare, the Arcadian Way, that proceeded to the theater. Excavations of the commercial market (agora), a Temple of the Egyptian Gods, the Library of Celsus, the Hadrianic Temple of Artemis, fountains of Trajan, and a lavish residential quarter reflect the great growth of the Roman city, especially from the 2nd century AD.

Capital of the Province of Achaea, Corinth held a unique position with its two ports either side of the isthmus (*map right*).

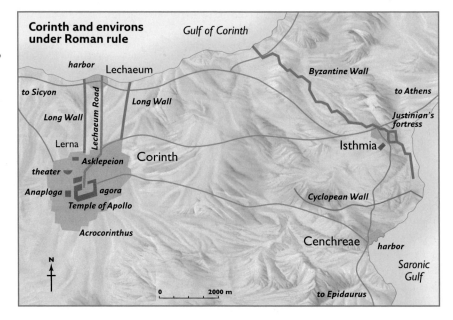

Corinth and environs under Roman rule

Gulf of Corinth
harbor — Lechaeum
Byzantine Wall
to Sicyon
Lechaeum Road
to Athens
Long Wall
Long Wall
Justinian's fortress
Lerna
Isthmia
Asklepeion
Corinth
theater
Anaploga — agora
Temple of Apollo
Cyclopean Wall
Acrocorinthus
Cenchreae
harbor
Saronic Gulf
N
0   2000 m
to Epidaurus

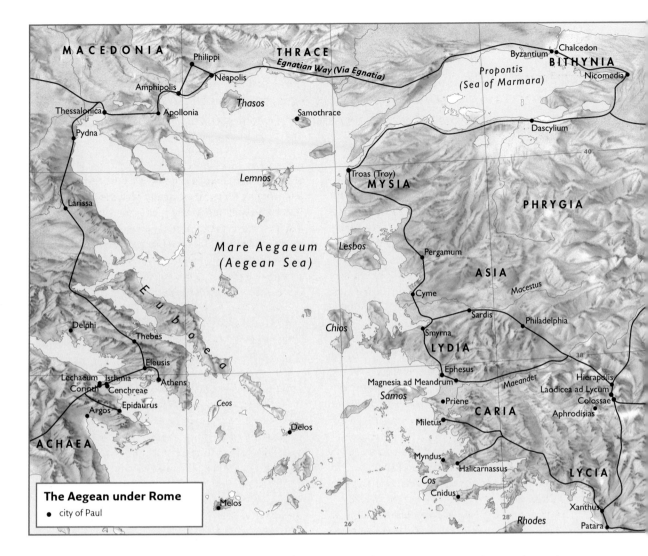

The Aegean under Rome
● city of Paul

Ephesus became Paul's base for several years during his Aegean mission. From there, he traveled and wrote many of his letters to other churches (1 Cor 16.5–8). Paul's preaching caused a riot, instigated by silversmiths who made statues of Artemis (Acts 19). Subsequently, he left Ephesus for Troas and Macedonia, before moving on to Corinth (2 Cor 2.12–13, 7.5–16).

Whereas Jesus' ministry took place against a largely rural backdrop, first-century Christianity was, predominantly, an urban phenomenon (map above). Traveling missionaries and teachers – such as Paul – traveled along the main roads and routes, setting up churches among cities from Asia Minor, Macedonia, and Achaea.

Thessalonica

Thessalonica is the main city on the Egnatian Way as it turns across the mainland of Greece. The city was the first capital of the Roman province of Macedonia (146 BC). It held a prominent position in the economy of the region. In addition to both local and foreign cults, Thessalonica boasted a major imperial cult center as well as Samaritan and Jewish enclaves. Paul's first letter (1 Thess) was written to Christians at Thessalonica (c. AD 50) to encourage and instruct them in his absence.

http://www.luthersem.edu/ckoester/paul/main.htm
Journeys of Paul
http://www.ntgateway.com/paul/
New Testament Gateway: Paul the Apostle

The journeys of Paul

The spread of Christianity to non-Jews was perhaps more the achievement of Paul than any other figure in the New Testament. While he was not the first Christian to work outside of Jewish networks, Paul the "missionary" (Greek *apostolos*) opened new doors in the urban environment of the Roman empire.

A Diaspora Jew from Tarsus, Paul had received a Greek education but also studied in Jerusalem as a Pharisee. He first comes to historical notice in the years after the death of Jesus. After initially persecuting the Christian movement, he was converted to "the way" (*Acts 9.1-9; 24.14, 22*).

Paul's first work occurred in and around the city of Damascus, but he soon moved back to the region of Cilicia and Syria. During this time, Paul had only limited contacts with the church at Jerusalem (*Gal 1.16-22; Acts 9.26-30*). He was later associated with Antioch, the capital of Syria and the center of a large Jewish community through which Christian groups had spread, and where the term "Christian" was first used (*Acts 11.26*). This phase is reflected in the so-called first missionary journey, in which he traveled with Barnabas through Pisidia and south Galatia (*Acts 13-14*).

The gentile mission

Concerns among the Jewish Christians of Antioch over the inclusion of gentile converts led to tension. Paul and a delegation from Antioch went to Jerusalem to consult with Peter and James (the brother of Jesus) on this matter (*Gal 2.1-14; Acts 15*). After this, Paul left Antioch for a new mission in the Aegean, heading west through Asia Minor, then going by boat across to Macedonia, landing at the port of Neapolis,

where he caught the Egnatian Way, the major overland route across Greece connecting the Levant with the Adriatic coast. Paul's travels in the coastal regions of western Asia Minor and Greece form the so-called second and third missionary journeys (*Acts 16-20*). Paul himself treats it as one phase, during which his efforts were directed toward gentile converts. It covers the period from about AD 49-60, during which most of the known letters of Paul were written. At the

> "Although I am the very least of all the saints, this grace was given to me to bring to the gentiles the news of the boundless riches of Christ, and to make everyone see what is the plan of the mystery hidden for ages in God who created all things... "
>
> **(Eph 3.8-9)**
>
> "In that renewal there is no longer Greek and Jew, circumcized and uncircumcized, barbarian, Scythian, slave and free; but Christ is all and in all!"
>
> **(Col 3.11)**

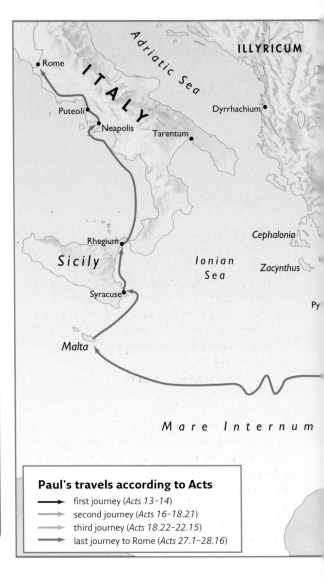

Paul's travels according to Acts

→ first journey (*Acts 13-14*)
→ second journey (*Acts 16-18.21*)
→ third journey (*Acts 18.22-22.15*)
→ last journey to Rome (*Acts 27.1-28.16*)

end of this phase, he had planned to visit Rome on the way to Spain, after stopping at Jerusalem with a collection for the poor (*Rom 15.22-29*). However, in Jerusalem Paul was arrested and eventually taken to Rome (*Acts 21-28*), where tradition holds that he was martyred under the Emperor Nero.

Travels and letters in the Aegean

It has been estimated that Paul logged some 10,000 miles during his missionary travels. The picture described in Paul's letters is one of a tireless worker who moves from city to city along the major highways of the Roman world. Acts portrays a series of individual stops during an extended travelogue. Paul's letters indicate that he followed the major highways to leading urban centers, where he then sought hospitality from which to begin his work of setting up local congregations of followers. Paul was concerned to keep in contact with his congregations, either through visits

or by sending his co-workers letters. Paul's letters in the New Testament reflect the widely used conventions of his day, but some aspects of his message - such as his statement that there was no difference between slaves and free (*1Cor 12.12-13*) - would have been highly radical at the time.

The map shows the missionary activities of Paul as depicted in Acts (*map below*). They lasted for some 16-18 years and carried Paul around the Mediterranean littoral beginning at Antioch, the capital of Syria. Paul's first missionary activities were carried on among gentile sympathizers in the areas around Antioch and Tarsus, his home town (*Acts 13-14*). Paul's own letters often give a different

or more detailed picture of his extensive travels. After leaving Antioch, Paul moved into the Aegean coastal regions, where he spent the rest of his known career. Although we treat the missionary journeys as distinct phases, Paul was almost continually on the move during the period AD 49-60, during which time he made numerous visits to congregations throughout the Aegean.

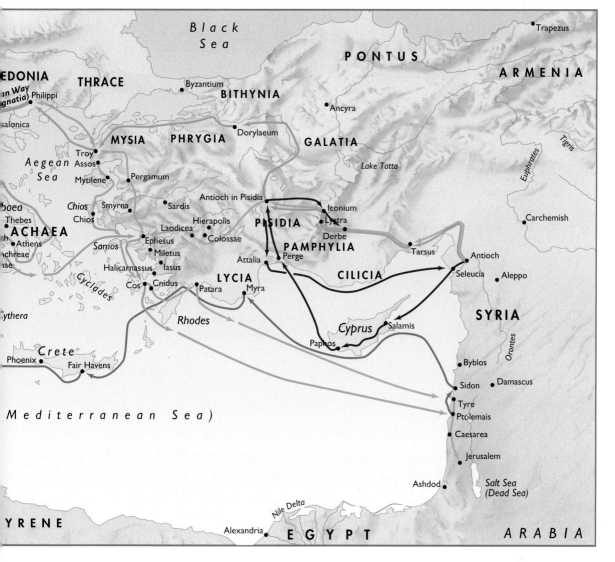

TEN

BEYOND THE TIMES
OF THE BIBLE

The Arch of Titus in Rome.
Erected in AD 81, the arch commemorates the sack of Jerusalem
in AD 70. The relief shows Roman soldiers carrying away plunder
from the Temple, including silver trumpets, the golden table,
and a seven-branched candlestick or menorah.

The First Jewish Revolt

Judaea was often racked by political unrest, fuelled by religious fervor and expectation of messianic deliverance. The First Revolt (AD 66–74) would result in the destruction of Herod's Temple (in AD 70). The Second Revolt (AD 132–135) dashed hopes of restoring the state and the temple. The disastrous outcomes forced both political reorganization under the Romans and religious reconstruction among Jews and Christians alike.

Much of the information for this period comes from the Jewish historian Flavius Josephus, who commanded the Jewish armies in Galilee. Following a decisive defeat and realizing the futility of the war, Josephus elected surrender rather than suicide. From Rome, he wrote his account of the revolts, *The Jewish War* and his voluminous *Antiquities of the Jews*.

The First Revolt

Roman procuratorial administration of Judaea produced resentment and resistance. Josephus places equal blame on the mismanagement of the last Roman procurators, Albinus (AD 62–64) and Gessius Florus (AD 64–66). In the late spring of AD 66, Florus confiscated the temple treasury, sparking riots. The high priest was killed and the Roman garrison in Jerusalem was butchered. The governor of Syria, Cestius Gallus (AD 63–66), marched to Jerusalem but could not recapture the city before winter set in. As he

withdrew, his forces were routed in an ambush near Beth-horon. The Jews took this as a sign of divine favor, and revolution swept through Palestine. The leaders divided the country into military districts, each with its own commander, among them Ananus the high priest (Jerusalem) and Josephus (Galilee).

They underestimated the strength of Rome. In spring AD 67, Nero despatched Vespasian, with 50,000 men. Galilee was first to fall, without much resistance. Josephus retreated to Tiberias, and then to the strongholds of Gamala and Jotapata, but resistance was futile.

Samaria was soon recaptured, and by the end of AD 67 Judaea and Peraea were left alone. Vespasian spent the next months "pacifying" the outlying territories, from Jamnia (Jabneh) to Idumaea and Peraea as far south as the Dead Sea. This may have been the occasion of the destruction of the Essenes community at Qumran (*see page 150*).

The fortress at Masada is described by Josephus in *The Jewish War*, book VII (*illustration right*). Situated on a rock surrounded by ravines, it became a last refuge for Jewish zealots after the First Revolt had been quashed by the Romans.

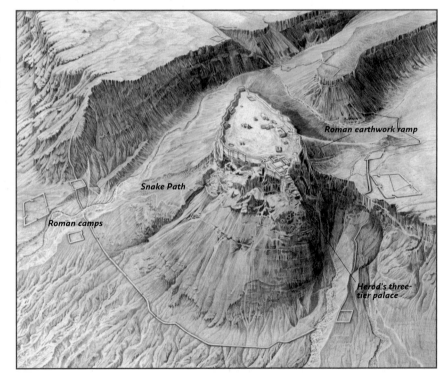

Roman earthwork ramp

Snake Path

Roman camps

Herod's three-tier palace

Vespasian had retired to Caesarea to plan the final siege of Jerusalem when news came that was to cause a temporary halt to the war: Emperor Nero had been killed and civil war was threatening Rome. Vespasian was recalled by the Senate to help restore peace. After the "year of the four Emperors" Vespasian himself was named emperor in July of AD 69.

The destruction of the temple

Responsibility for finishing the war fell to Vespasian's son, Titus, who resumed the war in AD 70. He laid siege to Jerusalem. The defenders were weakened by starvation and ravaged by infighting between the rebel factions. In August, Jerusalem fell in a final assault, during which much of the old city was destroyed and the population decimated. Most significantly, perhaps, the temple was destroyed - burned to the ground. The siege had lasted five months. The Roman senate honored Titus and Vespasian with a triumphal procession, and on the Arch of Titus in Rome can still be seen pictures of Roman soldiers carrying off the sacred candlesticks from the temple.

The first Jewish war against Rome resulted from nationalist fervor, exacerbated by the last Roman procurators (*map right*). Jerusalem was captured and destroyed by Titus in AD 70. Of the few remaining strongholds, Masada was the last to fall in AD 74.

From AD 71 to 73, the commanding general Lucilius Bassus subdued the fortresses of Herodium and Machaerus. Only the followers of Eleazar ben Jair held out in the imposing fortress of Masada. The Romans built a massive earthen assault ramp, but after the final assault (in spring AD 74), they found that the defenders had committed mass suicide rather than face capture.

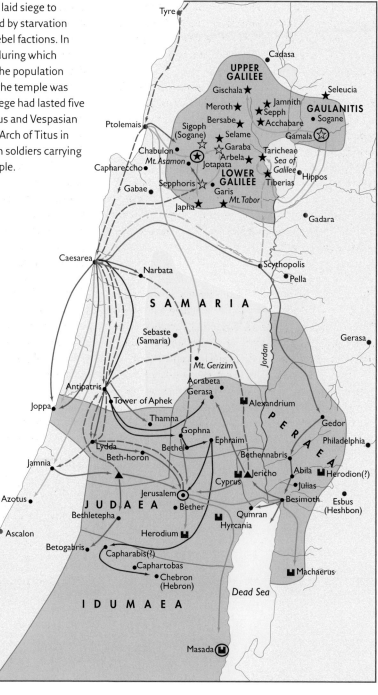

The first Jewish revolt

Roman military operations
- ⟶ Cestius Gallus, AD 66
- ⟶ AD 67
- ⟶ AD 68
- ⟶ AD 69
- ⟶ AD 70
- ⟶ after AD 70
- ---→ non-hostile troop movement
- ⟶ attack
- ▲ major Roman camp
- ◯ major siege

Jewish defenses
- — rebel military district
- ▨ primarily Jewish population
- ▨ primarily Samaritan population
- • gentiles attack Jews, AD 66
- • Jews attack gentiles, AD 66
- ▉ Hasmonaean or Herodian fortress used by rebels
- ★ site probably fortified by rebels
- ☆ site possibly fortied by rebels

The Second Jewish Revolt

The province of Judaea remained "peaceful" under Vespasian (AD 69–79) and his sons, Titus (AD 79–81) and Domitian (AD 81–96). The Jewish population was resettled, especially in Galilee. But the apocalyptic fervor of the First Revolt still persisted in some quarters.

In particular, new Jewish apocalyptic writings (*Ezra 4; 2 Baruch*) predicted coming messianic events. During the last years of Trajan (AD 98–117), there were uprisings among the Jews of Egypt, Cyrene, Cyprus and Mesopotamia.

The precise causes of the Second Revolt are uncertain, but Roman plans for Jerusalem certainly played a significant part. The accession of Hadrian (AD 117–138) brought a new period of imperial building, and, while visiting the east (AD 129–131), the emperor announced a plan to rebuild Jerusalem as a Roman city called Aelia Capitolina, with a temple of Jupiter built on the ruins of Temple Mount. Combined with other edicts against Jewish practices - a later writer attributed the revolt to Hadrian's prohibition of the practice of circumcision - this prospect sparked a new revolt.

Bar Kokhba

The leader of the revolt was Simon bar Kosiba, commonly called Bar Kokhba, a messianic title meaning "Son of the Star" (cf. Num 24.17). He was supported, according to tradition, by Akiba ben Joseph, the greatest rabbi of the time. The rebels took Jerusalem and held it for two years. Coins struck under Bar Kokhba are regularly dated according to the year "of the freedom of Israel" or "the freedom of Jerusalem." Hadrian viewed the situation with such concern that he summoned Julius Severus, one of his best generals, to command the legions. Severus had to

come from the other end of the empire; he was governor of Britain at the time. The final battle took place in AD 135 at Bether, south of Jerusalem. Both Bar Kokhba and Akiba were killed; many towns were destroyed and survivors deported as slaves.

Many caves have been found near the Dead Sea containing archives, coins, and other goods stored during the revolt. Four caves at Wadi Murabba'at yielded documents in Hebrew, Aramaic, Greek, and Latin. The Cave of the Pool at Nahal Dawid could have sheltered an entire family for some time. The five caves at Nahal Hever, however, yielded some of the most poignant remnants. The Cave of Letters contained letters of Bar Kokhba and the personal accounts of a woman named Babata, as well as 18 skeletons. In the Cave of Horrors, it appears that 40 persons - men, women, and children died of starvation - as a Roman camp sat on the ridge above.

The aftermath of revolt

After the revolt collapsed, Hadrian proceeded with plans for the rebuilding of Jerusalem (as Aelia Capitolina), and Jews were excluded from that immediate region of Judaea (from Acrabeta to near En-gedi). Under Antoninus Pius (AD 138–161), some of the restrictions were lifted, but the Jewish population shifted either to the Diaspora or to Galilee. From Usha, rabbis led the reconstruction, reflected in the codification of the Mishnah by Judah the Prince at Sepphoris in about AD 200.

> http://www.livius.org/ja-jn/jewish_wars/
> bk07.html
> The text of the Bar Kokhba letters
> http://en.wikisource.org/wiki/Wikisource:
> Open_Mishnah_Project
> Open Mishnah Project
> http://www.ntgateway.com/judaica.htm
> New Testtament Gateway: Judaica

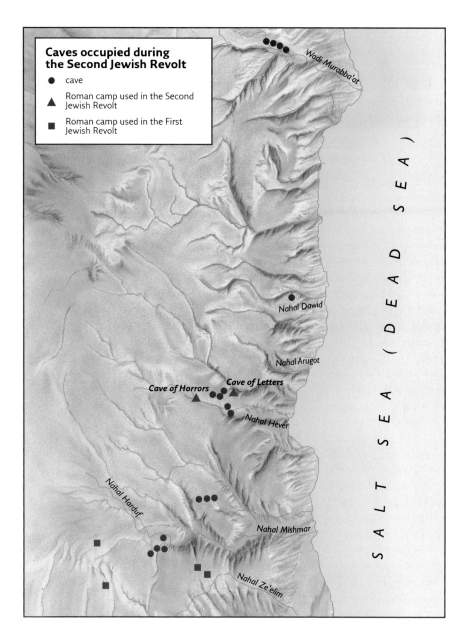

Wadi Murabba'at

S A L T   S E A   (D E A D   S E A)

Nahal Dawid

Nahal Arugot

Cave of Horrors   Cave of Letters

Nahal Hever

Nahal Harduf

Nahal Mishmar

Nahal Ze'elim

The only history of the Second Jewish Revolt written relatively close to the events was a brief account written by Cassius Dio at the beginning of the third century AD (*map above*). Historians therefore have to rely on archaeological, epigraphical, and numismatic remains. Archaeological remains are consistent with a fearful Jewish population taking refuge in caves and hiding places. Many caves have been found throughout the Judean desert where Jewish families and communities hid from the Romans. Elaborate tunnels and hiding places have also been found under many villages of the time, particularly south of Jerusalem in the Shephelah. Fragments from a large triumphal arch have also been found at Tel Shalem, near Beth Shean, indicating the importance the Romans ascribed to their victory.

Roman Palestine after the revolts

After Herod's death, his kingdom was divided among his three sons, but Judaea was under rule of a Roman military procurator who answered to the legate of the Province of Syria from AD 6-37. The First Revolt (AD 66-70) would precipitate major changes in the administration of the provinces, which continued into the 4th century.

Provincia Judaea

After the First Jewish Revolt, Judaea was reorganized as an independent province under a governor of higher rank (*legatus Augusti pro praetore*), with headquarters at Caesarea Maritima. A full legion, initially the Tenth Fretensis, which had served during the revolt, was assigned to the province and stationed at Jerusalem. Much of the area of Trachonitis was ceded to Agrippa II, while most of the region of the Decapolis was ceded directly to the Province of Syria. In AD 106, Trajan organized the remainder of the Nabataean kingdom into the Provincia Arabia.

Under Emperor Vespasian (AD 69-79), and later under Hadrian (AD 117-138), a program of "urbanization" was begun in the north, partly in recognition that many of the free cities had not supported the Jewish revolt. As these city-territories were organized, a growing class of provincial aristocrats and merchants helped in the administration through the collection of taxes. Vespasian restored Gabae, Apollonia, Antipatris (Pegae), Joppa (Flavia Joppe), Jamnia (Jabneh), Azotus (Ashdod), and, in Galilee, Sepphoris and Tiberias as autonomous, self-governing city-territories. Sebaste (Samaria) was reconstituted as Flavia Neapolis. Jerusalem remained the legionary headquarters until Hadrian reconstituted the city as Aelia Capitolina.

Provincia Syria Palaestina

During the Second Jewish Revolt (AD 132-135), Roman control was disrupted for a short time as a new state was established by Bar Kokhba. After the revolt was defeated, Emperor Hadrian reconstituted Jerusalem as a Roman colony called Aelia Capitolina. The provincial

administration was upgraded to the highest consular rank as Provincia Syria Palaestina and assigned two legions. One legion (the Sixth Ferrata) was assigned to the Valley of Jezreel, with headquarters at Capercotnei. Subsequently, the entire region, which became veterans' lands (*campus maximus legions*), was known as Legio, from which comes the modern name Lejjun.

Emperor Septimius Severus (AD 193-211) continued Hadrian's "urbanization" in the south. Idumaea was promoted to city status under the name Eleutheropolis, and the district of Lydda and Thamna became Diospolis. After a revolt under the legate of Syria, Severus reorganized the Province of Syria. Eventually, the coastal region was designated Phoenicia Prima, while the interior region, with its capital at Damascus, was designated Phoenicia Libanensis. In AD 220-221, Emperor Heliogabalus promoted Emmaus to the city-territory of Nicopolis. Thus, virtually the whole of Provincia Syria Palaestina was transformed into a net of larger and smaller city-territories.

After the death of Herod Agrippa I (AD 44), command of Judaea reverted to the Roman Procurators, although some of Agrippa's territories went to his son, Herod Agrippa II (c. AD 52-94). When he died the kingdom became part of the Province of Syria (*map right*).

Roman provincial administration, c. AD 70-193

- Roman administration, AD 44
- Agrippa II's kingdom, loyal to Rome
- area lost to insurgents, (AD 66-70) under Judaea after AD 70
- Judaea after AD 44
- Kingdom of Agrippa II, AD 54-92, later to Syria

The three Palestines of the later empire

Emperor Diocletian (AD 284–305) reorganized the entire Roman empire into four prefectures, divided into dioceses and subdivided by provinces. The Province of Palaestina fell under the Diocese of the Oriens in the Prefecture of the East. Diocletian established a strip of military territory called the Limes Palaestina along the southern border of Idumaea with the old Nabataean territories. During this period, Provincia Arabia was further developed in its urban centrers and reinforced with military garrisons against the eastern frontier, the Limes Arabicus. About AD 358, the region south of Idumaea was added to the province as Palaestina Salutaris, with its capital at Petra. Eventually, it was called Palaestina Tertia, after the remainder of the province was subdivided into southern and northern districts as Palaestina Prima (with a capital at Caesarea Maritima) and Palaestina Secunda (with a capital at Scythopolis), respectively. This organization of the region remained essentially intact throughout the Byzantine period and up to the time of the Arab conquests.

The administrative districts of the Roman province of Palestine in c. AD 400 (map right). Under the reorganisation of Diocletian (AD 284) Palestine was subdivided into three regions, governed as a consular province in the prefecture of the East. After the Bar Kokhba revolt, the use of Hebrew as the spoken language declined until, by around AD 300, it was surviving almost purely as a literary language.

Roman Palestine

- ■ important city
- ■ fortified city
- □ open city
- ● fortified small town/large village
- ● open small town/large village
- ○ fortified village
- ● open village
- ⚏ fortress
- —— Roman road (certain)
- – – – Roman road (uncertain)
- ·········· track
- —— provincial boundary, AD 400 (certain)
- – – – provincial boundary, AD 400 (uncertain)
- —— city territory boundary (certain)
- – – – city territory boundary (uncertain)
- ·········· boundary of territory (detached from city territory)

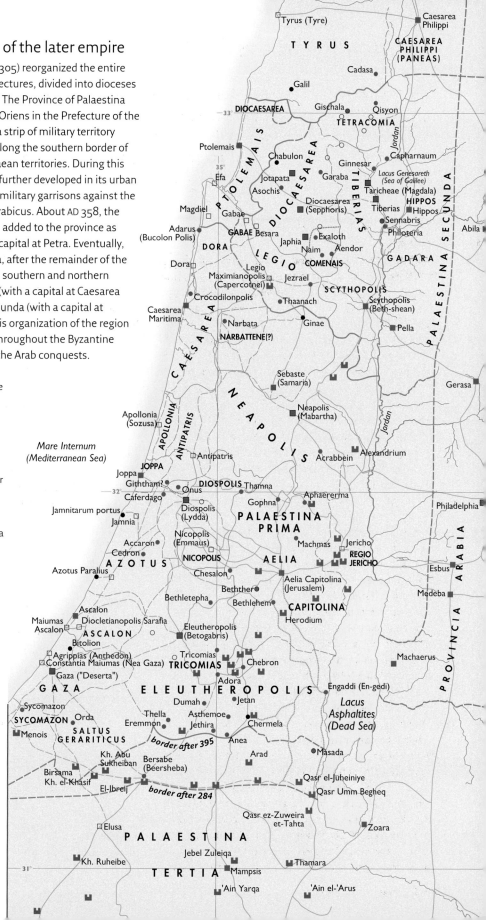

The growth of Christianity

The First Jewish Revolt against Rome (AD 66–74) was significant for the development of both Christianity and Judaism. The period of reconstruction following the war forced a new religious outlook and stimulated new missionary activities. During this period, the Christian movement would also begin to split apart from Judaism as a separate religion in the eyes of the Roman world.

The church in the Diaspora

When Paul wrote to the church at Rome, there were already several thriving Christian congregations, even though Paul had never been there. This church may have been founded by Diaspora Jews who, like Paul, moved about freely in the Roman world. Likewise, other major cities, such as Alexandria, had early Christian communities whose beginnings are now lost. Figures such as Peter (Cephas), Paul, and Apollos moved along the roads of Asia Minor spreading their message (*1 Cor 1.12, 3.22, 9.5*).

By the 2nd century, Christian groups were flourishing in Egypt and Syria. The impact of travel may be seen in the letters addressed to the seven churches of Asia Minor at the beginning of Revelation and in the proposed itinerary through Cappadocia, Bithynia, Galatia, and Asia of 1 Peter. Other writings such as the *Didache* (or *Teachings of the Twelve Apostles*) from Syria also reflect the importance of traveling Christian missionaries in the early 2nd century.

Persecution in the early church

In the first decades of the 2nd century, Christians faced the first "official" persecution since the outbreak under Nero following the fire in Rome. Christians, such as Clement of Rome and his wife Flavia Domitilla, faced persecution in the last years of Domitian (AD 81–96). Letters written by Pliny the Younger, as imperial legate of Bithynia-Pontus (c. AD 110–112), show the extent of Christian growth in those regions and the Roman response. Around the same time, the bishop of Antioch, Ignatius, was arrested and transported to Rome, where he was martyred. En route, Ignatius visited several churches in Asia Minor and wrote letters to churches at Philadelphia, Magnesia, Tralles, Ephesus, Smyrna, and Rome.

By the 2nd century, Christianity outside the Jewish homeland was becoming mainly gentile. Although it soon spread to other regions of the Roman empire, such as Gaul and North Africa, the dominant language continued to be Greek, through the 3rd century. North Africa was also the place where the Christian scriptures were first translated from Greek into Latin. They would eventually be rendered into Syriac, Armenian, and Coptic (Egyptian) versions as well.

Prior to the 3rd century, Jewish and Christian congregations still met in private homes or assembly halls. From the 3rd century onward, new, more elaborate religious architecture began to develop. The earliest known Christian building yet excavated, from Dura-Europos in Syria, illustrates the process of converting a house into a distinct place of worship.

With the spread of Christianity into yet more cities came further acculturation to the Roman world. Christian teachers - Justin Martyr at Rome, Clement and Origen at Alexandria, and Tertullian at Carthage - interpreted the scriptures in the light of Greek philosophy. Further interpretation also produced theological controversies as Christian thought was pulled in different directions. Greater growth produced greater diversity as the church went "into all the world."

The spread of Christianity between the 1st and 3rd centuries AD (*map right*). Between the reign of Constantine and the Muslim onslaught in the 630s, there was a spate of new religious buildings in Palestine. However, most churches and monasteries were built in the 4th century, becoming important centers during the 6th and 7th centuries.

Places of worship by the Byzantine period

distribution
- + churches
- • monastery chapels
- ★ Jewish synagogue
- ▲ Samaritan synagogue
- ■ church and synagogue

Bezet · Horbat Amud · Elijah's cave · Capernaum · Sea of Galilee · Zippori · Kafr Kanna · Tiberias · Bet Yerah · Caesarea · Bet She'an (Scythopolis) · Jebel et-Tor (Mt Gerizim) · Reshef · Gerasa · Joppa · Khirbet Seilun · Yavne · Sha'alvim · Jericho · Khirbet Imwas · Jerusalem · Ascalon · Bet Guvrin · Salt Sea (Dead Sea) · Gaza · Ma'on · Eshtemoa · Jordan

The spread of Christianity
- • Christian city by end of 1st century AD
- → route of Ignatius through proconsular Asia
- • Christian city during 2nd century AD
- • Christian city during 3rd century AD
- main areas of Christian growth, to AD 300
- areas largely Christian by AD 600

Pontus Euxinus · DACIA · Danuvius · Sinope · PONTUS · Neocaesarea · ARMENIA · Amastris · Parentium · ILLYRICUM · Salonae · Mare Adriaticum · Byzantium · BITHYNIA · Nicomedia · Caesarea Mazaca · Melitene · Samosata · ITALIA · MACEDONIA · THRACIA · Philippi · Pella · Neapolis · GALATIA · Antioch in Pisidia · Iconium · Edessa · Rome · Dyrrhachium · Thessalonica · Troas · ASIA · Thyatira · Tarsus · MESOPOTAMIA · Puteoli · Pergamum · Philadelphia · Lystra · Antioch · Dura-Europos · Apollonia · Larissa · Mare Aegaeum · Smyrna · Sardis · Hierapolis · Derbe · Apamea · Palmyra · Mare Tyrrhenum · Nicopolis · GREECE · Ephesus · Miletus · Laodicea · Colossae · Cyprus · SYRIA · Corinth · Patmos · Salamis · Damascus · Sicilia · Paphos · Sidon · Tyre · Cnossus · Gortyn · Crete · Pella · Carthage · Jerusalem · Malta · Mare Internum (Mediterranean Sea) · ARABIA · Alexandria · Naucratis · Cyrene · AEGYPTUS · CYRENAICA · Arsinoe · Nile · Euphrates · Holys · Tigris

Israel and Palestine today

In many ways, the "holy land" has an unholy history. Its geographical position - between Europe, Africa, and the Middle East - meant that it was always being fought over, whether by Egyptians, Assyrians, Babylonians, Romans, or Greeks. Its significance for three of the world's great faiths - Judaism, Christianity, and Islam, sees that it is still the subject of intense, often bitter conflict and division.

Visitors to Israel and Palestine today cannot escape signs of such division. There is Jerusalem, with its Christian, Muslim, Jewish, and Armenian quarters; the West Bank, peppered with Jewish settlements; the recently constructed and highly controversial Israel Defense Barrier, snaking through Israel for more than 112 miles. The political and religious issues facing the region today are complex and highly charged.

This complexity is reflected in the multicultural population. The two main groups - Israeli and Palestinian - contain many other people of different religions and from a huge range of geographical origins. There are, of course, many residents who belong to neither of these groups,

such as the Druze in the north, the Samaritans of Nablus and Holon, and the Armenians in Jerusalem.

Israel, as a modern state, dates from 1948, although settlers had been arriving from the 1870s onwards. During both the establishment of the nation and subsequent conflicts, large numbers of Arabs have fled or been displaced from existing settlements, and have either had to be resettled or have remained as refugees. The current boundaries - with all their concommitent problems – are largely the result of the so-called "Six Day War" of 1967, during which Israel gained control of eastern Jerusalem, the Gaza Strip, the Sinai Peninsula, the West Bank, and the Golan Heights. Israel returned Sinai to Egypt in 1978, and withdrew from the Gaza Strip in 2005.

Jerusalem contains a rich concentration of archaeological sites (*map right*). The Temple mount dominates the skyline, surmounted by the Dome of the Rock, built 687–691 AD by the Umayyad caliph Abd al-Malik. Below the dome stands the Western Wall, the only remnants of the temple complex built by Herod the Great. The Church of the Holy Sepulchre was built in 330 AD on the orders of Constantine, over the traditional sites of Golgotha and Jesus' tomb. The present church dates from Crusader times. Other significant remains include tombs in the Kidron valley and the early remains found in the city of David, including Hezekiah's tunnel and the "stepped stone" structure.

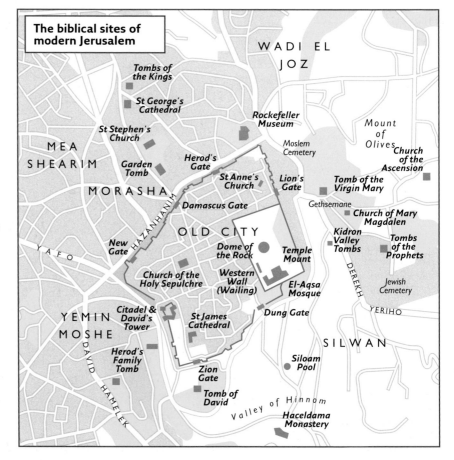

The biblical sites of modern Jerusalem

WADI EL JOZ

Tombs of the Kings

St George's Cathedral

Rockefeller Museum

Mount of Olives

Church of the Ascension

St Stephen's Church

Moslem Cemetery

MEA SHEARIM

Herod's Gate

Garden Tomb

St Anne's Church

Lion's Gate

Tomb of the Virgin Mary

MORASHA

Damascus Gate

Gethsemane

Church of Mary Magdalen

HAZANHANIM

OLD CITY

Kidron Valley Tombs

Tombs of the Prophets

New Gate

Dome of the Rock

Temple Mount

YAFO

Church of the Holy Sepulchre

Western Wall (Wailing)

El-Aqsa Mosque

DEREKH

Jewish Cemetery

YERIHO

Citadel & David's Tower

St James Cathedral

Dung Gate

YEMIN MOSHE

SILWAN

DAVID HAMELEK

Herod's Family Tomb

Zion Gate

Siloam Pool

Tomb of David

Valley of Hinnom

Haceldama Monastery

Yet it is not merely the geopolitical events that have changed the region. Commercial farming and irrigation have transformed the agricultural landscape. Irrigation has been the cause of some controversy; not only must Israel and Jordan divide the water from the river Jordan between them, but increased diversion of water from the upper Jordan has affected the flow of water into the Dead Sea. The result is that the level of water in the Dead Sea has shrunk at a drop rate of 1 meter per year. There are plans to replace this water with sea water from either the Mediterranean or the Red Sea, although this plan remains controversial.

The other significant issue is the growth in population. On Proclamation Day in 1948, the population of Israel was some 650,000; today it is over 7 million. This has led to the colonization of many previously empty areas and in some cases, rapid urbanization. Tel Aviv, one of the biggest cities of the region had 15,000 inhabitants in 1922; today it has well over a million.

The biblical sites of the modern Levant

Within Israel there are ancient sites such as Megiddo, Tel Jericho and Hebron (*map right*). Galilee contains sites such as Chorazin and Capernaum as well as Roman remains at Sepphoris, Caesarea Maritime, and Bet She'an. To the east, the fortress of Masada and the caves of Qumran draw many visitors to the Dead Sea. In Jordan there are sites related to Moab and Edom, as well as the famous Madaba map and the ancient Nabatean capital of Petra. Although Assyrian, Babylonian, and Persian sites are often rendered inaccessible either by conflict or by adverse political situations, in countries such as Egypt, Turkey, Italy, and Greece, archaeological sites continue to attract many thousands of scholars, archaeologists researchers and visitors every year.

Chronology

Assigning dates to the principal characters and events of the Bible is not an easy task. New discoveries, the reassessment of older evidence, and simple differences of opinion among scholars make it difficult to achieve a consensus. The dates for the archaeological periods in Palestine, for the kings of Israel and Judah, and for Babylonian, Assyurian, and Mesopotamian history are taken from the original edition of the *Times Atlas of the Bible*. The names of the Egyptian Pharaohs, and the dates of their reigns follow the preferred spellings and chronology of the Department of Ancient Egypt and Sudan in the British Museum. They can be found in *The British Museum Dictionary of Ancient Egypt*, by Ian Shaw and Paul Nicholson, 1995.

However, it must be remembered that other terms, dates, and chronological systems are also in use, so when it comes to dating events from before the seventh century BC this should be used as a framework rather than an absolute chronology.

Old Testament

Levant inhabited by small bands of hunter-gatherers	c. 90,000 BC
Microliths and bone tools introduced	c. 12,500
Wheat domesticated – oval houses	c. 8300
Agriculture – sheep herded – rectangular houses	c. 7500
Beginning of pottery in Syria	c. 6000
Copper metallurgy developed	c. 3500
Writing invented	c. 3800
Ebla archives	c. 2500
Potter's wheel in Palestine	c. 2000
Hammurabi's laws	c. 1792
Hyksos take control of Egypt	c. 1665
Kamose campaigns in Canaan	c. 1553
Ahmose expells the Hyksos	c. 1545
Amenhotep I campaign to Palestine	c. 1510
Thutmose III begins to build his empire in Palestine	c. 1457
Battle of Megiddo	c. 1457
Alphabetic writing at Ugarit	c. 1400
Beginning of Amarna correspondence	c. 1360
Setys I's campaign to the coastland	c. 1294
Battle of Qadesh	c. 1274
Ramesses II's treaty with the Hittites	c. 1260
Merneptah's battle with 'Israel'	c. 1208
Invasions of the Sea Peoples	c. 1200
Phoenician trade begins in the Mediterranean	c. 1000
Solomon assumes the throne in Israel	c. 965
Division of the Hebrew Kingdom	931
Shishak invades Palestine	924
Ahab defeated by Shalmaneser III at Qarqar	853

Jehu pays tribute to Shalmaneser III	841
Menahem's tribute to Tiglath-pileser III	738
Ahaz's tribute to Tiglath-pileser III	734
Tiglath-pileser III places Hoshea on throne	732
Fall of Samaria	722
Sargon II's campaign to Ashdod	712
Lachish attacked by Sennacherib	701
Manasseh pays tribute to Esarhaddon	670
Fall of Nineveh	612
Josiah slain by Necho II of Egypt	609
Nebuchadnezzar II conquers Jerusalem	597
Johoiachin deported to Babylon	597
Fall of Jerusalem and beginning of Exile	587
Release of Johoiachin	561
Cyprus becomes king of Persia	559
Fall of Babylon	539
Cambyses becomes king of Persia	530
Darius	522–486
Alexander the Great	336
Beginning of rule of the Seleucids	325
Beginning of the Ptolemies	305
Hasmonaeans	152

New Testament

Hasmonaean Civil War	67 BC
Arrival of Pompey	64
Assassination of Julius Caesar	43
Herod, King of Judaea	37–4
Death of Herod the Great	4
Judaea under Procuratorial control	6–41 AD

Tax census of Quirinius	6
Pontius Pilate, procurator	26–36
Crucifixion of Jesus	c. 30–33
Death of Herod Philip	34
Pogrom against Jews of Alexandria	37–39
Delegation of Philo to Rome	39
Removal of Herod Antipas	39
Herod Agrippa I	41–44
Judaea under Procuratorial control	44–66
Paul in Aegean	50–60
Herod Agrippa II	52–93
Neronian Persecution of Christians	64
Deaths of Paul and Peter	c. 65–67
First Revolt against Rome	66–74
Fall of Galilee	67
Death of Nero,	68
Year of Four Emperors	69
Destruction of Jerusalem	70
Fall of Masada	74
Death of Clement of Rome, John of Ephesus	c. 96
Ignatius of Antioch	c. 110
Pliny the Younger in Bithynia	c. 112
Revolt of Jews in Egypt	115
Second Jewish Revolt (Bar Kochbah) against Rome	132–35
Justin Martyr, Marcion, and Valentinus in Rome	144–64
Martyrdom of Polycarp, bishop of Smyrna	156
Year of Three Emperors	193
Persecution of Christians in Carthage	197
Persecution of Christians in Alexandria	203
Rabbi Judah the Prince codifies Mishnah	c. 200

Egyptian pharaohs

18th Dynasty c. 1550–c. 1295		
Ahmose **c. 1550–c. 1525**	Tutankhamun **c. 1336–c. 1327**	20th Dynasty c. 1186–c. 1069
Amenhotep I **c. 1525–1504**	Ay (II) **c. 1327–c. 1323**	Sethnakhte **c. 1186–c. 1184**
Thutmose I **c. 1504–c. 1492**	Horemheb **c. 1323–c. 1295**	Ramesses III **c. 1184–c. 1153**
Thutmose II **c. 1492–c. 1479**		Ramesses IV **c. 1153–c. 1147**
Thutmose III **c. 1479–c. 1425**	19th Dynasty c. 1295–c. 1186	Ramesses V **c. 1147–c. 1143**
and Hatshepsut **c. 1473–c. 1458**	Ramesses I **c. 1295–c. 1294**	Ramesses VI **c. 1143–c. 1136**
Amenhotep II **c. 1427–c. 1400**	Sety I **c. 1294–c. 1279**	Ramesses VII **c. 1136–c. 1129**
Thutmose IV **c. 1400–c. 1390**	Ramesses II **c. 1279–c. 1213**	Ramesses VIII **c. 1129–c. 1126**
Amenhotep III **c. 1390–c. 1352**	Merenptah **c. 1213–c. 1203**	Ramesses IX **c. 1126–c. 1108**
Amenhotep IV/Akhenaten	Amenmessu **c. 1203–c. 1200**	Ramesses X **c. 1108–c. 1099**
c. 1352–c. 1336	Sety II **c. 1200–c. 1194**	Ramesses XI **c. 1099–c. 1069**
Nefernefrauten (Smenkhkara)	Saptah **c. 1194–c. 1188**	
c. 1338–c. 1336	Tausret **c. 1188–c. 1186**	

Bibliography

Ackroyd, P. R. *Israel under Babylon and Persia*. Oxford: Oxford University Press, 1970.

Aharoni, Y., and A. F. Rainey. *The Land of the Bible: A Historical Geography*. 2nd ed. London: Burns & Oates, 1979.

Akurgal, E. *Ancient Civilizations and Ruins of Turkey: From Prehistoric Times until the End of the Roman Empire*. 6th ed. Istanbul: Haďset Kitabevi, 1985.

Albright, W. F. *The Archaeology of Palestine*. Rev. ed. Harmondsworth: Penguin Books, 1960.

Anati, E. *Palestine Before the Hebrews: A History, from the Earliest Arrival of Man to the Conquest of Canaan*. London: J. Cape, 1963.

Avi-Yonah, M., and E. Stern. *Encyclopedia of Archaeological Excavations in the Holy Land*. English ed. London: Oxford University Press, 1975.

Baines, J., and J. Málek. *Atlas of Ancient Egypt*. New York: Facts on File, 1980.

Baines, J., and J. Málek. *Cultural Atlas of Ancient Egypt*. Rev. ed. New York: Checkmark Books, 2000.

Baly, D. *The Geography of the Bible*. Rev. ed. Guildford: Lutterworth Press, 1974.

Baly, D., and D. Baly. *Basic Biblical Geography*. Philadelphia: Fortress Press, 1987.

Bancroft-Hunt, N. *Historical Atlas of Ancient Mesopotamia*. New York: Checkmark Books, 2004.

Bar-Kochva, B. *Judas Maccabaeus: The Jewish Struggle against the Seleucids*. Cambridge: Cambridge University Press, 1989.

Barnett, P. *The Birth of Christianity: The First Twenty Years*. Grand Rapids, MI: Eerdmans, 2005.

Bartlett, J. R. *Jews in the Hellenistic World: Josephus, Aristeas, the Sibylline Oracles, Eupolemus*. Cambridge: Cambridge University Press, 1985.

Bartlett, J. R. *The Bible: Faith and Evidence: A Critical Enquiry into the Nature of Biblical History*. London: British Museum Publications, 1990.

Bartlett, J. R. *Archaeology and Biblical Interpretation*. London: Routledge, 1997.

Beek, M. A. *Atlas of Mesopotamia: A Survey of the History and Civilization of Mesopotamia from the Stone Age to the Fall of Babylon*. New York: Nelson, 1962.

Ben-Tor, A., and R. Greenberg. *The Archaeology of Ancient Israel*. New Haven, CT: Yale University Press; Tel Aviv: Open University of Israel, 1991.

Bickerman, E. J. *The Jews in the Greek Age*. Cambridge, MA: Harvard University Press, 1988.

Biran, A. *Temples and High Places in Biblical Times: Proceedings of the Colloquium in Honor of the*

Centennial of Hebrew Union College–Jewish Institute of Religion, Jerusalem, 14–16 March 1977. Jerusalem, Israel: Nelson Glueck School of Biblical Archaeology of Hebrew Union College–Jewish Institute of Religion, 1981.

Bottéro, J., A. Finet, B. Lafont, G. Roux, and A. Nevill. Everyday Life in Ancient Mesopotamia. Edinburgh: Edinburgh University Press, 2001.

Bright, J. A History of Israel. London: SCM, 1960.

Campbell, J. G. Deciphering the Dead Sea Scrolls. London: Fontana Press, 1996.

Carcopino, J. Daily Life in Ancient Rome. New Haven, CT: Yale University Press, 1940.

Casson, L. Travel in the Ancient World. London: Allen & Unwin, 1974.

Casson, L. Ships and Seafaring in Ancient Times. London: British Museum Press, 1994.

Charlesworth, J. H. The Old Testament Pseudepigrapha. London: Darton, Longman & Todd, 1983.

Clements, R. E. God and Temple. Oxford: Blackwell, 1965.

Coggins, R. J. Samaritans and Jews: The Origins of Samaritanism Reconsidered. Oxford: Blackwell, 1975.

Connolly, P. Living in the Time of Jesus of Nazareth. Oxford: Oxford University Press, 1983.

Cook, S. A., F. E. Adcock, and M. P. Charlesworth. The Cambridge Ancient History. Vols. 8–11. Cambridge: Cambridge University Press, 1930–36.

Davies, W. D., L. Finkelstein, W. Horbury, J. Sturdy, and S. T. Katz. The Cambridge History of Judaism. Cambridge, New York: Cambridge University Press, 1984.

De Vaux, R. Ancient Israel: Its Life and Institutions. London: Darton, Longman & Todd, 1973.

De Vaux, R. The Early History of Israel. London: Darton, Longman & Todd, 1978.

Dothan, T. K. The Philistines and Their Material Culture. New Haven, CT: Yale University Press, 1982.

Dothan, T. K., and M. Dothan. People of the Sea: The Search for the Philistines. New York: Macmillan, 1992.

Ehrich, R. W. Chronologies in Old World Archaeology. 3rd ed. Chicago: University of Chicago Press, 1992.

Finegan, J. The Archeology of the New Testament: The Life of Jesus and the Beginning of the Early Church. Rev. ed. Princeton, NJ: Princeton University Press, 1992.

Finegan, J. Handbook of Biblical Chronology: Principles of Time Reckoning in the Ancient World and Problems of Chronology in the Bible. Peabody, MA: Hendrickson Publishers, 1998.

Freedman, D. N., ed. The Anchor Bible Dictionary. New York: Doubleday, 1999.

Freyne, S. Galilee, from Alexander the Great to Hadrian, 323 B.C.E. to 135 C.E.: A Study of Second Temple Judaism. Edinburgh: T&T Clark, 1998.

Fritz, V. The City in Ancient Israel. Sheffield: Sheffield Academic Press, 1995.

García, M., and Florentino E. J. C. Tigchelaar. The Dead Sea Scrolls Study Edition. Leiden: Brill, 1997.

Goldhill, S. The Temple of Jerusalem. London: Profile Books, 2006.

Grant, M. The History of Ancient Israel. London: Weidenfeld & Nicolson, 1996.

Gurney, O. R. The Hittites. 2nd ed. Harmondsworth: Penguin, 1990.

Hallo, W. W., and W. K. Simpson. The Ancient Near East: A History. New York: Harcourt, Brace, Jovanovich, 1971.

Hammond, N. G. L. Atlas of the Greek and Roman World in Antiquity. Bristol: Bristol Classical Press, 1992.

Haran, M. Temples and Temple-Service in Ancient Israel: An Inquiry into the Character of Cult Phenomena and the Historical Setting of the Priestly School. Oxford: Clarendon Press, 1978.

Harden, D. B. The Phoenicians. Harmondsworth: Penguin Books, 1971.

Hawkins, J. D. Trade in the Ancient Near East. London: British School of Archaeology in Iraq, 1977.

Hayes, J. H., and J. M. Miller. *Israelite and Judean History*. London: SCM, 1977.

Hengel, M. *Crucifixion in the Ancient World and the Folly of the Message of the Cross*. London: SCM, 1977.

Hengel, M. *Judaism and Hellenism: Studies in Their Encounter in Palestine during the Early Hellenistic Period*. London: Xpress Reprints, 1996.

Hengel, M., and J. Bowden. *Jews, Greeks and Barbarians: Aspects of the Hellenization of Judaism in the Pre-Christian Period*. London: SCM, 1980.

Hoehner, H. W. *Herod Antipas*. Cambridge: Cambridge University Press, 1972.

Horsley, R. A. *Galilee: History, Politics, People*. Pennsylvania: Trinity Press, 1995.

Horsley, R. A. *Archaeology, History, and Society in Galilee: The Social Context of Jesus and the Rabbis*. Valley Forge, PA: Trinity Press International, 1996.

Jeremias, J. *Jerusalem in the Time of Jesus: An Investigation into Economic and Social Conditions during the New Testament Period*. London: SCM, 1974.

Jones, A. H. M., and M. Avi-Yonah. *The Cities of the Eastern Roman Provinces*. 2nd ed. Oxford: Clarendon Press, 1971.

Jagersma, H., & H. Jagersma. *A History of Israel to Bar Kochba*. London: SCM, 1994.

Jones, A. H. M. *The Cities of the Eastern Roman Provinces*. New York: Oxford University Press, 1971.

Kenyon, K. M. *Archaeology in the Holy Land*. 4th ed. London: Benn, 1979.

Landels, J. G. *Engineering in the Ancient World*. Rev. ed. London: Constable, 2000.

Leick, G. *Mesopotamia: The Invention of the City*. London: Allen Lane, 2001.

Levy, T. E. *The Archaeology of Society in the Holy Land*. London: Continuum, 2003.

Leaney, A. R. C. *The Jewish and Christian World, 200 B.C. to A.D. 200*. Cambridge: Cambridge University Press, 1984.

Macqueen, J. G. *The Hittites and Their Contemporaries in Asia Minor*. Rev. and enlarged ed. London: Thames & Hudson, 1986.

MacMullen, R. *Paganism in the Roman Empire*. New Haven, CT: Yale University Press, 1981.

Mayes, A. D. H. *Israel in the Period of the Judges*. London: SCM, 1974.

Mazar, A. *Archaeology of the Land of the Bible, 10,000–586 B.C.E.* Cambridge: Lutterworth, 1993.

Mazar, B., M. Avi-Yonah, and A. Malamat. *Views of the Biblical World*. Jerusalem: International Publishing Co., 1958.

Meeks, W. A. *The First Urban Christians*. New Haven, CT: Yale University Press, 1983.

Meiggs, R. *Trees and Timber in the Ancient Mediterranean World*. Oxford: Clarendon Press, 1982.

Moldenke, H. N., and A. L. Moldenke. *Plants of the Bible*. Waltham, MA: Chronica Botanica, 1952.

Murphy-O'Connor, J. *The Holy Land: An Oxford Archaeological Guide from Earliest Times to 1700*. 4th ed. Oxford: Oxford University Press, 1998.

Murphy-O'Connor, J. *St. Paul's Corinth: Texts and Archaeology*. 3rd ed. Collegeville, MN: The Liturgical Press, 2002.

Negev, A., and S. Gibson. *Archaeological Encyclopedia of the Holy Land*. Rev. and updated ed. New York: Continuum, 2001.

Noth, M. *The History of Israel*. 2nd ed. London: Black, 1960.

Oppenheim, A. L. *Ancient Mesopotamia: Portrait of a Dead Civilization*. Chicago: University of Chicago Press, 1964.

Potter, T. W. *Towns in Late Antiquity: Caesarea and Its Context*. Oxford: Oxbow, 1995.

Pritchard, J. B. *The Ancient Near East in Pictures Relating to the Old Testament*. 2nd ed. with supplement. Princeton, NJ: Princeton University Press, 1969.

Pritchard, J. B. *Ancient Near Eastern Texts Relating to the Old Testament*. 3rd ed. with supplement. Princeton, NJ: Princeton University Press, 1969.

Ramsay, W. M. *St. Paul the Traveller and the Roman Citizen*. London: Hodder & Stoughton, 1908.

Reicke, B. I., & D. Green. *The New Testament Era: The World of the Bible from 500 B.C. to A.D. 100*. London: Black, 1969.

Riesner, R. *Paul's Early Period: Chronology, Mission Strategy, Theology*. Grand Rapids, MI: Eerdmans, 1998.

Robinson, E., & E. Smith. *Biblical Researches in Palestine and the Adjacent Regions: A Journal of Travels in the Years 1838 and 1852 by Edward Robinson, Eli Smith and Others*. 3rd ed. London: J. Murray, 1867.

Roller, D. W. *The Building Program of Herod the Great*. Berkeley: University of California Press, 1998.

Safrai, S., & M. Stern. *The Jewish People in the First Century: Historical Geography, Political History, Social, Cultural and Religious Life and Institutions*. Assen: Van Gorcum, 1974.

Saggs, H. W. F. *The Might That Was Assyria*. London: Sidgwick & Jackson, 1984.

Saggs, H. W. F. *The Greatness That Was Babylon: A Survey of the Ancient Civilization of the Tigris–Euphrates Valley*. 2nd ed. London: Sidgwick & Jackson, 1988.

Saggs, H. W. F., and H. N. Fairfield. *Everyday Life in Babylonia and Assyria*. London: Batsford, 1965.

Sandars, N. K. *The Sea Peoples: Warriors of the Ancient Mediterranean, 1250–1150 B.C.* Rev. ed. London: Thames & Hudson, 1985.

Sanders, E. P. *Jesus and Judaism*. London: SCM, 1985.

Simons, J. J. *Jerusalem in the Old Testament: Researches and Theories*. Leiden: Brill, 1952.

Simons, J. J. *The Geographical and Topographical Texts of the Old Testament: A Concise Commentary in XXXII Chapters*. Leiden: Brill, 1959.

Shanks, H. *Understanding the Dead Sea Scrolls: A Reader from the Biblical Archaeology Review*. London: SPCK, 1993.

Smith, J., and W. E. Smith. *The Voyage and Shipwreck of St. Paul: With Dissertations on the Life and Writings of St. Luke, and the Ships and Navigation of the Ancients*. London: Longmans, Green, 1880.

Stambaugh, J. E. *The Ancient Roman City*. Baltimore: John Hopkins University Press, 1988.

Stambaugh, J. E. B. *The New Testament in its Social Environment*. Philadelphia: The Westminster Press, 1986.

Stark, R. *The Rise of Christianity: How the Obscure, Marginal Jesus Movement Became the Dominant Religious Force in the Western World in a Few Centuries*. San Francisco: HarperSanFrancisco, 1997.

Stern, E. *Archaeology of the Land of the Bible, Volume 2: The Assyrian, Babylonian and Persian Periods (732–332 BCE)*. New York: Doubleday, 2001.

Stern, E. *Material Culture of the Land of the Bible in the Persian Period, 538–332 B.C.* Warminster, Wiltshire: Aris & Phillips Israel Exploration Society, 1982.

VanderKam, J. C. *The Dead Sea Scrolls Today*. Grand Rapids, MI: Eerdmans, 1994.

Van Der Meer, F., C. Mohrmann, M. F. Hedlund, and H. H. Rowley. *Atlas of the Early Christian World*. London: Nelson, 1958.

White, L. M. *Building God's House in the Roman World: Architectural Adaptation among Pagans, Jews, and Christians*. Baltimore: Johns Hopkins University Press, 1990.

Wilkinson, J. *Jerusalem as Jesus Knew It: Archaeology as Evidence*. London: Thames & Hudson, 1978.

Wiseman, D. J. *Peoples of Old Testament Times*. Oxford: Clarendon Press, 1973.

Wright, G. R. H. *Ancient Building in South Syria and Palestine*. Leiden: Brill, 1985.

Yadin, Y. *The Art of Warfare in Biblical Lands in the Light of Archaeological Discovery*. London: Weidenfeld and Nicolson, 1963.

Yadin, Y. *Bar-Kokhba: The Rediscovery of the Legendary Hero of the Last Jewish Revolt against Imperial Rome*. London: Weidenfeld & Nicolson, 1971.

Yadin, Y. *Masada: Herod's Fortress and the Zealots' Last Stand*. London: Phoenix Illustrated, 1997.

Zohary, M. *Plants of the Bible: A Complete Handbook to All the Plants with 200 Full-Color Plates Taken in the Natural Habitat*. Cambridge: Cambridge University Press, 1982.

Index

Bet She'arim 154
Beth-zechariah, battle of 135
Bethel 24, 38, 120
Bether, battle of 172
Bethsaida 154
Bible 22-3, 130, 176, 177
    Hebrew scriptures 130, 150, 163
    see also New Testament;
    Old Testament; Septuagint
Broad-room temples 82
Bronze, armor and weapons 57
Bronze Age
    settlements 17-19, 34-5, 46, 64
    temples 82-3
    see also Late Bronze Age; Middle
    Bronze
Byblos 69, 81

Caesarea Maritima 148, 174, 175
Caesarea Philippi (Paneas) 147, 154
Calah 80
Canaan
    as center of world 33
    Egyptian expansion into 44-5,
        48-53
    Israelite entry and settlement in
        53, 56, 62-5
    patriarchal routes in 36-41
    Proto-Canaanite script 20
    religions of 24-5, 46
    social structure 70
    temples and religion 24, 82, 120
    trade with Greece 54-5
Capernaum 154
Carchemish 100, 117, 118
Cassander 128, 132
Cassius Dio 173
Caves, used in Second Jewish Revolt
    172, 173
Celsus, Library, of at Ephesus
    158-9
Cestius Gallus 170
Chalcis 152
Chalcolithic period 30-1, 82
Chaldeans 109, 118, 120
    see also Babylonia
Chedorlaomer 39
Chinnereth, Lake (Sea of Galilee)
    154, 156
Christianity 164-7, 176-7
    see also Judaism; Pagan gods
Chronicles, book of 85, 114

Church of the Holy Sepulchre 157,
    178
Churches, Christian 157, 176-7, 178
    see also Jerusalem, Temple of;
    Temples
Cilicia (Khilakku) 119, 133, 166
Cities
    conquered by Shishak 92
    of David's kingdom 79
    earliest 34-5, 40-1
    Judean 110, 144, 147-8, 149
    Moabite 96, 97
    Paul's missions to 164-5
    renamed by conquerors 128-9
    Roman, in Palestine 154, 174
    Seleucid 133
    "unconquered" 66, 78
    see also Jerusalem; Samaria;
    Settlements; Ugarit
City-states
    Canaanite 48, 62-4, 65, 70
    Hittite 51
    Israelite 94
    Philistine 68
    Phoenician 86
Clans 70, 104-5
Claudius, Emperor 152, 162
Clay tablets 20, 21
cuneiform 38, 46, 48-9
Cleopatra VII 143, 144
"Client-kings" 142, 143, 152
Coele-Syria 130, 133
Coins, Jewish 172, 173
Copper Scroll 151
Corinth 164
Croesus 124
Crucifixion of Jesus 129, 156, 157
Cuneiform script 21, 47
Cuneiform tablets 38, 46, 48-9
Cyaxares 118
Cyprus 54, 55, 86, 130
Cyrus the Great 123, 124, 125

Dagon 14
Damascus 100, 103, 107, 142, 160,
    166
Dan, tribe of 68, 69, 70
Daniel, book of 125
Dating
    archaeological methods of 18,
        19, 22
    of the Exodus 58-9

David 68, 75, 76-9, 87, 90
Dead Sea 172, 179
Dead Sea Scrolls 150-1
Deborah 70, 71
Delilah 71
Demetrius II 132, 135, 136
Demetrius Poliorcetes 128, 132
Deportations 108, 109, 112, 122, 172
    see also Diaspora; Migrations
Deuteronomy, book of 58, 120
Diaspora, Jewish 138, 160-3, 176-7
    see also Deportations;
    Migrations
Diocletian 175
Diospolis 174
Documents see Texts
Dome of the Rock 178
Domestic animals 31
Domitian 172, 176
Dor 69, 107, 124
Dothan 40
Dura-Europos 162, 176

Early Bronze Age II-III
    settlements 17, 34-5, 64
    temples 82
Early Iron Age, settlements 66-7
Ebenezer 14
Ebla 38
Edomites 78
Egnatian Way 164, 165, 166
Egypt
    and Assyria 112, 116, 117
    and Babylonia 109, 118-19
    execration texts 40-1
    expansion into Canaan 44-5,
        48-53
    gods of 164
    hieroglyphic script 21
    Jews in 130, 161
    Joseph in 40-1
    and Judah 120, 121, 122
    the Ptolemies 128-9, 130-1
    Sea People's attempted invasion
        of 68
    see also Ancient Near East;
    Merneptah; Pharaohs;
    Ramesses II; Shishak
Ehud, and the Moabites 70, 71
Ekron 14, 68, 113
Elam 109, 116
Elasa, battle of 135

Israel
    and Aram 98–9
    Assyrian sovereignty of 106–7
    and Babylonia 108, 109
    conquests and settlement in
        Canaan 53, 56, 62–7, 70–1
    excavated sites in 91, 154
    and Moab 96–7
    in Old Testament period 22–3
    and Phoenicia 86–7
    present-day 178–9
    separation from Judah 90
    temples 83
    under Jeroboam II 104–5
    see also Jews; Judaea; Judah;
        Judaism; United Kingdom
Israel Defense Barrier 178
Israelite festivals 12, 58, 136, 156
Ituraea 144, 148, 152

Jabesh-gilead, battle of 74, 75
Jacob (Israel) 24, 38
James 152, 166
Jannaeus 136, 143
Japheth 32
Jason 134
Jebusites 76, 77
Jehoiakim 120, 122
Jehoram (Joram) 94, 97, 110
Jehoshaphat 110
Jehu 94, 100
Jephthah 70, 71
Jeremiah 120, 122
Jericho 23, 64, 82, 147
Jeroboam II 98, 104–5
Jeroboam ben-Nebat 90, 92
Jerusalem 41, 75, 84–5, 92, 113
    Babylonian destruction of 118, 122
    battles for 76–7, 114
    and Diaspora Jews 163
    and Herod the Great 146–7
    Jesus' entry into 156
    Paul in 166, 167
    Persian rebuilding of 125
    present-day 178
    Roman destruction and
        rebuilding of 171, 172, 174
    under Seleucids 133, 134–5
Jerusalem, Temple of 82, 85, 92,
    120, 122, 138
    capture and pillaging of 134,
        136

Herod the Great's new temple
    146–7
    Herod's temple destroyed 153,
        171
    rebuilding of under Joshua 125
Jesus 154–7
Jews
    culture 129, 130, 138, 154
    Diaspora 138, 160–3
    First and Second Revolts 150,
        151, 153, 170–5, 176
    Hasmonaean state 136–7, 143
    Jewish law 120, 125, 129, 134, 150
    synagogues 126, 138–9, 162, 163
    see also Israel; Judaea; Judah;
        Judaism; United Kingdom
Jezebel 86, 87, 94
Joab 77, 78
Joash 98, 110
John, Gospel of 129, 156, 157
John the baptist 156
Jonathan 74
Jonathan Maccabeus 129, 135, 136
Jordan, river 10, 92, 179
Joseph 40–1
Josephus (Flavius Josephus) 160,
    162, 170
Joshua 62–5, 67, 125
Joshua, book of 62, 64, 65, 66, 67,
    96, 104, 110
Josiah 114, 117, 120–1
Jotham 99
Judaea
    after Herod's death 148
    and First Jewish Revolt 170
    Hasmonaean period 136
    Roman period 142–3, 152, 154,
        174
    under Herod the Great 144, 145
    see also Israel; Jews; Judah;
        Judaism; United Kingdom
Judah, Prince of Sepphoris 172
Judah 81, 90, 92, 98, 99
    and Assyria 112–13
    and Babylonia 119, 125
    and the Ptolemies 130–1
    resurgence of 110–11
    and Seleucids 133, 134–5, 136
    under Hezekiah and Manasseh
        114–15
    under Jeroboam II 104–5
    under Josiah 120–1

    under Persians 124–5
    see also Israel; Jews; Judaea;
        Judaism; United Kingdom
Judaism
    of Babylonian exiles 119
    and Christianity 176
    and development of synagogues
        138
    of Diaspora Jews 163
    the Essenes 150–1
    replaces Canaanite paganism 120
    under Seleucids 134
    see also Christianity; Israel; Jews;
        Judaea; Judah; Pagan gods;
        United Kingdom
Judas Maccabeus 129, 134, 135
Judges, age of 70–1
Judges, book of 62, 66, 67, 70–1, 78
Julius Caesar 143, 144
Julius Severus 172

Karnak inscription 22, 92
Khilakku (Cilicia) 119, 133, 166
Khirbet Qumran 150, 151
Kings
    of Aram, Israel and Judah 98–9,
        106, 110–11, 114
    Assyrian 103, 116–17
    Babylonian 122
    "client-kings" 142, 143, 152
    Seleucid 132, 134–5
    see also Hasmonaean period;
        Josiah
Kings, book of 80, 81, 85, 90, 91, 94,
    95, 107, 109, 120
Kinship groups, and ethnicity 32–3
Kirhareseth 97
Kizzuwadna (Kue) 56
Kullania 106

Laban 24, 38
Lake Gennesaret (Sea of Galilee) 154,
    156
Late Bronze Age
    migrations and warfare 56–9
    settlements 46–7, 64
    trade 54–5
Latin 164, 172, 176
Law, Jewish 120, 125, 129, 134, 150
Leah 38
Legio (Lejjun) 174
Leontopolis 161

Acknowledgments and picture credits

Scripture quotations are taken from the *New Revised Standard Version Bible*, copyright © 1989 by the Division of Christian Education of the National Council of the Churches of Christ in the USA, and are used by permission. All rights reserved.

p.63 **The battle of Ai**: Based on *The Problem of Ai* by Z.Zevit in *Biblical Archaeology*

p.91 **Major excavated sites in Israel** and
p.93 **The division of the kingdom and the campaign of Pharaoh Shishak**: Based on the original material by Y. Aharoni, with permission of M. Aharoni, and Burns & Oates Ltd, Tunbridge Wells, England and The Westminster Press, Philadelphia

p.139 **Synagogue sites in Roman Palestine**: Based on *Ancient Synagogues Revealed* edited by L.I. Levine, published by Israel Exploration Society, Jerusalem

p.175 **Roman Palestine** and
p.174 **Roman Provincial Administration, c. AD 70-193**: Based on original material by M.Avi-Yonah, and used by courtesy of the Israel Department of Antiquities and Museums, Jerusalem

Picture Credits
Part 1: © Nick Page
Part 2: © Dean Conger/Corbis
Part 3: © Jose Fuste Raga/Corbis
Part 4: © Richard T. Nowitz/Corbis
Part 5: © Fred de Noyelle /Godong/Corbis
Part 6: © Nik Wheeler/Corbis
Part 7: © Gian Berto Vanni/Corbis
Part 8: © Richard T. Nowitz/Corbis
Part 9: © Larry Dale Gordon/zefa/Corbis
Part 10: © Nick Page